# SKY RIDER

PARK VAN TASSEL

SKY RIDER

AND THE RISE OF
BALLOONING IN THE WEST

GARY B. FOGEL     FOREWORD BY DICK BROWN

UNIVERSITY OF NEW MEXICO PRESS | ALBUQUERQUE

ISBN 978-0-8263-6282-7 (paper)
ISBN 978-0-8263-6283-4 (electronic)

Library of Congress Cataloging-in-Publication Data is on file with the Library of Congress.

Founded in 1889, the University of New Mexico sits on the traditional homelands of the Pueblo of Sandia. The original peoples of New Mexico—Pueblo, Navajo, and Apache—since time immemorial have deep connections to the land and have made significant contributions to the broader community statewide. We honor the land itself and those who remain stewards of this land throughout the generations and also acknowledge our committed relationship to Indigenous peoples. We gratefully recognize our history.

Cover illustrations: top photograph courtesy of Smithsonian National Air and Space Museum (NASM 89–920); bottom illustration courtesy of Vecteezy.com
Frontispiece: A portrait of Park Albert Van Tassel taken on July 4, 1883. Smithsonian National Air and Space Museum (NASM 89–920).
Designed by Felicia Cedillos
Composed in Adobe Caslon Pro 10.25/14.25

TO THE MEMORY OF PARK VAN TASSEL,
AND IN HONOR OF THE ALBUQUERQUE INTERNATIONAL BALLOON
FIESTA®, ITS ORGANIZERS, AND THE AERONAUTS WHO CONTINUE TO
KEEP HIS DREAM ALOFT IN THE LAND OF ENCHANTMENT.

# CONTENTS

# ILLUSTRATIONS

# FOREWORD

*Sky Rider: Park Van Tassel and the Rise of Ballooning in the West* is the first attempt to piece together the life and times of a long-forgotten aviation pioneer, a man who introduced ballooning to Albuquerque at a time when new inventions, mail-order catalogs, and transcontinental railroads were changing the face of the nation, and death-defying aerial exhibitions were just coming of age. That intrepid aeronaut was Park Van Tassel.

When his gas-filled balloon lifted off from a vacant lot in downtown Albuquerque on July 4, 1882, few had ever witnessed human flight. No one in the cheering crowd that day could have realized the importance of Van Tassel's balloon flight—a first for himself, a first for Albuquerque, a first for New Mexico, and a prelude to establishing aviation firsts in the skies above many foreign countries. Without this book, no one today would appreciate the impact of Van Tassel's many aeronautical contributions.

Author and aviation historian Dr. Gary Fogel traces Van Tassel's life journey and shows us how this charismatic barnstormer and his high-flying acrobatic troupe performed throughout the American West and beyond, added parachuting to his ballooning exploits, and, in a most spectacular way, introduced women to aviation.

The traveling showman had a stressful lifestyle, with constant money woes, pesky equipment failures, and relentless pressure to perform on schedule and to outdo burgeoning competition. Some daredevils who indulged in this risky business paid dearly, with their lives. But Van Tassel was a survivor, and after staging perilous yet successful exhibitions in the West, he ventured overseas—Australia, Southeast Asia, India—where the art and science of ballooning and parachuting were virtually unknown. In a real sense, he took ballooning from Albuquerque to the rest of the world. Ironically, now the rest of the world travels to Albuquerque for its annual Balloon Fiesta. The late Sid Cutter, founder of the Balloon Fiesta, had a dream—to create a world-class venue that celebrates the diversity and history of ballooning. Park Van Tassel also had a dream, a boyhood dream to float through the air in a balloon. His dream, like Sid's, also came true.

*Sky Rider* reminds us of Albuquerque's special place in sport ballooning history. The upcoming fiftieth anniversary of the Balloon Fiesta not only celebrates the city's long association with ballooning, but it salutes Van Tassel and the launching of his *City of Albuquerque*, landing the city on the world stage. It is no wonder Albuquerque is known as the Balloon Capital of the World.

Park Van Tassel has never been celebrated as a great American balloonist. He died in obscurity nearly ninety years ago, his life unheralded, his accomplishments unappreciated. Of the hundreds of thousands of fans who converge on Balloon Fiesta Park each year, only a few are remotely familiar with Albuquerque's first aeronaut. Fogel has launched *Sky Rider* to set the record straight and to serve as a tribute to a man with great courage, pioneering spirit, amazing foresight, and an uncanny ability to survive. It is his hope that future researchers will continue the task of unraveling the mysteries surrounding Park Van Tassel and his dubious associates.

As the 1979 winner of the Fédération Aéronautique Internationale's Diplome Montgolfier, the world's highest ballooning honor, for my literary contributions to sport ballooning, I can relate to the work Fogel has put forth in following Van Tassel's twisting, convoluted trails across the globe. And as one who has been involved in the Balloon Fiesta since its start in 1972, and as a member of its Hall of Fame, I believe Van Tassel's legacy will live on in this authoritative biography. In *Sky Rider*, Park Van Tassel finally takes his rightful place alongside other world-famous aviation pioneers.

DICK BROWN
Heritage Committee,
Albuquerque International Balloon Fiesta®
October 2019

# PREFACE

I first became interested in ballooning as a teenager. My father had the good fortune to attend a Balloon Fiesta in Albuquerque in the 1980s and returned to our home in San Diego with many photographs of what seemed like an endless sky filled with balloons of all shapes, sizes, and colors. Dad and I enjoyed flying radio-controlled model gliders together for many years. While gliders and balloons share a common theme of silent flight, there is something unique and inherently beautiful about balloons. Each flight is a new adventure, requiring smart pilots to think carefully about making use of the atmosphere and the energy it provides. I was naturally drawn to this way of thinking, as smart, continuous decision making is required to extend flight without motors.

At roughly the same time, a high school friend asked if I might be available to help as ground crew for a local ballooning company in San Diego, as it was short staffed at the time. I readily agreed, although I knew almost nothing about balloons and ballooning other than what my dad had shared with me about his experience at the fiesta in Albuquerque. Soon enough, I found myself in a field, helping inflate a very large balloon owned by the Skysurfer Balloon Company. The inflation was louder and hotter than I expected, and there was much to do. Soon we had the balloon and basket in their proper orientation, with paying passengers and pilot on board ready for their flight. Before I could really understand everything that was happening, the craft was off, rising rapidly like a toy balloon that had just escaped a child's grasp of the string.

My friend and I cleaned up the launch site, hopped in a van, and started the chase. We were in radio communication with the pilot and discussed likely landing zones on the way. Once a landing location was chosen, our task was to get there in advance of the balloon and then help with landing. I wasn't yet sure what that entailed. But chasing the balloon on the back roads of San Diego was its own new type of fun. With the sun just setting on this twilight balloon ride, we arrived at the landing zone, an empty field of bushes and grass. As the balloon came closer, our first job was to jump on the outside of the basket to serve as added ballast to keep the balloon on the ground. With a slight breeze, this wasn't going to be easy. We timed our jump on either side of the basket, held on for the landing, and scraped along the ground just a bit before coming to rest, with the passengers cheering a successful conclusion to their flight. Champagne followed, along with our packing away the balloon at dusk. Afterward, the company hired me to help with balloon chasing two or three times a week that summer. I was impressed by the skill of the pilots, their amazing ability to understand wind currents at different altitudes, and steer their way to the select landing zones available. On one landing approach, I hopped on as ballast, but the pilot realized the approach was going to go long and put us directly into a large patch of prickly pear cactus. He told me to hang on as he fired the burner just enough for us to glide over the cactus to a landing on the other side. I was even more relieved than the pilot.

I never did get a chance to go up in the balloon that summer, as it was always full of paying passengers. However, upon returning to San Diego after earning my PhD at the University of California–Los Angeles, my wife, Joanne, and I had the pleasure of taking a flight with the same balloon company. It had been a long time coming, but my familiarity with all aspects of the flight helped. Yet I remained unprepared for the silence and the majesty of the view from the basket. I was also unprepared for the noise and heat produced by the burner, a reminder that energy was required to extend the journey. But we landed safely and finally had the chance to enjoy sharing in the champagne.

From this modern vantage point, it can be difficult to process what ballooning must have been like in the past. We have become accustomed to the comforts of air travel, and we accept it as just another part of daily life. In just a short 250 years or so, we've managed to transform what was once considered an "impossible" art of flight into a reality. Commercial airliners whisk us around the world at nearly the speed of sound while we enjoy movies and drinks. Unpiloted aircraft can be flown by an operator half a world away or even controlled by a computer instead of a human. To people two centuries ago, our present-day reality would have absolutely seemed a futuristic pipe-dream.

The earliest hot air balloon flight occurred in Annonay, France, on June 4, 1783, manned by Joseph-Michel and Jacques-Etienne Montgolfier. Later that same year, on December 1, Jacques Charles, Anne-Jean Robert, and Nicolas-Louis Robert made the first gas balloon flight in a hydrogen balloon in Paris. Ballooning came to the United States soon thereafter in the form of unpiloted ascensions and tethered flights. Through the efforts of Benjamin Franklin and others to help popularize ballooning, European expert Jean-Pierre Blanchard came to Philadelphia in December 1792, selling tickets for his balloon ascension for $5 each (roughly $130 in today's dollars). Despite the cost, an enormous crowd, including George Washington, Thomas Jefferson, John Adams, James Madison, and James Monroe, gathered on January 10, 1793, to watch Blanchard's ascension. It was not only a spectacle of curiosity but offered interesting possibilities for the government. The crowd's astonishment must have been considerably greater than when I witnessed my first balloon launch, as I was already accepting of the possibility of both lighter-than-air flight and heavier-than-air flight at the time. The founders would have had no preconceived notion of what they would witness. Humans flying to the heavens? Who would have believed it possible! Blanchard's flight, the first untethered, piloted flight in US history, was a source of considerable inspiration, witnessed by thousands. Unfortunately for Blanchard, the flight also turned out to be something of a financial boondoggle, as he was unable to recoup his expenses.

At this dawn of piloted ballooning, a romantic "balloonomania" began to spread. Those who dared to sever their bond with Earth were celebrated as heroes after each flight. Children played with small model balloons made of paper. Intellectuals around the world became interested in the use of balloons for science, such as William Herschel's concept of taking telescopes high into the atmosphere with balloons for improved astronomical viewing. In the nineteenth century, poets and writers such as Percy Bysshe Shelley, Henry Mayhew, Samuel Taylor Coleridge, Edgar Allan Poe, and William Words-worth[1] helped popularize ballooning, culminating with French novelist Jules Verne's *A Voyage in a Balloon* (1851) and *Five Weeks in a Balloon* (1863), early

science fiction that further brought the excitement and possibilities of ballooning to the masses. Unlike the famous 1956 film adaptation of Verne's
*Around the World in Eighty Days*, the original 1872 novel did not in fact include
ballooning among its many modes of transportation.

Between the 1840s and the 1860s, Americans became increasingly interested in ballooning. As noted in *The Eagle Aloft*, Tom D. Crouch's compre-
hensive and authoritative history of ballooning in America, "a legion of
itinerant aeronauts, veterans and newcomers alike, crisscrossed the nation
during these years, flying in cities from Maine to California. Universally honored as 'Professor This' or 'Madame That,' their exploits were featured on the
front pages of great newspapers and the new illustrated magazines such as
*Harper's* and *Leslie's*. They were a breed apart, the first generation of footloose,
barnstorming aerial showmen."[2] This generation also included some brave
women who wished to prove themselves as aviators. Pioneer balloonist John
Wise and his associates were central in this new age of balloon exhibition.

Advances in ballooning coincided with a time of expansion in the United
States, as many migrated from East to West by covered wagon or boat to
make their pile during the gold rush. The First Transcontinental Railroad was
completed in 1869, providing Americans with a more efficient means of travel.
This monumental undertaking cost between $16,000 and $48,000 per mile of
track, depending on the topography (roughly $500,000 and $1,400,000 per
mile in today's dollars), over a total length of 1,868 miles. Before the transcontinental railroad, a trip from the East Coast to the West Coast took more than
four months. By 1876 the Transcontinental Express traveled from New York
City to San Francisco in just three and a half days. The railroad literally
opened up the West during the late nineteenth century, including the diverse
routes of the Union Pacific Railroad and the Atchison, Topeka & Santa Fe
Railway. Today we fly over this same route in a mere five hours through our
highways in the sky.

The first balloon flight west of the Rockies was arranged in Oakland, California, on August 28, 1853, by a certain Mr. Kelly.[3] This event didn't go as
planned, as the balloon had insufficient buoyancy to carry Kelly aloft. A
sixteen-year-old boy named Joseph Gates took his place and soared aloft
without much in the way of training. Two hours later, the balloon came back
to Earth and Gates hopped out 5 miles west of Benicia. Now relieved of its

weight, the balloon went skyward again, landing some distance beyond. Somewhat miraculously, Gates suffered a sprained ankle during the landing and also injured his hand while trying to cut a hole in the fabric at altitude to release some of the gas. He returned to San Francisco the following day. History fails to record if he ever flew again.

During the Civil War, both the Union and Confederate armies made use of balloons for reconnaissance. The efforts of Thaddeus S. C. Lowe are well documented in service of Union forces and for the War Department, leading to the formation of Lowe's Balloon Corps, which included multiple balloons, trained aeronauts, and a portable hydrogen generating system. His efforts with balloons continued after the war and included use of a gymnast performing stunts on a bar beneath the basket. He even staged the first aerial wedding in 1865, with the famous abolitionist clergyman Henry Ward Beecher officiating. As it turned out, the Reverend Beecher could not be persuaded to get into the basket. The couple was married instead at the Fifth Avenue Hotel before heading to Central Park for the balloon flight with Lowe.

During the mid-1880s, Americans also became interested in traveling exhibitions such as those offered by Phineas Taylor (P. T.) Barnum. These troupes often combined "science" with theater through unusual exhibitions of magic, animals, and an unnerving variety of human oddities. P. T. Barnum's Greatest Show on Earth began in 1871, touring the world in 1888. William F. Cody brought his Buffalo Bill's Wild West show to towns of the Old West starting in 1882. The show included shooting displays, rodeo events, and theatrical reenactments. A series of similar shows included Texas Jack's Wild West, Pawnee Bill's Wild West, and the 101 Ranch Wild West Show. The entertainers would travel from town to town, largely by rail, eager to provide performances that would offer a profit beyond the expense of transportation.

Prior to the Civil War, crowds in large cities were pleased simply to see experts go aloft in their balloons. After the Civil War and into the 1880s, aeronauts became more focused on exhibition and less on ballooning skill. Many learned through a process of trial and error, as experts in ballooning were uncommon. Errors on the ground led to ridicule and lost income. Errors in the sky proved far more dangerous and, for some, even fatal. The lack of mentors was most acute in the West. Those lucky enough to find one were taught how to make or buy a balloon and the basics of its operation. They were left to their own devices to try it. Just as the founders were amazed to watch balloons take to the sky, those who were brave enough to be the first in town to pilot a balloon were amazed just to fly and survive. Daredevils with the courage not only to fly but also to work a trapeze below the balloon, or even jump with a parachute, realized the opportunity to capitalize on the amazed audiences.

It is against this backdrop that we find a handful of western pioneers eager not only to enjoy the romance of leaving the bonds of an Earth-bound existence with a balloon but also to use balloons for entrepreneurship and to make their living as aeronauts. Unlike the pioneering spirits who came to the West to find gold buried in the Earth, these brave aviators would attain their wealth in the sky. Many westerners had only read about balloons in a newspaper or seen a rare photo. The opportunity to see a traveling balloon exhibition in person would have been the nineteenth-century equivalent of Richard Branson launching suborbital spacecraft from Spaceport America near Truth or Consequences, New Mexico, to carry space tourists on the ride of their lives. Those who were brave enough competed to see who could fly higher or farther or be first to launch from a specific town. These newfangled balloon exhibitionists traveled by rail from place to place to enthrall paying audiences. One of the most prominent of these aeronautical pioneers was Park Van Tassel.

I was introduced to the story of early balloonist Park Van Tassel by Albuquerque Balloon Fiesta pioneer Dick Brown and Rick Van Tassel, an indirect relative of Park. Together they had spent time researching his history. While certain facts were clear, other parts to this story were quite confused. Park Van Tassel's lifetime of travels and balloon launches across wide geographic distances, from the American West to the rest of the world, left a scattered trail. Arranging these pieces into a cohesive story was going to require considerable effort. Yet the more I researched the story, the more fascinating it became. Van Tassel not only introduced New Mexico to flight, but he also helped introduce flight to millions around the world and helped introduce women to ballooning and parachuting during the tumultuous women's rights movements of the late nineteenth century. Reporters in one city after the next hailed him as a hero, but few understood his past, fewer still knew where he would head next, and Van Tassel clearly sometimes embellished the truth. His often frenetic pace from town to town, state to state, country to country, and continent to continent left little in the way of a coherent history. As a result, his journeys have been largely forgotten. This biography aims to piece together these many disconnected anecdotes into one complete account of this early aerial showman of the West, Park Van Tassel.

Wherever primary source information has been possible to obtain, I have made use of it. But in many cases I have had to rely on multiple secondary sources to tease out Van Tassel's life story. I have researched as many contemporary versions of each event as possible and provide them all here in the references for future historians. Park Van Tassel's amazing story was the result of fortitude and good timing: the opening of the American West by rail, the popularization and accessibility of ballooning, a willing and interested public eager for entertainment, with newspapers helping to market events in advance of the next stop on the tour. Balloons have maintained their magic, much as they did for me back in high school. I hope this book will help you understand why.

# ACKNOWLEDGMENTS

I would like to thank various individuals for their assistance in the development of this book. First and foremost, Rick Van Tassel and Dick Brown are to be thanked for the initial suggestion to research this story, for supplying many critical references, and for helping interpret material along the way. This book would not have been possible without their help. In Albuquerque, I would like to thank Diane Schaller (Historic Albuquerque, Inc.) for assistance with reference materials. In New Orleans, Heather M. Szafran (reference assistant, the Historic New Orleans Collection) helped provide material regarding Van Tassel's association with the 1884 World's Fair. In Australia, special thanks go to Debra Close (learning and information officer, CityLibraries Townsville), Chris Brimble (learning and information officer, CityLibraries Townsville), and Ella Morrison (Reader Services, National Library of Australia). I was very fortunate to interact with each of them in search of material regarding Van Tassel's exhibitions in Australia. A very special thank-you goes to Fiona Spooner (ephemera officer, National Library of Australia), who provided excellent assistance from afar regarding specific material in the National Library of Australia collection. It was a pleasure to work with each of them as well as Cindy Abel Morris (pictorial archivist, Center for Southwest Research, University of New Mexico Libraries) and Katrina Pescador and Alan Renga with the San Diego Air and Space Museum. With regard to Van Tassel's time in China and Japan, thanks go to Howard and Norma Lee, Tomoko Bialock (Japanese studies librarian, University of California–Los Angeles), Sophie Arab, and especially Masako Ogawa and her students at Macquarie University for their assistance in finding articles and translating them into English. Thanks also to Erica Peters for her rapid research into early balloon exhibitions in Indochina and to Eliza Binte Elahi and Shameem Aminur Rahmanin in

Dhaka for their interest in Van Tassel's time in Bangladesh, as well as Roland Sommer and Rolf Stunkel for efforts to research portions of the story in Germany.

Park Van Tassel's story is not one of just New Mexico or the American West. It is truly international. To gather primary and secondary source material, I used many resources, including the Albuquerque Historical Society, Ancestry.com, the British Library, the British Library Business and Intellectual Property Reference Service, the fabulous California Digital Newspaper Collection of the Center for Bibliographical Studies and Research at the University of California–Riverside, the Center for Southwest Research at the University of New Mexico, Historic Albuquerque, Inc., the Historic New Orleans Collection, the Library of Congress, the Los Angeles Public Library, the Museum of Flight, the National Archives of Australia, the National Library of Australia, the National Endowment for the Humanities, Newspapers.com, the Richard C. Rudolph East Asian Library at the University of California–Los Angeles, the San Diego Air and Space Museum, the San Diego State University Library, the Save Our Heritage Organisation, the Smithsonian Institution, the Stanford University Library, the State Library of Victoria, and the University of Melbourne.

Special thanks go to Stephen Hull, Michael Millman, and others at the University of New Mexico Press for understanding the importance of this story not only for New Mexico but for the history of aviation in the United States and other nations. Thanks also go to Peg Goldstein for her valued copyediting of the manuscript. I would also like to thank Marilee Schmit Nason and Tom D. Crouch, who served as expert reviewers for the book's first draft and whose suggestions have helped immeasurably. Added thanks go to Joanne and Sabrina Fogel for putting up with my obsessions; to Eva Fogel, John McNeil, Charles Norris, David Hall, and Craig Harwood for helping review portions of the manuscript; and to Amie Hayes and Bruce Coons of the Save Our Heritage Organisation in San Diego for their many efforts to promote local aviation history. Lastly, very special thanks go to Ana Loyola for her assistance in helping me find Park Van Tassel's grave in Oakland, California, a process that required considerable research and effort.

# 1. ASCENSION

PARKER ALBERT VAN TASSEL was born on July 25, 1853, in Cass County, Indiana, the son of Rufus Van Tassel[1] and Nancy Connor.[2] Nicknamed Park, he was the third of five children, with older sisters Eliza J.[3] and Clarissa A.[4] and younger sisters Effie E.[5] and Lillie.[6] It remains unclear what happened to Nancy; however by 1875 Rufus had remarried, wedding Phebe Lorinda Smith,[7] and they had four children together. Rufus was short and stocky, with dark red curly hair and a genial disposition. He sang folk songs and often accompanied them with music played on a saw. Rufus's father hailed from New York, his mother from Virginia, but Rufus was from Tipton, Indiana, near Terre Haute.[8] Little is known about Park's mother, Nancy Connor, other than that she was born in Indiana in 1828 and was probably the daughter of John[9] and Elizabeth Connor,[10] both of Hoover, Indiana.

Park encountered his first balloons at a young age at a village fair in Ohio. This event instilled a passionate desire to be an aeronaut. With the help of friends, he proceeded to make model hot air balloons out of paper.[11] On October 19, 1872, teenage Park married his sweetheart, Elizabeth Spencer, in Franklin, Indiana.[12] They had one son together, Guy Van Tassel, born July 28, 1873. Although it is clear that Park remained in Ohio at least until 1876,[13] the marriage to Elizabeth did not last much longer, although no records of divorce have been confirmed. It also isn't clear precisely what Park did for the ensuing three years.

In 1879, thirty years after the gold rush, Park moved to Stockton, California. He married Ella Block[14] on June 10, 1879, in the city of San Joaquin, California. At the time, Park was twenty-six and Ella was only sixteen.[15] Park ran a cigar shop in Stockton but quickly tired of that work.[16] They had a son named Harry,[17] but it isn't clear what became of him. Within a year of his marriage to Ella, Park once again began experimenting with balloons, but these were now full-size passenger-carrying balloons rather than merely toys. It is not known for sure, but he might have obtained a balloon measuring 30,000 cubic feet, and some rudimentary instruction, from Forestus Fordyce Martin[18] of San Francisco, a well-known distributor of balloons during this period. F. F. Martin had migrated to California from St. Louis and partnered with James H. Whiteside of Sacramento in making balloon ascensions in the 1870s.[19]

Operating under the stage name Professor Van Tassel,[20] on August 14, 1880, Park attempted his first ascension in a balloon from Stockton's Hunter Square in front of several thousand spectators. Unfortunately, Park's balloon refused to ascend, and the throng of spectators considered Van Tassel's performance a "big fizzle."[21] Another attempt was made on the afternoon of September 5, 1880, from Sacramento's Agricultural Park. However, there are no reports of any successful ascension.[22] Ballooning was surely harder than it seemed. Park made a trip to San Francisco in January 1881, staying at the Baldwin Hotel, perhaps to obtain further instruction in ballooning from Martin.[23]

In 1881 Park and Ella decided to leave Stockton. It remains unclear what caused this decision, but they boarded a train on July 22 and headed south, first through Fresno and then to Arizona Territory, stopping in Tucson.[24] The railroad itself was rather new to Arizona, as the first train ever to stop in Tucson did so on March 20, 1880. The famous gunfight at the O.K. Corral would take place in nearby Tombstone in October 1881, only a few months after the Van Tassels continued on the train to Albuquerque, New Mexico Territory, where they made a new start on life in what was then a small town of only two thousand people.

After settling in Albuquerque, Van Tassel shipped the large balloon he had likely purchased from Martin from Stockton to Albuquerque by train.[25] The balloon arrived in time for the gas lines at the center of the city to finally be in operation, a key ingredient for balloon inflation.[26] Despite his difficulty with balloons in Stockton and Sacramento, in May 1882 Van Tassel expressed interest in making a public ascension for the citizens of Albuquerque.[27] During this time, Park and Ella began to socialize with others in Albuquerque. They helped the Albuquerque Guard celebrate George Washington's

Putney's Warehouse at First Street and Railroad Avenue (now Central Avenue) near what was then the center of New Town Albuquerque, 1882. This is close to the location of Van Tassel's balloon launch. Cobb Memorial Photography Collection, Center for Southwest Research, University of New Mexico (000–742–0494).

birthday on February 22, 1882, three years before the day was adopted as a federal holiday.[28]

Park Van Tassel owned The Elite tavern, located in the Albuquerque Opera House. Local newspapers routinely let their readers know when new shipments of whiskey were expected at the saloon.[29] As would be the case for the rest of his life, rather than correct people who misspelled his last name, Park simply adopted the spelling "Van Tassell," even in some of his own advertising. Albuquerque could be a rough town. On the moonlit evening of Sunday, May 7, 1882, a great excitement was generated in Albuquerque's Old Town. High from a telephone pole just outside of Van Tassel's saloon was the form of a man hanging from a noose. The coroner was called, and a crowd gathered in the area. But in the end it was revealed that the man was merely an effigy made of straw, either a practical joke or a message to others.

An advertisement for Park Van Tassel's The Elite saloon from the *Albuquerque Journal*, May 25, 1882. Digital images, newspapers.com.

While New Mexico remained only a territory of the United States, on July 4, 1882, the citizens of Albuquerque celebrated Independence Day in a large way with decorations, parades, bands, burro races, sack races, wheel-barrow races with blindfolded contestants, firecrackers, and a baseball game between the Albuquerque Browns and a hand-picked team from the Opera House. In the late morning, the crowd focused its attention on Second Street between Railroad and Gold Avenues in New Town. There, Park Van Tassel's balloon was being inflated. Despite the use of the city's new gas system, the inflation took far longer than expected. However, the citizens were so excited over the prospect of a balloon launch that during the two-day inflation, local gas customers volunteered to go without gas service. An inflation such as this used coal gas, originally designed for commercial use as illuminating gas.[30] The gas offered some mild buoyancy but only about half of the equivalent volume of hydrogen gas.[31] Without an understanding of the mechanics of balloon inflation, the spectators became increasingly restless, believing that there was no way Van Tassel's balloon would ever fly. As it became clear that the balloon was, at best, going to be launched in the late afternoon instead of the morning, the crowd headed for other events in Old Town. The streetcars headed for Old Town were full for the next two hours.

At 5:00 p.m., however, word spread quickly that the balloon would lift off at 6:15. The crowds once again flooded the streetcars, heading back for New

The initial balloon ascension by Park Van Tassel in Albuquerque on July 4, 1882. It was the first flight in the history of New Mexico. Cobb Memorial Photography Collection, Center for Southwest Research, University of New Mexico (000–119–0743).

Town. Van Tassel, who stood 6 feet tall and weighed 225 pounds, did not want to disappoint the crowd, but even after two days of inflation, the balloon remained at only two-thirds its total capacity. At 6:15 he stepped into the newly christened *City of Albuquerque*, only to find that his weight plus the 45 pounds of ballast was well beyond its lifting capacity. When all the ballast was removed, the balloon was coaxed to begin its slow ascension with only Van Tassel on board. A wayward bag of sand thrown overboard struck a spectator, who later filed suit.[32] The balloon floated to the south and continued skyward to the clouds to a maximum height of 14,207 feet above sea level, as measured by Van Tassel using a barometer. At apogee he pulled on the release valve rope to allow gas to escape and initiate his descent. Soon after, the balloon began to descend with increasing speed, and from the fairgrounds, a posse headed out on horseback for the likely landing location, with a wagon to help bring the balloon back to town. In a mild panic to slow the rate of descent, Van Tassel was busy throwing everything he could overboard, including his coat, lunch, and water. He managed to land uninjured in a cornfield near Old Town. By the time the horsemen arrived, they found Van Tassel releasing the remaining gas from the balloon. The balloon was loaded on the wagon, and the successful aviator finally arrived back to the point of takeoff at 9:00 p.m. Upon arrival at The Elite, Van Tassel was greeted by a hero's ovation, with everyone in agreement that the ascension had been a complete success. Van Tassel's flight was not only the first successful balloon launch and piloted flight in Albuquerque history, but it is also credited as the first piloted flight of any kind in New Mexico.[33] Park Van Tassel's adventures in ballooning had just begun.

A unique firsthand accounting of the events of July 4, 1882, was captured in a series of letters between William B. Lyon and his fiancée, Corie Bowman. On June 29, William wrote, "The balloon is here sure enough. I caught a glimpse of the basket one time but have not seen the monster itself."[34] He continued on July 3: "As I write, they are inflating the balloon to go up tomorrow. It is a mammoth affair, but I couldn't care to trust myself in it in this country. I think I will not go to S. F. but stay to see the balloon."[35] And on July 4, he wrote,

> This evening at 6 P. M. we had a most beautiful balloon ascension which was advertised to come off [between] 10 & 12 this morning. I waited all day for the confounded thing and missed thereby a dinner at Mr. F. and an engagement to go with them to the Old Town to see the races etc.
>
> There was some trouble about the gas which could not be supplied in sufficient quantity. That was the alleged reason though it was generally believed that it was a concerted arrangement to keep the crowd away from the Old Town for the benefit of the saloon here. But finally everything was arranged and the renowned Prof. Van Tassel, who ordinarily is a whiskey slinger in one of the numerous musical palaces under my window, stepped in the basket and after one false start, cut the rope that held him down, and the immense dome softly and easily mounted into the air. There was a gentle current of air blowing to the S. E. and the balloon at first took that direction, rising more rapidly as the Prof. emptied a bag of ballast over the heads of the crowd. Higher and higher it went, the Prof. industriously waving the flag of his country

Spectators at the 1882 balloon ascension follow the balloon on its voyage through the sky. Unfortunately, the balloon itself is not seen in the photo. Cobb Memorial Photography Collection, Center for Southwest Research, University of New Mexico (000–119–0744a).

Newspaper advertisements for Van Tassel's balloon launch, such as this one from the *Albuquerque Morning Journal* on July 2, 1882, ran for a week prior to the event. Digital images, newspapers.com.

and scattering advertisements. I wonder if there ever was a balloon or balloonist that went up without waving the conventional flag.

When about goodness knows how high, the balloon entered into a current of air going N. E. and of course went along, seeming to pass almost directly over the Old Town and towards the river. There was something grand, majestic and awe-inspiring in the sight, and I enjoyed a sensation rarely experienced in this country where awe-inspiring visions are not an everyday occurrence.

I have just heard, 10 P.M., that the Prof is back, but have heard nothing more. There is a brass band playing and a big bon fire burning in front of his saloon.[36]

After the balloon events left their mark, on July 5 he wrote, "I saw the balloonist a few minutes ago, but heard no particulars of his ride." In the top margin he wrote, "I couldn't tear myself away from the balloon and so missed the pleasure of sitting in the broiling sun and seeing the noble game of base ball butchered as I hear it was."[37] Albuquerque was now as captivated with the majesty of ballooning as was its new hero, Park Van Tassel.

# 2. ALBUQUERQUE

AFTER HIS INITIAL success at Albuquerque, Park Van Tassel was put in touch with several prominent citizens of Las Vegas, New Mexico, eager to host a similar ascension at that location. Van Tassel and a gentleman named H. Umbrea traveled to Las Vegas and were met with great enthusiasm at the Plaza Hotel for a proposed launch in mid-August.[1] The *City of Albuquerque* was transported to Las Vegas on August 2, 1882, by train. Considerable time and effort went into distributing marketing posters all over town, helping to generate interest.[2] However, locals wondered why the balloon wasn't named *City of Las Vegas* instead of *City of Albuquerque*.[3]

Given that this was the Old West, anything could happen at any time. On the afternoon of August 4, a noted horseman by the name of Kennedy rode on horseback into The Elite saloon in Albuquerque. This was apparently one of Kennedy's favorite pastimes, as he had succeeded in doing it a few times previously without being apprehended. With Park away in Las Vegas, the replacement barkeep, Jack Stuner, ordered Kennedy and his horse to leave the saloon immediately. Seeing no effect, Stuner seized the reins and pulled the horse out of the saloon, closing the doors. Kennedy immediately turned the horse around and used it to break the doors open, quickly arriving at the rear of the saloon, unwilling to budge. With this second intrusion, Stuner found his way to a revolver and fired three shots at Kennedy in rapid succession. The first missed entirely, the second hit Kennedy in his left side, and the third grazed the head of a bystander sitting near the door of a store opposite the saloon. Those who saw the altercation believed that Stuner was justified in his actions. With non-life-threatening injuries, Kennedy swore vengeance on Stuner.[4]

Upon learning of the altercation, Park returned to Albuquerque on

August 7.[5] However, by August 9 Park and Ella had returned to Las Vegas, staying at the St. Nicholas Hotel.[6] The situation calmed, and on August 13 it was announced that Park had hired the New Mexican Brass Band to play at his balloon ascension, now scheduled for August 15.[7] Filling of the balloon began on August 14 at 9:30 a.m., but all the available gas in Las Vegas was used up by the time the balloon was half-filled with 16,000 cubic feet of gas. The valves were closed until more gas could be manufactured. Sandbags and ropes were used to secure the balloon. However, increasing afternoon winds kept the balloon tossing about. At 3:00 p.m., a dark thunderstorm loomed on the horizon, a product of the regular monsoon season in the Southwest. Park and others began to watch the clouds closely. Within an hour, the afternoon breeze had strengthened to a gale due to the nearby storm. The balloon moorings were insufficient, and soon the *City of Albuquerque* set itself loose, bounding along the ground until being caught by fencing on the east side of the field. The fence punched large holes that kept the balloon from bouncing all the way to Texas but unfortunately allowed all the gas to escape.[8] Repairs commenced immediately. Only two days later, on August 16, the balloon was once again ready for flight. However, the city's high altitude, roughly 6,500 feet above sea level, made it difficult to attain any buoyancy at all. Reporters noted, "The balloon is full of gas, and she look like she ought to move off majestically, but she don't."[9] Another issue may have been the type of coal gas used for inflation. (Later balloonists used hydrogen generated on-site by adding iron filings to sulfuric acid.)[10] One newspaper noted that "ordinary illuminating gas is too nearly the same weight as our atmosphere to be a perfectly reliable medium for balloon ascensions."[11] Van Tassel made several attempts to launch but with no avail, much to the disappointment of the throngs of spectators.[12] Another attempt was made on the morning of August 17. Unwilling to disappoint the crowd, Park conned a man who weighed less to serve as the aeronaut and prepared him for the flight. When the balloon was released from its mooring, it began to rise, but the new pilot failed to throw sandbags over the side to increase the vertical rate of climb. Instead of continuing on its grand ascension, it rather quickly returned to Earth. Park and the pilot had a heated exchange, leading several other men to become engaged in the dispute.[13] In the ensuing ruckus, Van Tassel lost his treasured barometer and his gun, which were last seen in the basket, but he managed to collect $500 in donations from Las Vegas patrons and received an invitation to conduct balloon ascensions at an exposition in Denver. Van Tassel returned to Albuquerque without further attempts in Las Vegas.

On the morning of Sunday, September 10, 1882, Park was involved in another unfortunate altercation in Albuquerque. He and two others, including Lou Blonger,[14] were out late in a portion of town of ill repute near the intersection of Fourth Street and Railroad Avenue. The area was known for its opium dens and "houses which sell virtue by retail." One of the houses was operated by a woman associated with Blonger,[15] and Van Tassel and the woman began to talk. During the conversation, Van Tassel made a remark that so angered Blonger that he struck Van Tassel with his fist and then hit him over the head with a .45 revolver. Blonger cocked the gun, pointed it at Van Tassel, exclaimed, "You s—of a b—, you can't talk to my woman in that way," and then threw the gun at Van Tassel. Van Tassel was taken to a doctor to recover from his wounds, while on September 12 a warrant was issued for Blonger's arrest for assault with intent to kill. He was arrested and held on $3,500 bail pending a court case in October.[16] The results of the court case remain unknown.

Yet again, Van Tassel prepared for a balloon ascension in Albuquerque, as a part of the Second Annual New Mexico Territorial Fair, which began on September 18, 1882, and continued for roughly a week.[17] Calm air greeted Van Tassel on the morning of September 20, and the balloon was inflated at the corner of Third Street and Gold Avenue. The inflation took more than one day to complete, ending near noon on September 21. Once it was filled, approximately one hundred men and boys pulled the balloon by rope to the city exposition grounds, where it was to be launched. However, during the transfer, the main rope holding the balloon disconnected, likely due to someone's carelessness. Those closest to the basket jumped on to keep the balloon fixed to the ground. Despite their efforts, the *City of Albuquerque* took to the sky, unpiloted. With very calm air aloft, the balloon reached apogee almost directly above the exposition grounds, roughly 1 mile high. Everyone at the exposition grounds was left wondering how and where the balloon would descend on its own. The balloon eventually burst as the gas inside it continued to expand, with no means of pressure relief, leading to its rapid descent. The partially filled balloon acted like a large parachute, floating off to a landing

For his second ascension, Van Tassel continued with advance advertising, such as this one from the *Albuquerque Journal* from September 20, 1882. Digital images, newspapers.com.

about a quarter of a mile north of the point of launch. It was brought back to the exposition grounds in a wagon. Van Tassel felt terrible about these events, and given all the recent difficulties in Las Vegas and Albuquerque, he was left wondering if he should continue in ballooning at all.[18] There was word that he would try again on September 23, but it remains unknown if he had any success.[19] Van Tassel and Frank Norris set off for San Francisco to obtain a new balloon to replace the now destroyed *City of Albuquerque*. They intended to return from San Francisco with a balloon christened *El Montezuma* and fly it at Chihuahua, Mexico.[20] However, there are no known reports of balloon flights by Van Tassel in Mexico.

In early October, Van Tassel returned to Albuquerque. He continued running The Elite saloon in the Albuquerque Opera House, which had opened as the city's first theater on June 13, 1882. For a time in October 1882, Park, Sam Truer, and Charley Robinson were on the bill as local talent performing on its stage.[21] But it seems Van Tassel backed out of this opportunity at the last moment. Growing weary of Albuquerque and perhaps out of growing discontent in his marriage with Ella, in November Van Tassel sold The Elite to Harry Post, a well-known Albuquerque resident and bartender.[22] Ella had spent several weeks in October visiting her parents in Stockton, and she returned to Albuquerque on November 7, 1882.[23] She left Albuquerque for San Francisco via the Newhall Pass near Los Angeles in late January 1883, apparently without Park. Their marriage was strained.[24] Van Tassel had difficulty paying his bills, and criticism came from all directions. A Las Vegas newspaper noted, "If Las Vegans had considered this sufficient cause to thump him, he would now be sleeping where balloons and flying machines do not trouble the wicked."[25] The *Las Cruces Sun News* commented, "Park Van Tassell, the Albuquerque aeronaut, has disappeared, owing over $1000. Gone up in a balloon."[26] John Koogle of the *Las Vegas Daily Gazette* noted on February 13, 1883, "PROF. PARK VAN TASSEL has at last disappeared. He has skipped to parts unknown. He has collapsed his business, but he seems to have been filled with better sailing gas than his balloon was, at this city, last summer. Park is certainly a magnificent fraud."[27] The concerns continued to resonate all the way into spring 1883, when a reporter in Las Vegas noted, "The citizens of that city would do well to buy Park a balloon that would go to the sun. He would be appreciated then."[28] In early February 1883, Park found himself in an altercation with a Mexican, a fight that ended with Park "thumping" the Mexican over the head.[29] Despite being lauded as the first aviator in New Mexico's history, Van Tassel now found himself entirely unwelcome. He moved to Peach Springs, a very small town on the Atchison, Topeka & Santa Fe Railway in northwestern Arizona, feeling remorse about the way newspapers treated him in Albuquerque.[30] From there, he wrote to the editor of the *Albuquerque Journal*, stating for the record that he did not owe the large sums that were implied and that small bills still owing would be paid as soon as possible. The journal editor responded that "Van is going into business out there and if his friends here are in luck he will make money and pay them what he owes them."[31] Sadly, in just one year after his greatest ballooning success, Van Tassel had lost his second wife, his first balloon, his saloon, and his connection with Albuquerque. Another change of scenery was needed.

## 3. TOURING THE WEST

PARK DID NOT stay in Peach Springs for long. The Salt Lake Athlete Association contracted Van Tassel to make a balloon launch at Salt Lake City for Independence Day festivities at Washington Square. He moved on to Los Angeles[1] and then briefly to San Francisco, staying at the Baldwin Hotel on March 15, 1883, perhaps to pick up supplies.[2] His new *City of Albuquerque* was shipped to Salt Lake City and rechristened the *City of Salt Lake*. Many Utahans were excited by the opportunity to witness a balloon ascension in person, something they had only read about in the newspapers. A reporter from Montana made arrangements to travel all the way to Salt Lake for the opportunity to fly in the balloon with Van Tassel.[3] The balloon arrived via train on June 13, 1883, while the community was already preparing in earnest for Independence Day (which also included bicycle and footraces and a baseball game between the Ogden and Salt Lake clubs).[4] He made preparations on the balloon at Pitts' Pleasure Gardens in various states of inflation and deflation.[5] On Friday June 23, with the balloon in a state of inflation, several men were seen meddling with the balloon while Van Tassel was away. The balloon broke loose from its moorings, and the ensuing movements of the balloon carried some of the men into the air as they clung to the ropes. But eventually the balloon was secured.[6] On July 4, officials told crowds to avoid the area near Second East and Second South Streets, where the balloon was to be filled. Citizens were also kindly reminded to refrain "from burning fireworks in close proximity to the balloon."[7] The area was carefully guarded by local police to ensure safety. Large crowds gathered around the balloon as it was inflated in the afternoon. Between 2:00 and 3:00 p.m., the filled balloon was taken to Washington Square. Newspaper reports indicated that George A. Meears's popular monkey, named Jack, would accompany Van Tassel as his first passenger. After the release, the balloon rose and drifted slightly to the east in the direction of Fort Douglas. It then encountered a different current and floated to the northeast, finally coming to a nice landing in Red Butte Canyon. While the balloon was nearing Fort Douglas, the barometer indicated a relative altitude of 15,700 feet above sea level, high enough to warrant concern over hypoxia, but perhaps Van Tassel was unaware of the risk. The descent was made rapidly to avoid going over the Wasatch Range.[8] This flight was hailed as the first gas balloon ascension in Utah's history.[9] A man named O. P. Arnold raced after the balloon on his horse and was the first to reach Van Tassel after his landing, which had already startled a group of picnickers nearby.[10] On July 11, the *Deseret News* published a letter to the editor by Van Tassel:[11]

> *Editor Deseret News:*
> Please permit me through your columns to thank the many citizens who kindly aided me during the preparation for the balloon ascension. To Mr. Geo. A. Meears I am especially indebted, as without his aid I could not have kept my contract with the public.
> I have been solicited to make an ascension on the 24th inst., and should take pleasure in doing so, if I can be assured of liberal encouragement, otherwise I must accept other propositions, as my late ascension paid me very little indeed.
> Respectfully,
> Prof. Van Tassel, Aeronaut
> Salt Lake City, July 7, 1883.

Arrangements were made for Van Tassel's next balloon ascension, on Pioneer's Day, July 24, 1883, also at Washington Square. The *Salt Lake Herald* admonished those Utahans who had watched the July 4 flight without paying the fair entry fee, encouraging them to pay for this next event.[12] The newspaper also noted that a Mrs. Fannie Hoyt was going to accompany Van Tassel on this flight.[13] Some members of the public complained in the paper that it was improper for a man to take another man's wife for a balloon ride.[14] Not to be outdone by Salt Lake City, the city of Ogden made hasty arrangements for Van Tassel to perform an ascension there, also on July 24.[15] However,

H. J. Stone sued Van Tassel to recover $182, which he claimed was owed to him for some unknown reason, and the case was to be heard before a Justice Home on the morning of July 25.

Meanwhile, Van Tassel continued his arrangements for the launch. When the day arrived, a large audience gathered at Washington Square. While many expected Hoyt to back out at the last minute, she persevered. Together Van Tassel and Hoyt launched skyward. The balloon floated to the southeast, eventually to a safe landing in Mill Creek Ward, south of Parley's Canyon.[16] This flight was so perfect that it motivated Van Tassel to consider longer cross-country flights. He noted, "One of the longest trips I ever made . . . I started at Salt Lake City and crossed the Wasatch mountains, a distance of 143 miles. I reached an altitude over 15,000 feet above the level of the sea and it was a wonderful trip, taking six hours and a half to make it. An hour of this time was spent hanging over the Great Salt Lake in a calm. A young lady accompanied me and she displayed nerve and heroism."[17] Later, in 1884, the *New York Times* reported that the memorable flight had had a duration of six hours and thirty-two minutes.[18] On July 29, 1883, having had much success, Van Tassel left Salt Lake City on the early train bound for San Francisco, arriving at the Baldwin Hotel on August 3.[19] He spent the remainder of August planning his next tour.

In September 1883, Van Tassel traveled to Portland, Oregon. An ascension was made on September 5, 1883, with a reporter from the *New Northwest* as a passenger. The flight was a complete success except that Park and the reporter were forced to dump every possible type of ballast during their descent, including their drinking water. However, the people of Portland were delighted; this was reportedly the first balloon ascension in Portland, possibly the first in Oregon.[20] Park made several more ascensions in Oregon, including a flight in late September from Portland, with his balloon flying over a forest fire. He made yet another successful ascension from Portland on the afternoon of November 5, 1883, in front of an "immense crowd" at the Oregon State Fair.[21] Traveling about 5 miles in fifty minutes, he reached a maximum altitude of 9,000 feet, ending with a perfect landing near the Columbia River after flying over the Willamette River.[22] With this string of very successful and well-publicized launches, things were finally starting to click for Van Tassel.

# 4. WORLD'S FAIR

SINCE THE TIME of his departure from Albuquerque, Park and Ella were largely out of contact yet still married. In January 1884, Van Tassel returned to San Francisco with the *City of Salt Lake*.[1] A planned ascension for Sunday, January 27, was postponed by a week due to weather.[2] Newspapers reported that Van Tassel planned to fly from San Francisco to the east and over the Sierra Nevada. But it is unlikely that he ever made a flight in January 1884, as it was quite a rainy and cold time. In fact, one of San Francisco's rare snowstorms occurred on February 7, 1884, when two inches fell in the city. The *Las Vegas Daily Gazette* in New Mexico still tracked Van Tassel's doings and noted, "Park Van Tassell, the busted balloonist, and Harry Pratt, a former hotel 'worker,' both well known in New Mexico, are living off the good citizens of San Francisco."[3] An ascension was attempted on Sunday, February 17, at Recreation Park, with no clear documentation of success.[4]

Van Tassel traveled to Ella's hometown of Stockton and made a successful ascension on Saturday, April 19, 1884, but for unknown reasons managed to rise to only 1,000 feet before landing several miles to the east of town. After landing, Van Tassel lost control of the mooring, and the unmanned balloon continued on without him, coming to rest 16 miles from town.[5] Stockton never was all that forgiving. However, through these travels and ascensions with varying degrees of success, Van Tassel's exploits were becoming well-known in the West.

It remains unclear if he tried to patch up his marriage while staying in Stockton, and he did not stay long in the area. In May 1884, Van Tassel traveled to Los Angeles, and in early June it was announced that he would make an ascension on Saturday, June 7. Despite the growing size of Los Angeles, balloon flights were still rather uncommon there, and large crowds were expected.[6] On June 15, 1884, it was announced that Van Tassel would make another ascension as a part of a bicycle race.[7] However, instead of making this flight, Van Tassel hopped on a train for San Francisco via Mojave and Tehachapi, arriving on June 16.[8] He immediately started building a new, larger balloon, with work extending throughout the fall of 1884. The resulting silk balloon named *Eclipse*, measuring 58 feet in diameter and 110 feet high, was built under the direction of Van Tassel and F. F. Martin at the Sutter Street Railroad Company. The *Eclipse* was completed in November 1884, with eight seamstresses sewing it together over a period of ten days.[9] Billed as the largest balloon on the West Coast or in the United States, depending on the newspaper, the *Eclipse* held 65,000 to 85,000 cubic feet gas, sufficient to carry an estimated 2,800 pounds aloft.[10] The *Eclipse* was built especially with the New Orleans World's Fair in mind.[11] Van Tassel now dreamed of tremendously long cross-country flights. Whereas in the past he had voiced grandiose plans to fly over the Sierra Nevada, his new desire to fly from San Francisco all the way to New Orleans made those earlier dreams appear rather tame. Van Tassel also sought to have couples be married in the balloon basket in flight, "provided a priest or Justice of the Peace can be found who will be willing to risk his life on such a trip."[12] Descriptions of the *Eclipse* were carried nationally in the *New York Times*, *Washington Post*, and other newspapers.

The *Eclipse* was test flown at Central Park,[13] a baseball yard in San Francisco, on November 30, 1884. San Francisco had been a center of ballooning in the West for two decades, with heightened interest beginning in 1874. However, on October 5, 1879, a tragic balloon accident at Woodward's Gardens resulted in the deaths of two balloonists: a Professor Colgrove and Charles H. Williams. Van Tassel's test flight in 1884 was the first well-publicized launch since that tragedy and was considered a rebirth of ballooning for the city. Spectators turned out to watch balloon launches with a morbid curiosity—perhaps they might witness a disaster. Newspapers noted that at "about noon the nucleus was formed of an immense crowd that desired to see the bag soar aloft and explode and murder some of its passengers."[14]

As preparations were being made for launch on November 30, Van Tassel noted that the balloon was only about three-quarters inflated owing to some error with the gas supply. This lack of lifting capacity meant that only two passengers could go up with him rather than the expected three. Those who wanted to fly had been invited to fill out cards in advance; Van Tassel would select the lucky passengers. He reviewed these cards, eliminating kids who simply looked forward to getting away from their parents for a short time. After the review, he announced that E. K. Dunlap would make the trip, as he was a government employee interested in balloons. Van Tassel looked to others in the crowd to see who else might join them. Among the applicants was a heavyset woman who weighed more than Van Tassel could afford. A newspaper recounted the banter:

> "You can't go," said Van Tassell.
> "I will," was the reply.
> "You can't, you weigh too much. Take her away somebody." And she subsided.
> "Can I go?" asked a reporter.
> "How much do you weigh?"
> "Only 140 pounds."
> "Too heavy; can't take you."
> "Can I go?" said Eugene Hahn.
> "What weight?
> "About 104."
> "All right, jump in. Now, then, gentlemen, let her up slowly. Now then all ready; let go, let go."[15]

Another newspaper noted, "A round, rosy, plump, pretty young woman was among the disappointed candidates for a peep into heaven, she having had the promise of a front seat from the earliest inception of the 'Eclipse.' When firmly informed that it was impossible for her to go she shed a few pearly tears, looked mad enough to bite a nail in two, and then suffered herself to be led away by her young man, who was evidently as highly elated as she was disconsolate."[16]

At 3:00 p.m. the ropes were released, and slowly they rose, at first drifting toward the southwest. Given the typical westerly afternoon breezes, this was very atypical and immediately caused concern that the balloon would head out to the Pacific Ocean. At a height of about 2,500 feet, Van Tassel secured an opposing current, taking the balloon back over the park and from there over San Francisco Bay toward Black Point and Alcatraz. After Park dumped some sandbags over the Bay, the *Eclipse* rose and changed course again, heading toward Mount Tamalpais. By this time, most in San Francisco had lost sight of the balloon as it floated high and away, reaching its apex of 9,400 feet.[17] At 5:00 p.m., however, arriving ferry passengers from Sausalito stated that the balloon had been seen descending in the hills behind their town. This was soon contradicted by ferry passengers from Tiburon, who stated that the balloon had landed in Raccoon Strait in San Francisco Bay and that the aeronauts were being rescued. There was a great deal of confusion.

In reality, after hovering near Tamalpais, the *Eclipse* floated toward Angel Island and Alcatraz and over Point Tiburon. There it remained rather motionless for quite some time. The balloon slowly began to deflate and descend into the cold waters of Raccoon Strait. Without being able to alter their course, Van Tassel and Dunlap stripped down to their undergarments and prepared for a swim, while Hahn chose instead to climb the balloon rigging. The balloon eventually impacted the water and was dragged by a light wind for about 500 yards across the Bay before all three were rescued by small boats that had put out from Sausalito. Captain Charles Brown, with his tugboat *Annie Hart*, made considerable haste to provide a rescue. He "opened the furnace doors, threw in a box of hams, a paper of matches and several cords of pitch pine, and in short order the tug was speeding toward the wrecked balloonists."[18] In the course of events, Van Tassel lost most of his clothing; Dunlap lost most of his clothing, a gold watch, and other jewelry; and Hahn lost his coat. The rescued aviators were taken to Angel Island, where soldiers provided them with dry clothes. The aeronauts and the waterlogged but flight-tested *Eclipse* returned to San Francisco by tugboat in the dark.[19] News of these exploits and Van Tassel's exceptionally large balloon spread across America,[20] through newspapers and scientific journals such as *Nature*,[21] even around the globe to India.[22]

On January 1, 1885, Van Tassel was scheduled to make an ascension in San Jose,[23] but the flight was postponed to January 8, when Van Tassel made a successful ascension, taking off at 8:15 a.m. with passengers R. B. Reedy and A. E. Blanchard. They landed without issue in a wheat field near South Fremont in Alameda County, 11 miles north of their point of takeoff. They returned as a group to San Jose at 7:00 p.m.[24] After becoming romantically interested in Clara Coykendall of San Jose during this time, in early March 1885, Park finally provided Ella with a divorce decree at Stockton.[25] He continued with his ballooning, typically not charging any admission to event attendees but charging a fee to event organizers and asking the public for donations to help offset costs.

At this time the World's Industrial and Cotton Centennial Exposition (1884–1885) was being held at Audubon Park in New Orleans. Management arranged for Van Tassel to bring the *Eclipse* to New Orleans for demonstrations at the exposition. To help pay for this journey, Van Tassel wrote to cities and towns along the way to see if other exhibitions would be possible. One letter was written to a Major White, superintendent of the gasworks in Houston, to determine if it would be possible to obtain 50,000 cubic feet of coal gas for a balloon ascension there.[26] But there is no record of balloon flights along the way, so it is assumed that he went directly to New Orleans.

On March 14, 1885, a newspaper announced that Van Tassel's large balloon would soon be making captive ascensions at the New Orleans fair.[27] This was further advertised on March 18: "No instance has ever occurred in the South of more absorbing, thrilling interest, than the aerial journal to be taken by Prof. Van Tassell and companions on Thursday afternoon, 3:33 o'clock, from Exposition Grounds."[28] At the exposition grounds, a high boarded enclosure was prepared near the St. Charles Avenue entrance for preparation of the balloon. On Wednesday, March 18, the top of the balloon could be seen "rising like the convexity of an enormous yellow pumpkin" above the fencing. Park was described as a "hale, athletic, large-sized and pleasant-faced man."[29]

Spectators were advised to arrive early for the ascension at 3:30 p.m. on March 19. However, when they began to arrive, the balloon was still only partially inflated. According to the gas meter, 65,000 cubic feet of gas had been put into the balloon, but somehow the balloon was just slightly more than half-full, probably owing perhaps to an issue with the gas meter. This generated concern, and the gas supply was shut off during the discussion. While Van Tassel had intended to take several members of the press along for the ride, with the balloon half-filled, he resorted to flying solo. The fencing around the balloon enclosure was knocked down, and the balloon with all its netting and its large circular basket, 8 feet in diameter and 5 feet deep, stood at the ready. According to a reporter, inside the basket were, "a bottle or two of wine, a bottle of water, a number of printed bills advertising Minnesota spring wheat, and an overcoat."[30] Van Tassel climbed aboard armed with a knife in his hand and a small barometer in his breast pocket.

At 5:00 p.m., only one hour and thirty minutes behind schedule, the balloon was released from its moorings and began its ascent, drifting to the east, away from the setting sun, in a good westerly breeze. At about 1,000 feet it leveled off, continuing to the east. The crowd that had gathered cheered in excitement and watched as the balloon sailed off, becoming the size of a dot in the sky. Meanwhile, Van Tassel scattered the Minnesota wheat advertisements overboard and they sailed to Earth.

Park Van Tassel had intended to land near plantations that lined the Mississippi River. Instead, he had quite a harrowing experience. After about fifty minutes of flight, and reaching a maximum height of about 4,000 feet, the balloon began a rapid descent. Despite efforts to manage the descent properly with ballast, the balloon and its cargo landed "very rapidly" in a swamp on the west side of the Mississippi near Algiers.[31] Upon impact, Park opened the valve to release the remaining gas, but the strong wind made it impossible to drop his anchor to slow his rate of progress. He pulled the collapsing cord, which tore the top of the balloon open and immediately let all remaining gas escape. But with Park still stuck in the swamp, the wind continued to blow the decaying balloon across the Mississippi River. It came to rest at a plantation on the other side. Park dragged himself out of the swamp and swam across the river in search of the balloon, finding it already "attacked by the natives, the netting cut to pieces and all the property divided out and confiscated."[32] He refused an offer to hire a horse for $10 for just a few miles and finally recovered his property, hired a wagon, and brought the remains of the *Eclipse* back to New Orleans, where he arrived at about 10:30 p.m.

Van Tassel's balloon may have been wrecked, but the flight caused considerable notoriety. His ascension at the fair made national news,[33] with many considering it to be the "event of the day."[34] On the return journey to the West Coast by train, Van Tassel passed through Galveston, Texas, staying at the Tremont Hotel on March 27.[35] Continuing on, he passed through Mojave, California, on March 30, arriving back in San Francisco on March 31.[36]

Only two days later, on April 2, 1885, Park Van Tassel (age thirty-one) married Clara A. Coykendall (age twenty-four)[37] at San Jose.[38] Clara came from a prominent local family; her father was a partner in the firm Andrews & Coykendall, a popular local importer of the best ham, cured beef, and lard. Hoping for more for their popular socialite daughter, both of Clara's parents were reported to be "violently opposed" to the marriage. Park was a previously divorced man without much savings and with what they viewed as a crazy profession. They did not attend the ceremony.[39] Undeterred, Van Tassel continued with all the arrangements, including a special enclosed cab from the Auzerais House to a Presbyterian church. There they were married by the Reverend Minton in a private ceremony with only two witnesses present.[40]

Continuing with the wedding theme, Margey Dabney, a young aerobatic performer, and his fiancée, Kate Myers, were married in Van Tassel's balloon over Stevens' Park in Oakland on Saturday, May 30, 1885. Some reports suggest that once the vows were said, the balloon rose above the park, with the married couple tossing chunks of cake over the side.[41] However, a report in the *San Francisco Examiner* relayed quite a different story. It seems that just before Margey Dabney stepped into the balloon, his elder brother Lee stepped in front of him in protest of the marriage, backed up by both their parents. A man named Stevens, the owner of Stevens' Park, asked Lee to step aside, and when he did not, Stevens hit Lee. A free-for-all ensued, with a dozen participants combating about the balloon. Police officers finally restored peace, and it was resolved that Margey and his fiancée would go up in the balloon but would not be married aloft, as the minister had fled the scene. By the time Margey, Kate, and Park all were established in the basket, a lot of gas had escaped, so the balloon could carry only one person. So Park Van Tassel made the flight on his own.[42] In just a short time, Van Tassel had toured Utah and Oregon, provided demonstrations at San Francisco, and gained national attention with his large *Eclipse* at New Orleans. Once again he was married. His life was on the rise.

# 5. SAN FRANCISCO

ON JULY 22, 1885, Van Tassel christened a new balloon, the *City of London*, at Central Park.[1] The large balloon could hold 60,000 cubic feet of gas. A test flight was arranged for July 26 at the park.[2] The concept was for Van Tassel to launch in the *City of London* with Clara and a reporter. However, when the time came for the launch, Van Tassel determined that the atmosphere was "very heavy,"[3] so he launched unaccompanied in the basket due to the lack of buoyancy. After the launch at 3:30 p.m., the balloon took a southeasterly course into the thick marine layer at 100 feet above ground level. Park unfurled an American flag from the basket before disappearing from view. Climbing steadily up through the clouds, and clearing them at 3,000 feet, he was unable to see any landmarks through a cloud break other than a ferry crossing the Bay to Oakland. Soaring over the Bay, he topped out at 7,000 feet and then cruised to a nice landing at Walnut Creek at approximately 5:34 p.m.[4]

On Sunday, September 6, 1885, Van Tassel was scheduled to make another ascension in the *City of London*, from Agricultural Park in Sacramento for the opening of the California State Fair. The inflation was to commence thirty-six hours before the ascension to make sure the balloon would be ready in time. To attract additional attention, Van Tassel donated a $100 prize to the winner of a baseball game between the Alta and Knickerbocker clubs to be on the same field later that afternoon. The ascension was perfect, and the balloon rose to 9,750 feet, remaining in the air for one hour, thirty minutes, coming to a landing on the Norris property, 4 miles west of Arden-Arcade, California. The flight was observed by a very large crowd of spectators at the park, as well as residents of Sacramento and the general vicinity. The weather was also perfect, with only light winds aloft, and the balloon sat over Yolo County and

Sacramento for much of the duration of the flight. Park's skills as a balloonist were solidifying.[5]

On September 20, 1885, Woodward's Gardens in San Francisco arranged for a benefit for F. F. Martin, the well-known area aeronaut and likely maker of Van Tassel's first balloon, *City of Albuquerque*, as well as the *Eclipse*. The day prior, Martin had been given a special gold medal as a token of appreciation by the employees of W. W. Montague & Co., a hardware store specializing in iron and brass products, where he worked as a foreman. The medal featured his name on one side and a depiction of the Golden Gate, with Martin's balloon flying above it on the other side.[6] The benefit included a balloon race between Van Tassel in the *City of London* and James H. Whiteside in the *Eclipse*, now repaired after its New Orleans ordeal, for a purse of $200 to the aeronaut with greatest distance from the launch point. Eight thousand spectators came to witness the dual balloon ascension, which was said to be "a graceful sight." The *Eclipse* drifted southward while the *City of London* drifted southeast. The *Eclipse* was a larger balloon, and Whiteside had invited Charles Nye to be a passenger during the trip. After the launch, the *Eclipse* raced to an altitude of 8,700 feet while the *City of London* stabilized at 6,000 feet. Whiteside had lost more gas from his bag than expected, and despite making distance, he and Nye soon found themselves in a descent and eventually floating at just 200 feet over the Alvarado marshes of the Bay. They threw ballast overboard to avoid a watery landing. When this barely worked, they threw over everything, including lunch baskets, bottles of soda water, and anchor rope. Despite the effort, the balloon continued to slowly descend, perhaps a result of a temperature inversion, a leak, or a gas valve that had not been seated properly. Soon enough, the pair was looking to jump before impact. They were on the edge of the basket, prepared to do so, when all of a sudden the balloon jerked violently, expelling both passengers without warning as it impacted the marsh. Whiteside fell about 6 feet and hit the ground hard, breaking his leg just above the ankle. Nye tumbled and escaped merely with bruises. Whiteside had clung to the collapsing cord and pulled it in time to rip the balloon wide open, but it still managed to hop and skip for a mile before coming to rest within 3 miles of Alvarado. Nye went for help and returned with a pair of hunters, who built a makeshift chair out of their gun barrels to carry the injured Whiteside to a nearby ranch.

Meanwhile, Van Tassel found a suitable breeze at a lower altitude than Whiteside and made good distance. Along the way, he dropped advertising cards for a Sacramento sewing machine company. One side of the card gave information about the company; the other side included a strongly worded message: "Dropped from balloon City of London—September 6, 1885— Among the clouds this little messenger . . . has been nearer the source of inspiration than most of you, and the words should be heeded." However, as the sun began to lower in the sky, Van Tassel's balloon also lost its buoyancy. About halfway across the Bay, he too began to throw everything from his basket. Despite the effort, the balloon continued to descend. Van Tassel yet again stripped to his underwear and climbed onto the edge of the basket. And yet again the balloon impacted the water, proceeded to dunk Van Tassel, and continued jumping and sailing along on the water, carrying Van Tassel along for the ride. This lasted for approximately ten minutes, until the balloon reached the mudflats on the eastern shore. "The basket ploughed its way at the tail of the balloon, leaving a trail as though a steamer had cruised inland,"[7] wrote a reporter. Van Tassel and the balloon finally came to rest at the Pacific Salt Company near Mount Eden. He managed to coax some Chinese workers to grab the anchor line to bring everything to a standstill. While they held onto the balloon, Van Tassel went back into the mud to retrieve his missing shoes. Van Tassel returned home with badly cut feet and hands, a cold, and the knowledge that he had lost the race. For all his pain and suffering, Whiteside had beaten Van Tassel for the longest flight by roughly 7 miles.[8]

In early 1886 Van Tassel made an ascension in another new balloon, *Fredricksburg*, one of the largest balloons ever flown in the Bay Area. The initial flight was scheduled for Telegraph Hill on January 10, 1886.[9] Inflation began on schedule on Friday afternoon, January 9, and continued through to Saturday afternoon. Large crowds filled an auditorium nearby and eight thousand more packed the hill, with another ten thousand in the general area. But cold temperatures and a lack of sunshine made it impossible to get the required buoyancy for lift. The gas condensed as fast as inflation progressed, with no warmth to expand it.[10] Duncan C. Ross, the manager/advertiser of the exhibition, was incensed when it became clear that there would be no launch and did his best to understand why. They would try again on January 11.[11]

On January 11, the balloon was filled by noon, and Van Tassel lifted off at

2:40 p.m. The atmospheric density "considerably reduced the balloon's lifting power," and Van Tassel gave his position as aeronaut to a lighter-weight amateur pilot, W. E. Blanchard (probably of no relation to the famous French aeronaut Jean-Pierre Blanchard). Blanchard had made only two prior ascensions under the instruction of experts. Van Tassel provided considerable instruction before liftoff. Thousands of spectators cheered when the balloon was finally cut loose. Blanchard piloted it solo to an altitude of 2,000 feet before finding a current, first toward the southwest and then east over Hunter's Point. Ballast was dumped, and the balloon again drifted southwest, making a landing near San Bruno.[12]

Van Tassel returned to Telegraph Hill for a successful flight on Sunday, January 31, 1886, this time accompanied by a young woman named Frankie Eceelle.[13] Two weeks later, he again rose from San Francisco from a point near the Haight Street cable car terminus. This time another young woman, seventeen-year-old Ollie Wilson, was his passenger, and they carried an additional 150 pounds of ballast. Directly after launch, a current carried the balloon west toward the Pacific Ocean. Van Tassel immediately released 50 pounds of ballast (a risky strategy, as this meant there would be hardly any ballast remaining to help control the final descent) and climbed to 3,400 feet, but there was no current headed in the opposite direction. Instead of risking a landing at sea, he opened the release valve on the balloon and landed at Golden Gate Park, only about 500 to 600 yards from the starting point. It was a short but phenomenal flight given the lack of total distance made.[14] Later that same day, Van Tassel launched in the *City of London* at 3:35 p.m. from Telegraph Hill, and the balloon drifted to the east out over the Bay. Van Tassel "amused the spectators by standing on the edge of the basket and performing hazardous antics."[15] After ascending to approximately 2,000 feet, the balloon began descending over Goat Island to a mere 500 feet over the Bay. Van Tassel tossed ballast overboard. The balloon rose again but then began another descent, and this process repeated several times. He passed over an Oakland-bound ferry and held a conversation with its passengers, who suggested he land near the boat to make an easier rescue. But with 50 pounds of ballast remaining, he decided to continue on. Nearing the East Bay, air currents began to reverse his course back toward San Francisco. As he frantically tossed the remaining ballast over the side, landing in the Bay became the inevitable outcome. The tugboat *Relief* was nearby and saw the landing at roughly 4:40 p.m., about a half mile from the Harrison Street wharf in Oakland. Van Tassel was once again plucked from the Bay, with the balloon towed to the Spear Street wharf at San Francisco. A large group of onlookers had witnessed the splashdown.[16]

On February 21, 1886, Van Tassel was at it once more, this time launching from Golden Gate Park using gas from the city gas mains. Launching promptly at 2:30 p.m. in the *City of London*, he immediately took an easterly course and rose to a height of 2,000 feet. He then encountered a wind from the northeast, which blew the balloon back toward the ocean. He descended, hoping to find the former westerly wind, but he could not find it and instead came down over the foothills south of Golden Gate Park. After landing, the balloon was not well secured and rose back into the sky without an occupant. It did not travel far, and Van Tassel recovered it soon thereafter at the Almshouse farm.[17]

Van Tassel was increasingly dissatisfied with the lack of sufficient buoyancy. He sought a balloon that was even larger than the *Eclipse* so he could carry multiple passengers. In March 1886, he began drafting plans for a massive balloon with more than 600,000 cubic feet of volume to make a complete crossing of North America, something considered rather foolhardy at the time.[18] Construction began in March and was completed by early May 1886. At the same time, Van Tassel and J. H. Love, an amusement manager at Woodward's Gardens, secured a short lease of space for flight testing.[19] At Woodward's Gardens they also arranged for a company of comedians to entertain the public on March 14, 1886.[20] The new *Monitor* was billed by newspapers as the "largest balloon ever built in the United States" and christened by Estelle May Thompson in front of invited guests at the Mechanics' Pavilion.[21] This impressive building was a wooden exhibition hall of approximately 18,000 square feet located on the block surrounded by Hayes, Polk, Grove, and Larkin Streets in San Francisco and built in 1857 for the Mechanics' Institute Fair.[22] The capital required for the development of the balloon came via a new company, the Pacific Captive Balloon Company, led by Van Tassel. The balloon was 119 feet tall and 180 feet in circumference, held 150,000 cubic feet of gas,[23] and required 23,000 yards of cloth made in strips and then triple-sewn.[24] The basket measured 9 feet in diameter, with a depth of nearly 4 feet, and was designed to hold up to fifteen people. The first ascension was scheduled for May 30, with a stated goal of crossing "the Sierra Nevada by the close of the first day."[25] This ascension would be, according to news reports, Van Tassel's thirty-eight balloon flight.[26] Van Tassel showed up at Woodward's Gardens on May 23 to erect the balloon, and a large throng of spectators also arrived at Woodward's Gardens. They were disappointed when Van Tassel carted the balloon away for unknown reasons.[27] But Van Tassel had his reasons: he was off to make another balloon exhibition tour of the West.

# 6. ON THE ROAD AGAIN

PARK AND CLARA VAN TASSEL quietly left San Francisco via train for Los Angeles. Park had secured the opportunity to make an ascension in Los Angeles as a part of Independence Day celebrations, and he wished to make additional income through a series of captive flights for paying customers ahead of July 4. They traveled with the *Monitor* and arrived in Los Angeles in the latter half of June 1886.

A test flight of the *Monitor* was arranged for June 26. Taking off at 5:00 p.m., they made the ascension together, perhaps for the first time. As for their landing, they first came down on Morgan Lane but then bounced back into the air and came down on the house of former Los Angeles mayor Cameron E. Thom, then in his backyard, then on a house at 240 South Main Street, demolishing a chimney in the process. They finally came to rest in a vacant lot.[1]

Park offered tethered flights in the *Monitor* from the arena grounds at the corner of Main and Fourth Streets.[2] Flights were made to an altitude of 1,000 feet, using a strong cable and winch.[3] Newspapers reported that the "amusement is a most novel one, and probably no more dangerous than baseball."[4] As a part of Independence Day celebrations, Van Tassel made his ascension in the *Monitor* accompanied by E. R. Cleveland and J. M. Hale. They enjoyed a serene flight in calm conditions, landing roughly 3 miles west of Los Angeles an hour or so after takeoff.[5]

On July 5, Van Tassel went up in the *Monitor* again, this time with a passenger named Moody of Pasadena. They launched from the arena grounds after the balloon was filled with hydrogen gas provided by the City Gas Company. Park had been using coal gas predominantly to this point, and the higher lifting power of hydrogen gas would have been a pleasant relief. Rather quickly they ascended to 7,200 feet, making a grand tour of the Los Angeles

Basin from Cahuenga Valley (now Hollywood) to Glendale, finally coming to a landing not far from the home of Superior Court justice K. M. Rose.[6]

The *Monitor* was "seized" at Los Angeles on July 6, "on an attachment for $100, but was afterward released."[7] Van Tassel had held a $100 debt, which he paid to secure release of the balloon. It is possible the payment was for damages caused by his landing on June 26. Articles in the *San Francisco Chronicle* and the *Los Angeles Herald* describing Van Tassel's "monster" balloon were duplicated nationally,[8] including in *Scientific American*[9] and even internationally,[10] especially in Australia.[11] This process began in mid-August 1886 and continued through the end of October 1886, with more reprints in July 1887. The stories generally focused on the *Monitor*'s very large capacity and Van Tassel's desire to complete a transcontinental flight across America at high altitudes that would allow for unheard of speeds above 100 miles per hour.

With increasing notoriety, Park Van Tassel traveled from California to Denver and then Kansas City, Missouri. It is unclear if Clara accompanied him. In Denver, Van Tassel was scheduled to make an ascension on August 1, 1886, with the *City of London*, accompanied by passenger Lute Wilcox, a local newspaper reporter. Already familiar with Van Tassel, the papers in Albuquerque noted, "When he [Wilcox] gets up to the highest attainable altitude he had best grab onto the edge of a cloud and stay there. He will never get nearer heaven."[12] The flight was moved to August 6, to take place from Jewell Park.[13] Van Tassel connected the balloon to a local gas main at 2:00 a.m., but filling took a far longer than expected. By 3:00 p.m., the balloon was only half-full. Locals wondered if the entire affair was a hoax and grumbled that refunds should have been offered to cover the cost of the train ride to the launch location.[14] The flight was postponed to August 8. While Van Tassel did briefly take to the sky that day, the ascension was considered a failure by most.[15] The *Herald Democrat* wrote, "The greatest elevation reached by the aeronaut would not have permitted him to see across the Colorado range. He could have reached a higher point on a narrow-gauge train."[16] Van Tassel made another attempt on Sunday, August 13. Before a large crowd, the ascension proved difficult. Van Tassel gained only a few hundred feet before landing very close to where he had started. The *Colorado Daily Chieftain* wrote that the balloon ascension was "as tame as the flight of a pet buzzard.... The problem of practical aerial navigation is still among the unsolved possibilities."[17] Despite the difficulties, some modern historians credit Van Tassel with the first balloon flight in Colorado.[18]

Park moved on to Kansas City. There, on August 27, he spoke with a reporter from the *Kansas City Times* about his career as an aeronaut. A planned ascension at League Park was arranged for August 29. Van Tassel boasted that he had been flying for eight years (it was likely closer to four) and that he had made forty ascensions (in actuality there were more).[19] Van Tassel felt that the previous fifty years hadn't offered many technological improvements to ballooning, with the exception of small devices, such as a rip cord to open a panel on the side of the balloon for deflation:

> My balloon, the "City of London," in which I will make my ascension Sunday is a gas balloon and not a hot air one. I know nothing about the latter, which I believe to be utter[ly] worthless. The "City of London" contains when filled about 80,000 square [*sic*] feet of gas and it is made of a patented cloth especially for balloons. The cloth is constructed of muslin woven in with linen and raw silk. It is very light but remarkably strong. The cloth is cut into a pattern to conform with the shape of the balloon, and then sewed together by a machine using the lock-stitch. The top of the balloon is much stronger than the other part, because it has to bear the strain. It is arranged in tapering layers of cloth, the next seven feet three layers and so on tapering down. The inside and outside are then coated with a preparation formed of turpentine and boiled oil. Two such coats are put on and after the balloon has been used once another coat is added. This renders it perfectly air tight.
>
> The netting of a balloon adds more than anything else to its strength. That over the City of London is made of the very finest Italian cord and the basket is formed of the best rattan and willow. The collapsing cord I spoke of runs up the side and is so arranged by loops in the seam that by pulling it the whole side of the balloon can be opened right out. It is only used in stormy weather when there is danger in landing.
>
> The gas is put in the pipe by means of a hose leading from the main to the neck of the balloon where an upright arm is inserted. I never fill my balloons full so that the neck and all bulge out because I think it is

dangerous and I am as careful of my life as you would be of yours even
if folks do call me a balloonatic. When I go up I generally carry plenty
of ballast because that is my greatest reliance—lots of little pieces of
tissue paper to tell the course of the balloon and whether it is moving or
not. Then with something to eat, and plenty to drink, in an emergency,
I feel almost as safe on land, although I would have mighty little to
catch on to 7,000 or 8,000 feet above the ground in case anything happened.[20]

Van Tassel's balloon ascension from the baseball park in Kansas City was a
fine one, although the crowd outside the park, watching the event for free, was
about ten times larger than the number of paying attendees inside. This was
quite frustrating. When the appointed time for the launch arrived, Van Tassel
asked a nearby officer, Dan Kane, to remove some people near the entrance
to the park who were making a fuss, but Kane would not do so. Van Tassel
demanded that the officer take action and that it was his right as a citizen to
ask for the officer's assistance. But Kane later noted that Van Tassel seemed
very angry, that the number of people who had failed to pay was large, and
that Van Tassel was intoxicated at the time of his request. People were merely
blocking the entrance rather than being rowdy, so Kane refrained from inter-
fering and told Van Tassel that it would be impossible for him to disperse a
crowd of three to four thousand people. According to Kane's accounting,
upon hearing this, Van Tassel swore at him and told the officer that if he did
not assist, he would have Kane removed from the grounds. Kane felt threat-
ened, and when Van Tassel reportedly came toward him in a menacing way,
Kane struck Van Tassel on the head with his club and arrested him. This
altercation delayed the launch by an hour while Van Tassel arranged for bail,
but he still managed to launch in his balloon.[21]

Following the flight, Van Tassel was charged with disturbing the peace.
The case came before Judge Worthen on August 31, 1886. While Kane brought
four witnesses to represent his side of things, Van Tassel brought seven witnesses. Park's witnesses swore that Kane had struck Van Tassel before Van

(*Opposite page*) An example of a tethered balloon from the period, the large multi-
passenger *City of San Francisco* is prepared for ascension from the Central Park baseball yard in San Francisco in 1894. San Diego Air and Space Museum.

*City of San Francisco* floats above Central Park at Eighth and Mission Streets, giving passengers a panoramic view of the city. The balloon was raised and lowered by winch. San Francisco History Center, San Francisco Public Library.

Tassel had abused the officer. The court could not reach a verdict and the case was dropped in favor of Van Tassel.[22]

Without much luck in Denver or Kansas City, Park Van Tassel returned to San Francisco to make captive balloon ascensions for paying customers at Central Park in October 1886.[23] Tethered by a 1,200-foot rope, 2 inches in diameter, the very large *Monarch* held 115,000 cubic feet of gas and could be raised to an altitude of roughly 1,100 feet.[24] Rides lasted about seven minutes before the balloon was pulled back to Earth. The large basket under the balloon had a maximum capacity of sixteen people, with passengers charged $2 for the experience.[25]

Park announced a desire to fly from Woodward's Gardens in San Francisco to Sacramento in November 1886, but the unknown large sum of money required to perform the feat could not be raised, so the launch never took place.[26] An ascension was planned for November 14 at Central Park to carry

Van Tassel; the assistant superintendent of the California Street Railroad, John Ferguson; and two others, Charles Chapman and J. C. Tice. But the winds were so strong that Van Tassel elected to pull the release valve on the balloon during inflation rather than risk additional damage to the balloon or its passengers.[27] On November 19, a Mr. Marion and a Mr. W. H. Hart paid Van Tassel a sufficient sum to make their own flight in the *Eclipse*. Neither Marion nor Hart had ever flown in a balloon before; the stunt was the result of a saloon bet that Marion would not go up in a balloon.[28] They launched at 1:00 p.m. from Central Park, opposite City Hall in San Francisco, and soon rose more than 2 miles into the sky. They drifted south, descending to a landing at Millbrae at 4:00 p.m. without injury. The balloon was returned by train to Van Tassel the following day.[29] For the rest of 1886, the inventive Van Tassel began a series of experiments that would change his direction in aviation considerably.

# 7. FALLING WITH GRACE

IN THE EARLY 1880s, other daredevils were practicing their art in San Francisco. For instance, tightrope walker Thomas Scott Baldwin[1] created quite a sensation by walking a high wire between the Cliff House and Seal Rock, over the waves of the Pacific below. This amazing feat gave Baldwin considerable notoriety as well as the realization that people would pay considerable sums to watch his death-defying exhibitions.[2] In 1885 and 1886, he began to contemplate more extravagant ways to entice the public.

In Europe, more than one hundred years earlier, daring aeronauts had already jumped from tethered balloons with parachutes, returning to Earth safely. At first the parachutes were largely rigid, with ribs to help support the structure. Then André Garnerin jumped from a balloon with a flexible parachute made of silk on October 22, 1797, in Paris. His wildly oscillating journey came to a successful end, but not long thereafter, French astronomer Jérôme Lalande introduced a vent in the canopy to improve airflow and reduce the oscillation of a parachute during its descent. Louis Charles Guille made the first parachute descent from a balloon in the United States in New York in 1819.

It remains unclear if Park Van Tassel was aware of these advances or not, but with the hope of launching a new series of exhibitions for the public, in 1886 he began experimenting with flexible parachute designs that included a vent at the top of the chute. Hearing that Van Tassel was planning to make such exhibitions, Baldwin met with Van Tassel and convinced him to join in a series of controlled experiments and jumps to test the designs. These experiments were conducted at the Mechanics' Pavilion in San Francisco in the fall of 1886.[3] It is likely that Van Tassel saw a courageous, lighter-weight "test pilot" in Baldwin, while Baldwin saw a creative opportunity in Van Tassel. No

Thomas Scott Baldwin, circa 1886.
San Francisco History Center, San
Francisco Public Library.

one in the United States had jumped with a flexible parachute since Guille's
flight in 1819. Van Tassel and Baldwin were working on something that would
revolutionize aerial exhibition.

Initial indoor tests with sandbags below the parachute indicated that a
lightweight, flexible parachute would open quickly if given sufficient distance
to fall. Increasingly larger parachutes were developed and tested. Prying
reporters for the *San Francisco Examiner* made their way to the Mechanics'
Pavilion after receiving word that someone was going to kill himself by jumping with a parachute inside the building.[4] Reports indicated that the first
jump was made by Baldwin and then at least one jump was made by Van
Tassel, from heights of about 80 feet. A reporter noted, "On Van Tassell's
occasion, his 250 pounds tugged so fiercely at the parachute as to send the air
rushing through the small hole at the top with a loud hissing noise."[5]

In the fall of 1886, a small dog strapped to a parachute was dropped by Van
Tassel and/or Baldwin from a tethered balloon at an altitude of 3,000 feet at
Seal Rock Park near the Cliff House,[6] without injury to the dog. According
to historian Howard Lee Scamehorn, Baldwin then made a successful jump

inside the Mechanics' Pavilion to test a human-size parachute.[7] In 1889 Van Tassel recalled,

> One day when I was at work in the Mechanics' Pavilion in San Francisco, I got to thinking about jumping from a balloon and I rigged up a parachute and attached weights to it. Well, to make a long story short, I experimented until I got a parachute that would let 210 pounds down easy; then I built a big one, about the time I met Baldwin, and he coaxed me until I let him make the first jump ever made in the world from a balloon. Since then he has become famous and I have kept up jumping.[8]

The parachute was made of canvas and manila rope and could be attached to and detached from a balloon by way of a rip cord.[9] Unwilling to wait further and sufficiently convinced of the parachute's safety, Baldwin went immediately to the office manager of a local streetcar company and proposed to jump from a balloon via parachute at a cost of $1 per foot from whatever height the manager cared to choose. The manager agreed to a 1,000-foot jump on January 30, 1887.

When January 30 arrived, people took the streetcars, gathering at the Haight Street cable car terminus, and made their way to Golden Gate Park in the vicinity of the music pavilion, where Van Tassel's *Eclipse* was in the process of being inflated. Roughly ten thousand to twelve thousand people gathered, although later estimates place the number at thirty thousand. Baldwin arrived on the scene at 3:00 p.m. wearing pink tights. He checked the parachute, which measured 24 feet in diameter and had been affixed to the side of the *Eclipse*. The rigging was automatic: Once Baldwin jumped from the balloon, his mass and the force of his weight would pull the rip cord, causing the parachute to fall away and open. A tethered ascent of Van Tassel's *Eclipse* was made with both Baldwin and M. Blanchard in the basket. Blanchard controlled the paying out of the rope with voice and hand signals,

(*Opposite page*) Thomas Baldwin rising over the skies of San Francisco on January 30, 1887, in the basket of Van Tassel's *Eclipse*, with a parachute tethered to the side. San Francisco History Center, San Francisco Public Library.

*My first jump from Captain ... San Francisco ...*

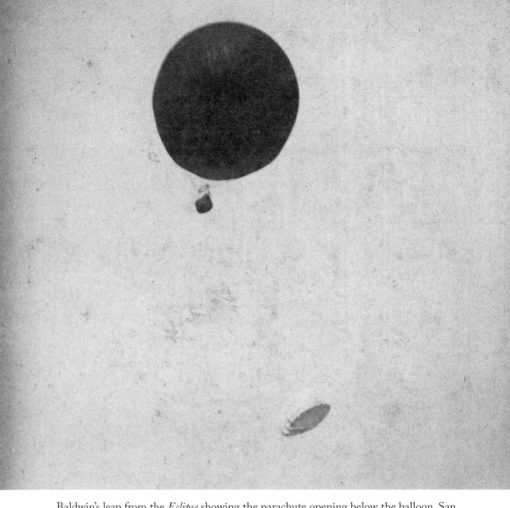

Baldwin's leap from the *Eclipse* showing the parachute opening below the balloon. San Francisco History Center, San Francisco Public Library.

indicating when it was time to stop. At the desired height of 1,000 feet, Baldwin grasped the trapeze bar with both hands and dropped over the side of the basket. Several onlookers screamed in panic, but the parachute opened, although not fully. With increasing speed, after a total descent time of 4.5 seconds, Baldwin landed in a lot attached to a small cottage, having crashed through some small wattle trees. Immediately, the crowd came to see if he was injured. He was not, and after a hearty congratulations by Van Tassel, Baldwin made a back somersault and a short sprint for onlookers.[10] News of this accomplishment traveled as far as Europe.[11] Baldwin's leap was the first successful public parachute jump in the West, billed as the first of its kind in the United States—without reference to Guille.

After the initial excitement, the *Eclipse* was brought back down. Not one to waste a fully inflated balloon, Van Tassel launched with an "adventurous bystander," Joseph M. Masten, and landed approximately an hour later, about 3 miles south of Redwood City, at about 4:30 p.m. He had reached a height of 13,000 feet.[12]

Another demonstration was arranged for April 3, 1887. At Central Park, Baldwin, William Ivy (performing as "Ivy Baldwin," Thomas's "brother"),[13] and Van Tassel prepared the *Eclipse* for flight. However, nearing the appointed time of 2:30 p.m., the crowds were scant, so Van Tassel thought it best to postpone the launch until after a baseball game between the Vallejo and Damiana teams. After the game, however, strong gusty winds arrived, making the *Eclipse* difficult to restrain. As the balloon swayed from side to side in the wind, an assistant grabbed the canvas, hoping to help, but instead put a large hole in the balloon's side. Rather than provide further risk to the balloon and the people nearby, Van Tassel pulled a rope to release the gas from the balloon. As a reporter later noted, "In a minute more the proud bubble lay in a disorderly heap on the ground, and the exhibition was declared an end."[14]

Shortly after this, Baldwin departed the Bay Area for Quincy, Illinois, to make parachute jumps from considerably high altitudes using untethered balloons. These were successful and led Baldwin to take the concept to New York City and then London, England, making many leaps and generating a considerable monetary reward. Van Tassel, meanwhile, was left entirely out of the equation, despite his initial collaboration. The resulting split between the two aeronauts was deep. Baldwin was surely the more courageous daredevil, and without this additional source of income, Van Tassel was left to ponder other ways to make money from balloons or muster the courage to make jumps on his own.

In early 1887, Van Tassel finally secured additional funding through the *San Francisco Daily Examiner*. He took a reporter/artist from the *Examiner* and a photographer up in the *Monitor* to take pictures of San Francisco at altitudes of 1,000, 1,500, 2,800, 5,500, and 7,200 feet. The results were then printed in the Sunday paper, showing the general public what the city looked like from high above for the first time. The reporter noted that up high, it was easy to hear sounds from the ground, including clucking chickens when floating high above the Jersey farms.[15] The photographer for the flight on April 15, 1887, was Edwin H. Husher of J. W. Talber & Co., working on behalf of the *Examiner*. The camera measured 10 by 8 inches and was affixed to a swivel. When held over the side of the basket, it could be aimed in different directions. Husher believed that these would be the first aerial photos taken in the United States, unaware of a photo taken by James Wallace Black and Samuel Archer King over the skies of Boston on October 13, 1860.[16] However, Husher's images were likely the first aerial photos taken over California. Several homing pigeons were also carried on board to send messages back to Earth.

The launch was well attended by a large crowd, including F. F. Martin and M. Blanchard. Twelve photo plates were taken, resulting in six good negatives. W. K. Burton, a writer for *The Photographic News*, noted, "Some difficulty was experienced in landing, Husher contriving to get out of the balloon on the top of a tree with his plates unbroken, with the natural result that the balloon, with its two other occupants, bounded into the air again, and only landed for the second time at a considerable distance."[17] The resulting photos and their publication in the *Examiner* helped catapult the career of young editor William Randolph Hearst.[18]

On May 27, 1887, Park traveled to Sacramento to discuss the opportunity for a balloon ascension on July 4 with the city's Fourth of July Committee.[19] On June 1, he attended a meeting of the committee at the Sacramento Court House, with Mayor Eugene Gregory as committee chair. Van Tassel offered to make a balloon ascension for the cost of $600 or a balloon ascension and parachute jump for the price of $1,000. The committee decided to pursue neither offer, as the prices were considered quite high. However, the newspapers on June 9 suggested that he would in fact provide a balloon ascension on July 4.[20] Perhaps in an attempt to pressure the committee to change its decision, Van Tassel provided a balloon ascension on the afternoon of June 9. There is no record of a parachute jump.

Van Tassel was hired by the *Los Angeles Examiner* to fly the same large balloon used for Husher's photography in San Francisco, now renamed the *Daily Examiner*, to take photos of Los Angeles, Pasadena, Santa Monica, and other locations. The ascension on Sunday, June 26, 1887, was coupled with a baseball match between Los Angeles and San Luis Obispo for a pennant offered by the *Examiner*. Special trains brought people from all over southern California to Sixth Street Park in downtown Los Angeles. For instance, someone from San Bernardino could take a train and witness the baseball game and balloon ascension all for $3.40.[21]

At 6:00 a.m. on June 26, a team began to inflate the balloon for the ascension. However, they quickly realized that the flow of gas was far less than expected and that something was wrong. They discovered that someone had placed sand and rocks in a pipe running from the gas main on Sixth Street to the balloon to tamper with the process of inflation. Rumors spread that perhaps the culprit was from a competitor newspaper. Very carefully, the crew assembled 2-inch piping to circumvent the damaged portion. While this improved the flow, the inflation was already far behind schedule; there was no way to fill the balloon properly prior to the baseball game at 2:00 p.m. The launch was scrubbed, much to the dismay of the roughly two thousand people who had shown up early to see the balloon ascension and game. Van Tassel considered launching after the game, but a Mr. McDowell, who was in charge of the event for the *Examiner*, announced that since the goal of the flight was to take photos of Los Angeles, this had to be done in the proper lighting of the height of the day. The launch was postponed to the following day, Monday, June 27, with photographer Husher scheduled to leave for Montana the day after. Accompanying Van Tassel and Husher was Frank Ward of Pasadena, who was in charge of making sure that the various points of interest in the community were noted to Husher during the flight. The balloon used for these photography trials was 65 feet high when fully inflated and had a basket of about 5 feet in diameter and 3 feet in depth. On the baseball diamond, the Los Angeles team beat the team from San Luis Obispo by a score of 9–8.[22]

About twelve hundred people returned the following day, June 28, 1887, to the Sixth Street baseball field to witness the balloon ascension. At 7:00 a.m., the superintendent of the gas company, J. S. Kaneen, showed at the park and turned on a valve that allowed gas to flow from the main to the balloon. Four hours and fifteen minutes later, the valve was shut off, but the balloon was only about three-quarters full. Despite this, Van Tassel set to work to prepare the balloon for flight. The photographer hopped in, but there was insufficient lifting capacity to include Frank Ward, so he was left behind. Van Tassel and Husher launched at 11:33 a.m. The balloon rose, passing up over the Belmont Hotel and Brea Ranch beyond the city. The course then shifted to Cahuenga Pass, toward Santa Monica, passing to the north of Vicente Ranch and then to the east again along the mountains, in the direction of the San Gabriel Valley. The balloon finally landed at 1:40 p.m. in the San Fernando Valley, having been in the air for a little more than two hours and having reached a maximum altitude of 14,300 feet. Van Tassel and Husher were considered heroes for making the flight, as these were the first aerial pictures of Los Angeles.[23] Interviewed by reporters from the *Tribune* that evening, Van Tassel said,

> We went up in a bee line to an altitude of 8,000 feet, and after hovering over the city for a while we struck a current which carried us over the San Fernando Valley, where we reached the highest altitude ever reached by any aeronaut on the Pacific slope viz. 13,000 feet which great height was reached by throwing out ballast. Mr. Husher, during our flight, took the plates, which he considers the most perfect ever taken by any living being from a balloon. The ascension was the most successful I have ever made, never having reached such a great height before, for everything was in our favor, and I was never so near to heaven as to-day. Mr. Husher is the most enthusiastic balloonist I ever had up with me and he never had a better opportunity of photographing the country. After taking all the plates needed we found ourselves hovering over Burbank. Up to this period I had not pulled the collapsing cord, but the natural escape of gas caused the balloon to gradually lower to the earth. After passing Cahuenga pass the balloon grazed the earth, within ten feet. At a given signal we got out of the balloon, but hung on to the basket like grim death, as there was nothing underneath for us to jump on except cacti. We both let go together, Mr. Husher being rolled for several feet up in the cacti. After jumping out, the balloon being relieved of its weight, arose to a distance of several hundred feet and landed out of sight a couple of miles distant. A boy raced on to us and wanted to know if any one was killed. He afterwards brought us to the balloon, which was found grunting and suffering from the effects of the cacti. The young lad brought us to his father's residence, where we were royally entertained, the boy afterward driving us into town. It was 5:45 o'clock when the balloon landed at Cahuenga Pass, fourteen miles distant. The ascension was a success beyond the greatest expectation, and a

graphic account of the trip, together with all the plates, will appear in Sunday's Examiner.[24]

Edwin Husher remained in the Bay Area until 1890 and then continued with his career in photography in Detroit, Michigan, through 1903. He later sold his interest in a photography-related company and returned to southern California, first as a farmer and then as a real estate agent.

As a part of the July 4, 1887, celebrations, Van Tassel made a balloon ascension from Capitol Park in Sacramento. At 2:15 p.m., he and two passengers, Jerry Payne and Ralph Donohue, went aloft. The balloon was barely able to ascend due to weight, and despite Van Tassel releasing bags of ballast and pouring sand from a sandbag off the side, it just cleared the rooftops of buildings on the north side of L Street. The balloon drifted to the northern limits of the city and then encountered reverse winds at 2,000 feet. These brought it back to the southeast and then directly east, bound for Brighton. A successful landing was made at 3:30 p.m., 1 mile south of state senator Joseph Routier's farm in a field owned by William Criswell.[25] Meanwhile, fifteen thousand people attended an open-air concert at Capitol Park that evening, with the event capped by a fireworks display.[26] Van Tassel left Sacramento on July 6 bound for San Francisco, staying at the Pacific Ocean House hotel in mid-July.[27]

# 8. SEPARATION

BY MID-1887, VAN Tassel had finally worked up enough courage to jump from a balloon via parachute. With Baldwin now an international sensation for his parachuting in England, Park was increasingly eager to capitalize on their invention. He proposed making his first jump to the directors of the Agricultural Society in San Jose as a part of the twentieth annual fair of the Santa Clara Valley Agriculture Society,[1] scheduled for August 15–20, 1887. The plan was to have Van Tassel ascend to a height of about 7,500 feet on August 18 at 1:30 p.m. and then jump, simultaneously pulling the rip cord to collapse the balloon and deploying his parachute to land safety.[2] The directors agreed to share 75 percent of any gate receipts over $800 (roughly $25,000 in today's dollars) with Van Tassel. In 1930 he recalled, "I built my first parachute from a picture in a dictionary. Parachutes had been known of course for years. In fact, men had made descents in them in France, but these were so frequently fatal that the parachutes were known as man-killers and balloonists restrained themselves with dropping at most a live pig. But I figured, if a live animal, why not a live man. Needless to say my parachute and my jumps with it were successful."[3]

On August 18, a huge crowd assembled at Agricultural Park. It was believed to be one of the largest crowds ever at the park, second only to a visit by President Ulysses S. Grant as a part of his world tour. At 2:00 p.m., Van Tassel and Charles Oliver (performing as Park's "brother" Charles Van Tassel) stepped into the basket. Although it isn't clear through newspaper reports, plans had apparently changed; Charles was on board to guide the balloon back down to Earth after Park's jump rather than Park releasing the rip cord at altitude. Just as the ropes were being cut for launch at 2:20 p.m., a fifteen-year-old "demented youth" named Rosenthal jumped into the basket. His additional weight brought the balloon back down to the ground. Rosenthal lay in the bottom of the basket, refusing to leave. The reasons for his choice to climb aboard are unknown, but perhaps he simply felt that by doing so, he would save the life of the man who would be jumping from aloft to his certain death. Rosenthal was finally forcibly removed from the basket by Deputy Sheriff Kamp.

The balloon was re-prepared for flight. However just at liftoff, the precariously attached parachute detached itself from the balloon and fell to the ground. As the balloon was already ascending, no parachute jump would be made. They continued in the balloon, over the southern portion of San Jose at an altitude of roughly 2,500 feet. At a distance of 5 miles from Agricultural Park, the duo prepared for a landing. Park climbed outside the basket, hanging at arm's length to help with the landing, but just as they neared the ground, a sudden thermal updraft carried the balloon skyward for 500 feet. Park hung on to the outside of the basket, unable to climb back in. Charles opened the exhaust valve and they descended rapidly to a landing, dumping both "Van Tassels" and all the sand ballast out of the basket. Having released its load, the much lighter balloon raced skyward again, continuing on to the southeast, to the very limit of their vision. Nearby farmers heard a very large bang that was mistaken for thunder. The balloon had burst, perhaps due to the pressure of the expanding gas, descending in shreds to the ground. The *Eclipse* was no more, an estimated loss of $1,600 for Van Tassel. Strips of oiled silk were found scattered over an area of about 10 acres.[4]

Van Tassel's activities for the remainder of 1887 are a mystery. However, by January 25, 1888, things were back on track with a new balloon, the *National*, inflated for the first time and christened with champagne by C. F. Townsend at the Mechanics' Pavilion in San Francisco in front of friends. Including the basket, the *National* stood 105 feet tall, with a diameter of 45 feet.[5] In February 1888, the *Los Angeles Herald* advertised that Van Tassel was to make a balloon ascension on February 21 at 2:30 p.m. in Los Angeles.[6] On that date, local newspapers reported that two seats in Van Tassel's new balloon were available for purchase, for an ascension at Los Angeles's Agricultural Park.[7] It remains unclear if there ever was a flight on February 21. However, at least according to one report, a successful flight was made on February 23 with a druggist from the Stewart Hotel as Van Tassel's only passenger.[8]

Van Tassel had flown balloons at many locations in California but never at San Diego, as the railroad had only recently been completed to that town of about forty thousand. The general manager of the Coronado Railroad Company, E. H. Story, reached out to Van Tassel to arrange an ascension on March 25, 1888. Van Tassel came to San Diego to work out the deal, staying at the Horton House downtown on March 9–10.[9] The ascension was arranged for Coronado Heights, an area of newly auctioned lots just north of what is now Imperial Beach and south of where the Hotel del Coronado had opened its doors earlier that year, on February 19. Initially, organizers suggested that Clara would jump by parachute from the balloon, but Park put a quick end to those thoughts. To fill the balloon in a reasonable time, gas from the nearby San Diego Gas and Electric Light Company was used. The filled balloon would then be transported by boat across San Diego Bay. Filling started on Saturday for a launch on Sunday. To accommodate the expected crowds, the city arranged for two ferries instead of one to make the harbor crossing between Coronado and San Diego. But as the date for the ascension approached, it became rather clear that there weren't enough ferries to accommodate everyone. The launch was postponed a week to provide additional time for preparation.[10] On March 31, newspapers described the filling and the crossing of San Diego Bay with the inflated balloon on a barge. It was towed to the Coronado Heights wharf, where it was to lift off at 2:30 p.m. on April 1. Van Tassel assured organizers that if he did not ascend to an altitude of 1.5 miles, he would refuse payment.[11] Although plenty of clean, light gas had been secured in advance for filling the balloon, Van Tassel noted that the gas that was supplied was instead a mix of "water, wind, and tar." With a severely reduced lifting capacity, the balloon went nowhere. Van Tassel's pride was once again on the line.[12] San Diego Gas and Electric Light personnel expressed their regrets and vowed to supply "the real article: unadulterated coal gas" on Sunday, April 15. The San Diego and Coronado Ferry Company and the Coronado Railroad Company guaranteed to refund all fares if Van Tassel didn't ascend and reach 1.5 miles above Earth.[13]

On April 15, a large portion of San Diego traveled by ferry across the harbor to Coronado and from there south to Coronado Heights to witness the great balloon feat. There, Van Tassel's large balloon could be seen, filled and ready to fly. Yet again, the gas simply did not provide the required buoyancy, and the sun remained behind clouds, which did not help in heating and expanding the gas further. As it was clear that no passengers were going up with him, Van Tassel began emptying the basket of ballast so that buoyancy might be sufficient for liftoff. Finally, with only a few pounds of sand remaining, Van Tassel slowly took to the sky. He threw the remaining ballast overboard and climbed, much to the pleasure of the large crowd. A newspaper reported that the balloon looked "no bigger than a man's hand" before it drifted off to the northeast, across the bay toward Chula Vista, where Park fortunately landed safely, despite having no ballast remaining to adjust the descent rate. Spectators and newspaper reporters considered the flight "a brilliant success," and transportation of the large crowd, estimated at well over twenty thousand, also went off without a hitch.[14] As it turned out, that same day the town of Ocean Beach, to the west of San Diego, held a celebration for its first anniversary, including a balloon launch by Emil Melville. Both events were advertised side by side in the local papers. Much of San Diego and National City were left empty that day as most everyone attended one of the launches. Watching balloon launches had an unusual effect on some. Two days later, San Diego police officers arrested a disturbed man. After witnessing Van Tassel's flight, he became sure that his body was filled with gases sufficient for liftoff. He ran around town asking everyone to hold him down and wouldn't stop until they complied. The police labeled him a "balloonatic."

Meanwhile, Baldwin continued to make tremendous income with his daring high-altitude parachute leaps from balloons in England. Dismayed by this, during the spring of 1888, Park and Clara Van Tassel continued to think of ways make a living by ballooning. Park arranged to provide an ascension on July 4, 1888, at Los Angeles as part of Independence Day festivities, under the auspices of the well-known Fredericksburg brewery near Agricultural Park.[15] However, this wasn't going to be a typical arrangement. As the date drew closer, newspapers announced that both Park and Clara would ascend together in the balloon, but from a height of 1,000 feet, Clara would be the one leaping from the basket to return to Earth via parachute, not Park. No woman in the West had ever made a parachute jump from a balloon. Although history suggests that the first woman to jump via parachute in the United States was Louise Bates in August 1860, at Cincinnati, Ohio,[16] Los Angelenos in 1888 were obviously not aware of the prior history and were utterly

perplexed by the proposition. Why would any woman consider Independence
Day, of all days, as the appropriate date to commit suicide by jumping from a
balloon?[17] But the marketing plan worked well, as the controversy surrounding the attempt generated significant interest.

On July 4, 1888, Los Angeles was in the midst of a heat wave, and its citizens took an early start on their festivities. By 9:00 a.m., an estimated one
hundred thousand people crowded Agricultural Park. Fearing for Clara's life
should she actually be crazy enough to follow through with the parachute
jump, someone sent a message to the chief of police, demanding that Clara
be prohibited from launching. Chief Cuddy agreed and ordered Detective
Tom McCarthy to be pre-positioned for the launch at 1:00 p.m. McCarthy
was given orders to stop Clara from going up in the balloon unless she gave
her word of honor not to make the leap. However, long before 1:00 p.m., word
of the police arrangement made it back to the Van Tassels. They decided to
launch as quickly as possible to avoid the detective. By 10:00 a.m., the crowd
got word that the wind was favorable and Park Van Tassel was preparing his
balloon with gas at the Haymarket. A rush of spectators made their way to
the Haymarket to see the balloon in the finishing stages of being filled as it
swayed back and forth in the gentle breeze. The race was on.

The Van Tassels had also arranged to be accompanied on this flight by
D. E. Barclay, deputy county recorder for Los Angeles County. Barclay was
also a balloonist and had shared at least one previous ascension in Los Angeles with Park Van Tassel, in 1886. However, with the rush to fly, word was sent
to find Barclay as quickly as possible and get him to the balloon so they could
launch. Barclay was located and ran to the Haymarket to find the Van Tassels
already seated in the balloon and ready to go. Barclay hopped in. The balloon
was tethered to Earth with just one rope. When Park gave the order to "cut
her loose," the balloon rose quickly into the sky at 10:47 a.m., roughly three
hours ahead of the well-advertised launch time.

Affixed to the side of the balloon was a parachute, ready to spring to life
like an umbrella when required. The balloon took a northeasterly heading,
with the crowd below following its path, making their way back to the city
streets and forming a large throng at the corner of Seventh and Main Streets,
with mounted marshals maintaining crowd control.[18] The editors of the *Los
Angeles Herald* had asked Barclay to write an article about the events,

considering the rumors about Clara's proposed jump to be rather preposterous. Barclay later described the scene:

The balloon contained about 250,000 [cubic] feet of gas[19] when we started up. Incident to an ascension is an upward jump of the balloon immediately after it is cut loose from its moorings. The jump of our balloon was a memorable one. It carried us to an altitude of about 2,000 feet. Professor Van Tassel, Mrs. Van Tassel and myself were in the cage. When we had attained that altitude we found no clearly defined current of air. A calm, so to speak, was prevalent. Our height, we all agreed, was not sufficient to admit of the parachute jump being made with safety. Our ballast consisted of several bags of sand and numerous bundles of papers, dodgers, etc. Some ballast was tossed out, but we finally decided to release some gas. This we did and came to within about 1000 feet of earth when a good wind current was struck. We shut off the gas valve and rode with the current, taking a gradually upward course until we were about over, or a little to one side of the Jefferies place, and near the Arroyo Seco. At that time, I shall judge we were 5000 feet in the air. Van Tassell all along was extremely wary. Every moment he would glance up at the parachute we carried, swung from the cage. The 'chute, as he called it, seemed all right. Finally he said he guessed the time had come for the leap. Mrs. Van Tassell was cool and collected. Van Tassell pulled the 'chute down into the cage. The parachute is shaped much like an umbrella, and just about twenty feet in diameter at its mouth. Pendant from it are two ropes, provided with hand rings at their ends. To these rings Mrs. Van Tassell's hands were strapped. Also pendant from the center of the apex of the corner of the now inflated chute is a rope. About Mrs. Van Tassell's waist we fixed a stout strap in circingle [sic], and the end of this we attached to this rope. All was ready. Van Tassell bade his wife good-by, and so did I. She was cool as an iceberg as Van Tassell cleared the parachute from its moorings. She stepped on the edge of the cage, looked down once and then stepped off into space. We shot heavenward at once, a distance of about 500 feet. 'Van' was so nervous he crouched in a corner of the cage. I peeped down and saw

the parachute dashing toward the earth like a rocket. My heart was in
my mouth for a moment, but when I saw the old 'chute' fill out and
sail downward at an easy gait I knew that the first parachute descent
in the world by a woman was a complete success.

Van Tassell had arranged with his wife that should she reach the
earth in safety, she was to hail him by waving her handkerchief. As soon
as we could collect ourselves, Van Tassell told me to pull the valve cord.
This cord, when pulled, releases the valve, or plug, holding the gas in the
balloon. I pulled it with a will and we were soon descending at a fearful
rate. I tried then to release the valve but failed, and it looked as if we
were going to get the worst of it until we got within about 300 feet of
the ground. We were tossing out all the ballast left, when the balloon
lightened a little. When the cage was within about ten feet of the earth,
we both leaped out and landed in safety. As we carried no grapples or
anchor we had to let the balloon go scooting over the ground. We made
our way at once to Mrs. Van Tassell and found her standing on a sandy
heap. About her had gathered a half a hundred people, among them
being Messrs. J. D. Yoakum, Shumway, Jeffries, Poor, Smith and others
of Pasadena. Mr. Smith and Mr. Shumway had already released Mrs.
Van Tassell from the 'chute. She was a little bit jarred but not injured in
the least. All of us shook hands. Mrs. Van Tassell said the 'chute did not
work until she had fallen 200 or 300 feet, she thought. Her descent was
made easily and gradually. It was a grand feat and I think it but just to
Mrs. Van Tassell to say that she was the coolest and bravest of the party
of three. Mrs. Van Tassell reached the earth, I should judge, about a
mile the other side of the wagon road bridge over the Arroyo Seco.[20]

While news of this feat spread quickly in the West and across America, it
took time for it to reach the far corners of the world. For instance, in New
Zealand, the *Lyttelton Times* reported the event on February 14, 1889, a full six
months after it took place. However, the majesty of what had been accomplished was not lost to the New Zealand press: "Professor Baldwin, who has
been astonishing all the world by his perilous and daring descent from a
balloon, with the aid of a parachute, has been put in the shade by the exploits
of a woman—Mrs. Van Tassell—who quite recently performed the wonderful

feat of leaping from a balloon at a height of 4000 ft, steadied only by a parachute."[21] Reporters in London were so amazed that a woman would dare
attempt such a feat that they felt the reports must surely be untrue: "Those
yearning for new modes of being rid of their better-halves will please note
this latest invention. But then the story has travelled far."[22]

The following day, Park Van Tassel went to Pasadena to recover the balloon. He found it in a collapsed state and without much damage. Meanwhile,
congratulations flooded in to Clara for her brave feat. The Van Tassels immediately announced plans to travel to Seattle to repeat the remarkable parachute descent.[23] They left Los Angeles by train for San Francisco on July 12.[24]
Upon arrival in San Francisco, they were interviewed by a reporter from the
*San Francisco Examiner* at their home on Turk Street. The 165-pound Clara
was described in the paper as "big, young, handsome, and blonde." The
reporter wrote:

> "It is only a question of nerve," said Mrs. Van Tassell, when asked
> about her exploit. "I made up my mind that I could jump from a bal-
> loon as well as Baldwin, and when I make up my mind to do a thing I
> do it. Don't I, Van?"
>
> The Professor looked at the woman who wasn't afraid of a mile jump
> and meekly admitted that what she said was true.
>
> "So, when we were over a clear place," continued the lady, "they
> opened the valve to hold the balloon stationary and give the 'chute a
> start to open a little, and then I said good-by and jumped. I had been
> warned that my arms would be jerked from their sockets and expected
> a tug, but though I dropped thirty feet like a shot before the parachute
> was well open, there was no shock, and I felt no great strain on my
> arms.
>
> I often dreamed of falling immense distances, and I wanted to see
> how it really was.
>
> I ain't exactly a bird nor an angel, but it's just about what I imagine
> the sensation of flying is. It was beautiful! Though I went through that
> 6000 feet in five and one-quarter minutes, I didn't seem to be going
> fast, and never lost my breath. I swung hundreds of feet one side and
> the other for the first 4000 feet, but after that I just floated down an

incline to the ground, and alighted with no more shock than would be caused by jumping off a chair.

I wasn't the least bit frightened from the start. One arm was strapped to the parachute, and there was a belt around my waist, so I could not fall away from the parachute."

"Did you do any thinking while you were falling?" asked the reporter.

"I only thought about my landing, whether I would drop on a big tree that was just under me, or on a house that I saw. I luckily missed both.

I was anxious to get a reputation, and I did, and I expect to make a fortune by jumping from balloons. Don't I, Van?"

Prof. Van Tassell meekly acquiesced.[25]

As a test before their trip to Seattle, the Van Tassels arranged for a parachute jump on Sunday, August 19, 1888, at Agricultural Park in San Jose. Clara's parents must have been in utter shock when reading the announcements in the local paper. However, the Van Tassels had difficulty even getting airborne. Just as the basket was being fitted to the inflated balloon, the balloon completely split open near the top and collapsed. The large paying crowd was far from amused. A boisterous mob soon made its way back to the ticket office, looking for refunds. Upon seeing the approaching angry mob, the ticket sellers threw a cash box containing only a few dollars in that direction while they ran in the opposite direction as fast as possible with the rest of the take. The mob then turned to follow the aeronauts instead. Clara was escorted from the park by Deputy Sheriff Jay Hall and Bob Anderson. After making their way to Hall's "buggy," they drove to Clara's home on Center Street near the park. The buggy was followed by the mob, and several hundred people remained in front of the house for thirty minutes. They were prevented from entering the house by special officers who guarded the gates. Eventually Clara's father came out to inform the mob that Park Van Tassel was not in the house and never had been. Upon hearing this, the crowd dispersed. While no one was hurt, Clara considered the angry mob to be far more dangerous than parachute jumping from a balloon. She spent the night at her parent's house.

Her husband had left the park in a different direction without attracting attention. Once Park and Clara had left the area, their manager/assistant, Frank Frost, returned to the scene, pulled out a pistol, and yelled at the crowd: "You're a nice set of cowards to stone a woman, ain't you? Now stone me, but stone hard and fast or I'll make some of you sick. You think I'm Van Tassell; well I ain't but I'll fight any two of you if the balance will see fair play. If you won't just look out, that's all. I am not afraid of a thousand cowards that would stone a woman."[26]

After that display, no one bothered Frank as he packed up the balloon. Park Van Tassel later blamed the incident on the gas company for supplying low-quality gas made of petroleum with very little lifting capacity. He said that the large tear in the balloon was caused by Van Tassel deflating it after realizing it would never fly.[27]

The event had other serious ramifications. A man named Otto Curdts had attended the balloon ascension. In the melee that ensued, another man, George Dibble, had pushed Curdts into Clara Van Tassel. Curdts was angered and told Dibble, "We'll have this out when we meet again." They met later at Santa Clara and got into a shouting match. A fight ensued, with several of Dibble's friends jumping on Curdts, hitting him in the face with either a knife or a pistol. With a broken nose, Curdts pulled his pistol to ward off further attack. As he held it with two hands, someone grabbed him from behind in a choke hold. His gun fired, hitting Dibble. Not long thereafter, Dibble died of his injuries. Curdts managed to escape the choke hold and fled the scene by jumping into a car, proceeding to Hestor Schoolhouse, where he washed the blood from his face. From there he went to his home on Lenzeu Avenue, changed clothes, went to Max Schmidt's saloon, and finally made his way to the Southern Pacific Depot, where he convinced a conductor that he needed to get away, and fast. He traveled by train to San Mateo, San Francisco, Alameda, and Stockton. Convinced that police were on his tail, he traveled to Pleasanton, where he was finally captured by Sheriff Sweigert and Constable Haley. It remains unknown what became of Curdts, but it is clear that the scene at the Van Tassel ascension was a violent one and not at all what the Van Tassels had in mind as preparation for their trip to Seattle.[28] The event also reinforced the divide between Clara's parents and Park Van Tassel, with Clara caught in the middle.

# 9. NORTH BY NORTHWEST

UNDETERRED BY THE fiasco in San Jose, the Van Tassels traveled by train to Portland, arriving on September 10, 1888, for a planned parachute jump with the repaired *National* on September 23.[1] The balloon was filled with gas in Portland and then transported by barge to a launch location at City View Park, 3 miles up the Columbia River. Yet again, disaster struck before launch. Van Tassel enlisted locals to help steady the filled balloon with guide ropes as it was being moved onto the barge, but some of them let go while crossing a slippery set of logs. In the ensuing chaos, Park Van Tassel and two helpers, John Murphy and David Kafka, became entangled in the ropes and fell into the river, with Murphy falling from a height of 30 feet. While no one was seriously hurt, the freed and unpiloted *National* rose on its own to an estimated height of 10,000 feet, drifting 9 miles to the southwest before catching on fire and descending rapidly to Earth. It was later surmised that one of the guide ropes had been too close to burning sawdust at the launch location, and over time an ember ignited the gas inside the balloon. The destruction of the balloon was an estimated loss of $2,000, with another $150 worth of gas wasted in one big "poof." According to a reporter, Van Tassel said, as he watched the balloon sail away,

> There goes my all. If all had gone well there is where we would have been sailing along as nice as you please, a perfect trip and a perfect day. If I had not fallen into the water and could have got near her I would have climbed into the car, and could have managed her . . . I think she will travel about forty miles. She is up about 8000 feet and there is a strong wind. If I can recover her I will make the ascent next week . . . there goes $2600 and all I have in the world.[2]

Van Tassel and a friend from the Merchants Hotel searched for the balloon, finally locating it several days later about 3 miles west of Taylor's Ferry. Van Tassel offered $50 to any local who would bring it to Portland, and five days later a rancher named R. Malloy brought the remains in. He noted, "I saw the thing light and followed it up. It took me the greater part of the day to extricate it from the brush and trees amidst which it fell. In coming down, the balloon broke a tree fifteen inches in circumference, and knocked the top off another."[3] It became clear that the stories of the balloon being lost to fire were incorrect.[4] Van Tassel examined the balloon and spread it out at the Gambrinus Gardens dance hall for repairs. He recalled, "The platform at Gambrinus Gardens is the best place I could get. I tried to engage the Mechanics' Pavilion, but they are working in there, preparatory to the fair. The Gambrinus hall is about eighteen feet too small for the balloon. I shall have to make several new sections, do about 3000 yards of stitching, have eight or nine people working at it, and will be put to an expense of between $600 and $700, not to mention my loss of business."[5]

He declared to the press that he would attempt another flight with the *National* after October 7.[6] The repaired balloon was inflated on a barge on October 13 and towed on the afternoon of October 14 to City View Park. From there the balloon was carefully moved with the help of twenty men "and nearly a hundred boys shouting and dancing about" to the judges' stand in the park.[7] There, Van Tassel and news reporter A. A. Ritchie climbed aboard in front of about twelve hundred to fifteen hundred spectators. They launched around 4:00 p.m., ascending to 12,800 feet over Portland and then moving in a southeasterly direction toward Willsburg. Passing 5 miles east of Milwaukie, the balloon finally landed 11 miles east of Rock Creek at 5:45 p.m.[8] A newspaper report suggested that the Van Tassels would "leave for London in a few days," although the reporter likely meant London, Oregon—not London, England. With all the difficulties, and with Park's trepidation about more parachute jumps by Clara, Park decided that from then on, if there were going to be parachute jumps, he would make them.

Together, they traveled to Seattle as planned, but their new balloon didn't go with them. A dispute arose with a Mr. Hodgson, who owned the depot in Portland where the balloon was housed. Hodgson would not release the balloon until he had received payment for the services of his band, which had likely played as a part of Van Tassel's ascension. Hodgson's attorney suggested that they ask the courts to see whether anyone wanted to buy it. If not, Hodgson would keep the balloon as his own and "go up myself."[9] The balloon ended up being sold to a musician named J. H. Ross for $100, with the sale handled by Constable Samuel Simmons.[10]

On November 2, 1888, Van Tassel arrived in Seattle, where it was announced that he was building a new 35,000-cubic-foot balloon, a relatively small one, similar to the balloon used for his inaugural flight in Albuquerque. Built at Turn Verein Hall,[11] the balloon was to be completed by the end of November. Van Tassel suggested that he'd make a test ascension to 600 feet from a barge in the bay.[12]

Meanwhile, following his sensational demonstrations of balloon-assisted parachuting, Thomas Baldwin embarked on a trip to Australia to make similar exhibitions there. Australian aeronauts had already caught on to the mechanics of the operation. For instance, a thirty-eight-year-old Australian watchmaker named J. T. Williams made his own ascension and parachute descent from 6,000 feet at Ashfield, a borough of Sydney, in December 1888.[13] Williams had never been up in a balloon before; nor had he made a parachute jump before. But the jump was a success and is often considered the first parachute jump in Australia's history. Another American aeronaut, known as Professor Bartholomew, had also reached Australia. He began making parachute jumps in December 1888.[14] Australia was hungry for American talent and a welcome market for the spectacle of trapeze work and parachuting from balloons. Baldwin was eager to capitalize.

On January 1, 1889, Park Van Tassel attempted to launch in his balloon at Seattle but failed due to a lack of sufficient gas. The next day, he launched at 1:00 p.m. along Jackson Street near the Seattle Gas Company's plant near Fifth Avenue. He launched with the intent of finding an air current that would carry him over the harbor, where he would leap and then land with his parachute in the water. However, after launch, no air current to take him over the harbor was found. He leaped from an altitude of 7,000 feet, hoping the parachute would do its job properly. The first 500 feet of the descent were made with a tremendous velocity, as the parachute took its time to open. When the parachute finally did open, the jolt was so severe that Van Tassel lost his handhold and for a time was secured to the parachute only by the strap around his waist. This was considered "indescribably thrilling" by report-ers for the *Post-Intelligencer*. He regained control of the hand rings and pro-ceeded to descend in a safe manner for two minutes, landing unharmed in waist-deep water at the foot of Denny Way. He was picked up by a small boat while his balloon came down eventually at Smith Cove. This death-defying leap was Park's first successful parachute jump.[15] Rather quickly thereafter, Park returned to San Francisco by train.

Once back in San Francisco, Park announced that he would make a parachute jump near the Cliff House for the city he called home.[16] On February 10, 1889, a crowd of ten thousand came to witness the feat. A light but unusual offshore breeze was blowing, so the launch was moved a half mile inland from the Cliff House to a sheltered location. Unfortunately, the gas at that location was insufficient to fill the balloon to its maximum capacity, something that was now becoming a routine problem. Rather than risk looking like a failure in front of ten thousand spectators, Van Tassel decided to remove the basket entirely and dangle from the balloon with only a rope as his seat. After taking the balloon aloft, he jumped at approx-imately 1,300 to 1,500 feet above the dunes near the Cliff House. For the first 200 feet, the parachute failed to open and he gained significant speed. It was clear to most on the ground that Van Tassel's legs had become entan-gled in a rope, preventing the parachute from opening fully. He gave a few quick jerks with his legs and finally the rope was freed. At an altitude of just 500 feet, the parachute opened fully, slowing Van Tassel down to a light landing on a nearby sand dune. The crowd was ecstatic. However, the initial high rate of speed was an overly concerning experience for Van Tassel, enough to make him seriously question any further parachute jumps. The press noted that "Van Tassell was a little pale and said that for a moment he thought he was lost."[17] His unpiloted balloon remained aloft and drifted west with the breeze, coming to rest in the Pacific, roughly 8 miles from shore near San Pedro Point. The balloon was picked up by the *City of Puebla* as it left San Francisco for Port Harford. Other than being soaked, the balloon was not damaged. It was returned by train from Port Harford. Meanwhile, reporters wondered how many jumps Van Tassel had left before the reaper would catch up with him.[18] The *Santa Cruz Sentinel* reported, "It is only a question of time when Van Tassell will drop out of existence."[19] He

A balloon prepares to launch from Ocean Beach just south of the famous Cliff House (on the left) at San Francisco. This is likely Van Tassel's 1889 jump or a similar event from the period. Note the advertising billboard for Eclipse champagne on the cliff face. The California champagne company may have paid to have Van Tassel give his balloon the same name. San Francisco History Center, San Francisco Public Library.

was wondering the same thing, but the income was too good to be ignored. Through the repeated stunts up and down the West Coast, Van Tassel had generated considerable notoriety, perhaps even more so when balloon launches or parachute jumps did not go as planned. The death-defying leap near the Cliff House further cemented his fame. The press reported, "It need hardly to be said that his thrilling jump has contributed largely to the name of the daring aeronaut."[20] News of his harrowing stunt was mentioned in various newspapers worldwide, sometimes in parallel with stories about Baldwin and other daredevils.[21]

Van Tassel arranged to provide a balloon launch and parachute descent for the grand opening of Kroncke's Park in Santa Rosa on April 6, 1889. The balloon was moved to the field the week prior for staging. As with previous launches, event organizers made arrangements for the transportation of large crowds, by rail to Santa Rosa and from there to the park. For unknown reasons, on April 6 the balloon launch was pushed to the following

Saturday, April 13. And on April 12 it was announced that the ascension would take place on April 20. It remains unclear whether the ascension ever happened.[22] What is clear is that Van Tassel was at the Bay District horse track on April 20. He attended opening-day races of the Pacific Coast Blood-Horse Association and did not make a balloon launch.[23] After that, Van Tassel once again set off on a journey through the West.

# 10. BACK TO UTAH

BY EARLY MAY 1889, Van Tassel made arrangements for an ascension and parachute jump at Garfield Beach,[1] on the shore of the Great Salt Lake west of Salt Lake City. With his previous ballooning success in Utah not forgotten, Park was hailed by Salt Lake newspapers as having "unrivaled daring and courage," with a jump that would be "the greatest test ever attempted in this territory." Newspapers also reported that Van Tassel had made more than three hundred balloon flights at various locations in America and was engaged to travel to London, England, with his wife to provide a balloon launch at the Crystal Palace grounds in July 1889.[2] While no reports of the Van Tassels actually providing exhibitions in London can be located, balloonist Eduard Spelterini and trapeze artist Leona Dare (whose real name was Susan Adeline Stuart) did perform balloon stunts at the Crystal Palace in July 1889.

Van Tassel arrived in Salt Lake City on May 20 accompanied by his manager, a Mr. Fenton, but without Clara.[3] Balloon launches were scheduled for May 26. The newly expanded Utah & Nevada Railroad announced that it was prepared to handle the larger-than-expected crowds with special trains departing Salt Lake at regular intervals, arriving in time for the ascension scheduled for 5:00 p.m. Reporters noted that Van Tassel was using a new smoke balloon and a parachute used only once previously, at Santa Rosa, California.[4] Donald McLaire, general manager of the Pacific Short Line Railroad, arranged for a special train to bring spectators from Ogden, Utah, to Garfield Beach for the launch.[5]

Filling of the balloon began on Saturday, May 25, at 4:45 p.m., about the time of the arrival of the last train. However, with the balloon nearly filled, someone managed to step on the sheet of iron that covered the tunnel carrying hot air from the coal fire to the balloon. This caused the tunnel to collapse

On May 26, 1889, the *Salt Lake Herald* announced that "The Great Van Tassell," "engaged at great expense," would provide balloon ascensions and parachute jumps at Garfield Beach. Digital images, newspapers.com.

and let the remaining hot air escape. A new trench was dug in haste. During the ruckus, the partially filled balloon was moved out of the way, and during that process, the canvas snagged and was damaged slightly. Van Tassel worked quickly to repair the trench, stoke the fire, and repair the smoke balloon to continue the inflation. By 8:20 p.m., the balloon was ready for launch, but by this time the atmosphere had begun to cool. A gust of cold air came to the field, and it became clear that a launch this late in the day in poor conditions was futile, so Van Tassel simply pulled a release valve to let the hot air escape. He and his organizers promised the large crowd that remained that they would try again the following afternoon.[6] The May 29 edition of the *Salt Lake Herald* noted that Van Tassel would remain in town to provide a full ascension and parachute drop, "even if it took him all summer."[7]

However, on May 26, the *Salt Lake Herald* reported that citizens could also see the ascension of "the largest balloon *City of Salt Lake*" and a parachute jump by "Professor" James William Price[8] at Lake Park.[9] Price was said to be trying to "beat the world's record," but it wasn't clear precisely which record that was. So here in Salt Lake City were two "professors" of ballooning and parachuting, determined to see whose jump would be the highest, fastest, or farthest, and which of them had the larger balloon. Price's exhibition included a woman, a daredevil parachutist who used the stage name Millie Viola. Unknown to most, her real name was Ruby Marana Hawker.[10] She hailed from Australia, and although it isn't clear how she came to the United States or became connected with Price, she often told the press she was his sister.[11] Price and Viola had made balloon ascensions and parachute jumps prior to their arrival in Utah. For instance, on May 4, 1888, at Paris, Illinois, Price (performing as Professor Sisk)[12] made his first parachute jump from a balloon for thousands of spectators.[13] He made a similar attempt a week later at Mattoon, Illinois, but just as the balloon was being prepared for launch it caught fire and was released, fortunately leaving Price safely on the ground.[14] Later, in the fall of 1888, Viola made her first parachute jump, with Price's assistance at Chicago, landing in Lake Michigan. On September 10, 1888, Viola and Price[15] made a spectacular dual ascension and parachute jump over Minneapolis as part of Minneapolis Day celebrations at the state fair.[16] At the time, Price was seventeen years old and Viola nearly fifteen.

Price made his ascension at Lake Park in Utah on Sunday, June 2, 1889, but the launch was delayed by an hour and a half, and Price failed to jump via parachute. He remained with the balloon for a safe landing after spending some time hovering over the Great Salt Lake. On June 5, Viola made a successful balloon ascension and parachute jump at Lake Park.[17]

It is conceivable that this set of crosstown rivals could have conspired to cause Van Tassel's inflation troubles on May 25. However, Van Tassel's troubles were all of his own doing. He had made the mistake of bringing the wrong balloon with him to Salt Lake—a smaller balloon, appropriate for his wife but not for him—and the delay on May 25 was related to this issue. The thirty-five-year-old Van Tassel now found himself in a considerable bind. He had promised a balloon ascension and a jump, and not only were people expecting him to fulfill the promise but the competition was making him look like a fraud. A jump had to be made, but he was unable to do so! What to do?

One accounting of what actually transpired came to light in 1900 in the pages of the *Nebraska State Journal*. A man named Dudley Cochran provided his version of the events:

> I came to make my first drop in a most peculiar way. My partner and I were doing trapeze work in Salt Lake City at Garfield beach when the Union Pacific was just opening it. We had good work and enjoyed it and got good salaries. One day we went into a restaurant and saw a bill of the first balloon ascension in Utah. It was to be made by Professor Van Tassel at the beach on the next day and it was spread out big, I tell you. My partner and I knew mighty little about the balloon business and pronounced the thing a fake and said so pretty loud in the hearing of a man who had entered after us and was taking our talk all in. I remember that I said I would make the ascent for $100. The show bills told of the immense sum that was being paid the professor and I made the boast that I would go up for the much smaller sum.
>
> The next day you better believe I felt like a monkey when I saw the man we saw in the restaurant approach while we were walking on the beach and especially when he began talking balloon. It turned out that he was the great Van Tassel, with a record a mile long and a pocket full of coin. And he was in a fix. He had come all the way from San Francisco to make the ascent and on opening up his canvas, he found that

his wife's balloon had been packed instead of his own. His wife was as accomplished an aeronaut as he and her balloon was much lighter than his, so much lighter that he could not make a successful ascent with it. He reminded me of my talk of the previous day and more as a poke at me suggested that I go up in place of himself. He thought he was giving me the merry ha-ha and offered me $400 if I would make the ascent. He was to get $1,200 for it, but he said he would have to throw up the contract as it was impossible for him to ride the light bag. I was making each week with my partner a fraction of what he offered me. I had my brags and a fellow in the show business feels like sticking to them. This was a poser of a proposition. There wasn't any hole to crawl into anywhere so I just stood and looked at column after column the professor had in newspaper clippings telling what he had done and which he kept shoving my way when he saw me weakening.

It was an actual fact that I had never seen a balloon ascension myself and that I simply knew they were possible and that parachute jumps were often taken. The upshot was that I decided to go it against the demands of my partner and against my own feelings, you better believe. The professor, who had no idea that I had nerve enough to take the offer, was a little dazed himself and he left me any number of chances to back out. I guess he didn't want to cart my bones home and take the responsibility but I hung on and I walked out of the dressing room on the eventful afternoon decked out in my prettiest tights and feeling as if I was going to my funeral. I wouldn't go through the preliminaries again for a family I had to feel everything I felt on that occasion. The balloon was a huge bag, even if it was Van Tassel's lightest. It was a ninety-footer, made to go higher than blazes for a spectacular fall. Maybe you think it didn't look big tugging away at the ropes. The professor gave me one more chance to back out and when he saw I was game, he shoved a $100 note in my hands as an evidence of good faith and got me in the harness while I was stowing the money away in my flashy garments.

Don't tell me anything about people getting afraid. I guess if I hadn't had the life belt strapped about me and if the ropes to the bag had not been allowed loosened, I would have thrown the $100 note at the professor and flew for the lake or anywhere to get out of sight of the monster that I was tied to. I was jerked up before I could hesitate. Instinctively I had followed advice carefully pumped into me, to run along and give a spring as the balloon was freed for the ascent. It was not one-tenth as bad as I thought. My limbs were through rope loops and the life belt around my waist would have held me if I had lost consciousness. But I actually began to enjoy myself though for a moment, I was limp. The earth spread out a huge saucer below me. Gradually I saw the lake below, from end to end. In a few moments, I looked over the mountains near and then across into the valleys beyond. Then I saw other lakes and other mountains. It was a fine day and the sight was so novel that when the signal pistol was shot from below for me to cut loose, I was simply wondering what held me up and how fine it was. The balloon had gone into a cloud and the hundred feet of rope that held me ran upward seemingly supported by nothing. Then I went into the cloud too and as the mist struck into me, I felt for the first time what I was there for.

The pistol shot suddenly recurred to me as a signal to drop. The trip had been so interesting that I had clear forgotten all about the end but you better believe I tumbled to myself then. The bag was still rising and I got out of the cloud and sent my hand out slowly for the rope which would cut me loose. I got it in my hand and stopped. If I had ever seen a parachute drop before and had known how long the old style chute takes to open, I never could have pulled the rope. As it was, I drew my hand back and thought, with my heart in my throat, Just one pull and—. Say, but it was all I could do to hang on for a minute. Just one little pull and—. I felt for my $100 to see if it was safe and reached out for the rope. I tried it and it was all regular. Then I determined to do the business and raised my hand to give it the jerk. That rope seemed to hold the future, my life, my death, a thousand terrors.

The aeronaut who tells me he can drop several hundred feet straight and know what is going on all the time, I would like to see for a few minutes somewhere alone. Ten thousand sea sicknesses in one wouldn't do it justice. Eternity in a jumble, dreams, horrors, then insensibility to everything but dread were my feelings. I didn't look up to watch the chute to take notes when the wind came in. I couldn't. No one can. I hung on like the devil and let her rip. I couldn't think. I couldn't move. I could just grip with a dying man's hold the slender ropes that seemed to support me no longer. If the chute had not opened, I would have been unconscious long before the mile between myself and the ground had been covered. The fall would not have hurt me a particle for a few more seconds would have made me dead to all pain and as it was, I expected the thud any moment with less and less certainty where I was or what I was doing.

Then in a moment, I was sailing down admiring the saucer of the earth once more in all its beauty. The chute had slowly opened and I was falling only a hundred feet or so a second. Off a little way the balloon was just turning over for its drop. Then the ground grew nearer and larger and I fell with a thud that nearly drove my legs into my body right on the lake beach. An offer of $25 had been made to the first man who would get me if I fell into the water and the first thing I heard was a hurry up call from a fellow making for the shore in a row boat. "Jump in the water and let me get you and I'll divvy." But I prized my green suit and ignored the offer and felt for the $100 as the professor came running up brimming over with congratulations. I was only a short distance from the starting point.

It seems that I had made a star ascension. I had tumbled from the clouds in earnest. When I cut the rope, I was entirely out of sight from below in the clouds. The time I sat holding the string in my hand thinking it over was so long that those below thought the gear had fouled.[18]

It remains unclear how many in the audience actually knew that it was not Van Tassel who had made the leap from the sky but another daredevil with the Van Tassell stage name.

Millie Viola made another jump on June 10 at Lake Park.[19] While clearly the two teams of ballooning parachutists were competitive in Salt Lake, additional reports suggested that Price made use of a Van Tassel balloon on his attempt of June 2, 1889.[20] But it remains unclear how those reports could be true if Van Tassel had brought just his wife's balloon with him, unless his larger balloon had also arrived by train. Van Tassel and Price would soon see each other again under more collaborative circumstances, so it seems they left Salt Lake in friendship, perhaps even with a future partnership already planned. However, after appearing at Salt Lake, Price and Viola continued on their planned tour, with a paired ascension from Columbia Gardens in Helena, Montana, on July 9. On July 10 they made another spectacular paired ascension, to an altitude of 6,000 feet, and leaped simultaneously from their balloons to return to Earth via parachute.[21] And while Price and Viola were in Montana, Van Tassel continued on to his more familiar stomping grounds of New Mexico.

# 11. BACK TO ALBUQUERQUE

VAN TASSEL RETURNED to Albuquerque on June 29, 1889, in preparation for a balloon ascension, with a reporter from the *Albuquerque Morning Democrat* newspaper, and a parachute jump as part of 1889 Independence Day celebrations. However, the jump would be made by the lighter-weight Joseph Lawrence, while Van Tassel would supervise the launch. Upon joining the Van Tassel team, Lawrence became known as Joseph Van Tassell, Park's "brother."[1]

Joseph Lawrence was born on May 4, 1864, in Hookstown, Pennsylvania. He attended public schools at Hookstown, Darlington, and Beaver, becoming a clerk in a hardware store in Beaver Falls. Lawrence led a very clean life as a child, without using profanity, drinking alcohol, or indulging in any other vice. While employed at the hardware store, he often slept there overnight to serve as a guard. One evening burglars entered the building, only to discover Joe in the store. They opened fire on him and Joe returned fire, with the burglars fleeing the scene.[2]

At the age of seventeen, in 1881, with the help of his brother Walter, Joe took a position in another hardware store, at Fort Scott, Kansas. From there he moved to Kansas City to work in yet another hardware store. He suffered from rheumatism and was advised to move to Texas, but he moved to East Las Vegas, New Mexico, working in the Coors Brothers hardware store, and then Albuquerque, where he once again took a position in a hardware store. Lawrence met Van Tassel in either Salt Lake City or Las Vegas, New Mexico, or more likely upon his arrival at Albuquerque.

Citizens from both New Town and Old Town Albuquerque came to watch the balloon ascension at the fairgrounds. Many in Albuquerque remembered Van Tassel's prior success and failure. And given his previous exodus, it is perhaps surprising that no one asked to collect on a long-lost debt. However, just when Van Tassel wanted to make right with Albuquerque, he arrived with his wife's balloon and was working with a new performer (Lawrence). He tried to launch with both gas and hot air/smoke, but many "difficulties" arose and no launch was made. Once again, Van Tassel found himself a persona non grata in his former town, frustrated that he could not perform and make amends. Locals, remembering how Van Tassel's balloon had escaped without him at the 1882 New Mexico Territorial Fair, were outraged. Folks who journeyed north from Socorro and south from Santa Fe felt they had once again been deceived by Van Tassel. An anonymous author commented in the *Santa Fe Daily New Mexican*, "Peague explains why the bear fight did not take place [as part of July 4 celebrations], but Van Tassell does not tell why the balloon did not go up on the 4th."[3] Both Van Tassel and the public in general were beginning to tire of missed ascensions.[4]

Van Tassel and Lawrence left Albuquerque behind, heading back to San Francisco, making risky but thrilling parachute jumps at cities along the way, with Lawrence as the jumper. It isn't clear if Lawrence received an equal share of the gate receipts or if he was hired by Van Tassel as his parachute jumper at a reduced rate. At Santa Monica, California, Lawrence (called simply Van Tassel in the papers) made an ascension on July 27, 1889. An estimated twelve thousand spectators watched as he launched in a smoke balloon from a bluff north of the pier at 3:30 p.m. and rose to an approximate altitude of 4,000 feet before leaping with the parachute. He fell quite fast for an estimated 400 yards before the parachute opened, and he landed on the ground safely. The balloon came back to Earth on Ocean Avenue near the home of US senator John P. Jones.[5] Later, Park Van Tassel noted to a reporter, "When he [Lawrence] sprang from the balloon over a mile and a half from the earth. He was clear out of sight, the clouds being very high, and a prettier sight you never saw then when the clouds opened, it seemed, and let him fall through." Lawrence added, "I came down terribly fast," to which Van Tassel added, "Yes brother, too fast."[6] But Lawrence finally had a successful parachute jump under his belt.

The duo stayed in the Los Angeles area for another week, promising another ascension on August 5, 1889. Prior to the attempt, newspapers suggested that Lawrence would leap from the tremendously high altitude of

10,600 feet and that it would be "the most sensational [jump] that he has ever attempted." However, on August 5 the afternoon winds were so strong that it was nearly impossible to launch. The crowds were large and patient, and slowly the winds subsided in the late afternoon. The balloon ascension began at nearly 7:00 p.m., and Lawrence leaped to a successful parachute descent, much to the pleasure of the spectators. Once again, papers reported this as a jump by "Van Tassell," still confused as to which "brother" was actually doing the jumping.[7]

Continuing on, the duo stopped in Fresno for a parachute jump. This was the first time Park made formal mention of Joseph Van Tassel as his "brother" to reporters.[8] Newspapers largely assumed that after Park's initial jump at the Cliff House, he was the one doing all the jumps. In Fresno, a reporter for the *Fresno Expositor* interviewed Park at the Hughes Hotel. The reporter described Park as weighing 200 pounds, "built like Apollo and very handsome."[9] When asked how many jumps he had made, Park answered that he had made twenty-eight jumps and that "Joe has jumped six times and Mrs. Van Tassell has jumped once."[10] (With the exception of Clara's one jump, these numbers were likely exaggerations.) When the reporter asked, "How does it happen that your wife has made but one jump?" Park replied, "Because, sir, I wouldn't endure the agony I suffered when she did jump for all the money on earth. I think I suffered a thousand deaths. She went up 5,600 feet, but she will never do it again."[11]

On August 18, 1889, their launch at Fresno was once again precluded by high winds. More than three thousand people had come from all over the San Joaquin Valley to see the ascension. Roughly one thousand of them had paid fifty cents to be inside the enclosure for the launch, and their money was returned to them at the gate. The remaining two thousand "stood up on their buggy seats and peered over the fence. Horsemen stood on their saddle; small boys glued their eyes to cracks and knot holes; ladies tiptoed in their carriages, and thus, from half-past 2 until 5 o'clock, they endured the heat of the sun, because they wanted to see the show."[12]

Determined to make an ascension for the citizens of Fresno, the team set a date of August 25 for the attempt.[13] On that date, with two thousand spectators gathered to watch the first parachute jump in Fresno County, the balloon ascended just fine, taking Lawrence to an altitude of roughly 7,000 feet.

But a problem with the rip cord prevented the parachute from detaching properly. As a result, Lawrence rode down in the balloon.[14] It was Lawrence's first miscue, but he played out the issue safely.

Park and Joe tried again in Fresno on October 3, 1889, as part of the county fair. At 2:00 p.m., all was ready. Fifty men held tight to the balloon to secure it in position. On the ascent, Joe released fifty thousand small colored cards, which floated down on what little breeze was aloft. At 6,500 feet, Joe cut loose and proceeded to make a perfect parachute jump, landing exceedingly close to the original point of takeoff.[15]

From Fresno, Park and Joe moved on to attempt another balloon launch and parachute jump at nearby Visalia, California. The balloon ascended just fine, but then Joe had trouble. Instead of the more typical arrangement of securing the parachute to the side of the balloon at its equator, Park and Joe had attached the parachute directly to the bottom of the balloon. A connecting cord passed through a box containing a knife to cut the cord. A jerk on a pull cord for this box should have severed the rope between the parachute and the balloon. Joe tugged away at this pull cord for minutes without success. Meanwhile, a large rent formed in the side of the balloon, causing it to descend. The rate of descent began to increase, and Joe was now in serious trouble of landing at high speed. A reporter wrote, "The last fifty yards seemed as though they were being traversed in a second and the crowd from the back of the grandstand made a rush to see what many feared would be a pulp. The aeronaut, however, was most fortunate. He fell in the softest spot in a wide meadow, on the top of a twenty-foot haystack, which seemed as though it might have been placed purposely to receive him."[16] Lawrence was lucky to survive, and the "brothers" postponed further ascensions until the balloon and the parachute release mechanism could be repaired.[17] They headed for San Francisco with loftier goals in mind.

# 12. HAWAII

ON OCTOBER 20, 1889, Van Tassel began a new phase of his life. He boarded the steamer RMS *Alameda* from Meiggs' Wharf in San Francisco, bound for Honolulu, Kingdom of Hawaii.[1] The *Alameda* was an iron-hulled steamship built in 1883 in Philadelphia for the Oceanic Steamship Company, in service between San Francisco, Hawaii, and Sydney. Park traveled with a purpose—to bring ballooning and parachuting to Australia and Asia as part of an eighteen-month touring show, in a manner similar to Thomas Baldwin's exhibition. Hawaii was the first stop.[2] Accompanying him on the *Alameda* were Frank Frost (the business manager who had so courageously handled the angry mob at the San Jose ascension) and Joseph Lawrence, performing as Joseph Van Tassell.[3] Together they departed San Francisco with two balloons, two parachutes, and Park Van Tassel's "patent gas generator." Their planned itinerary was to visit Honolulu and then Auckland, Wellington, Christchurch, and Dunedin, New Zealand, and from there Hobart, Tasmania, Melbourne, Victoria, and other points in Australia before going to Java, China, Japan, and India. Following India, the plan was to go to Ceylon (modern-day Sri Lanka), Mauritius, Madagascar, South Africa, and then Europe via Egypt and the Suez Canal and Turkey.[4] Considerable thought went into such a plan, indicating that the route may have been chosen while Van Tassel was in Utah. It is also notable that Clara was not a part of this lengthy trip, as their marriage was now likely strained. Park was quoted as saying, "I expect to be in New York about a year and a half from now. Whether I will give exhibitions in the East, or come back directly to San Francisco, I have not yet determined, but I expect by that time I will be so homesick that as soon as I am again on American soil I will make a bee line for California."[5]

They arrived in Honolulu on October 28, 1889.[6] Park was now absolutely finished with making parachute jumps. He would manage the troupe and prepare the balloon while Joe would do all the jumping. In Hawaii, all gate receipts were under the care of L. J. Levey.[7]

The Van Tassell Troupe, as it was now known, did not waste any time. At Kapiolani Park on Saturday, November 2, about five hundred people gathered to watch the balloon launch, but thousands more watched from other vantage points, such as the top of Diamond Head. A Hawaiian band played during the afternoon, and the lack of trade winds was perfect for ballooning. At 3:30 p.m. the balloon inflation began and remarkably was completed in just thirty minutes, indicating that this was likely a smoke balloon, although reports suggested they used a combination of hot air and gas. At 4:00 p.m. the balloon rose into the air with Joe aboard, sitting on a trapeze rope. The balloon rose about 1 mile, but on the ascent, several guide ropes entangled and Joe attempted to unwind them from his seat. While he made these adjustments, the balloon began to descend and Joe decided to jump. He managed to partially inflate the parachute and jump, which made the typical initial fall less abrupt. He landed roughly 200 yards from the point of takeoff, between a set of trees. The newspapers reported that while he was aloft, Joe could hear the band playing and said, "Diamond Head looked like a small saucer." The balloon drifted to the south and landed about the same time as Joe, but about 100 yards outside the park near Diamond Head. David La'amea Kamananakapu Mahinulani Naloiaehuokalani Lumialani Kalākaua, the king of Hawaii, was present for the exhibition and completely enjoyed the show. Lawrence's flight is considered the first fully successful balloon ascent and parachute descent in the history of Hawaii.[8] Emil Melville, the same aeronaut who had shared the skies over San Diego with Van Tassel in April 1888 had made three attempted balloon launches at Kapiolani Park in March and April 1889. His third attempt, on April 7, had him aloft over Palace Square, but strong trade winds blew him out to sea, where he was able to jump from the balloon near the surface and be rescued. The balloon was also recovered and towed back to port. Melville had intended to jump by parachute but never had the chance to do so, and his attempts were not considered a success.[9] Van Tassel described his balloon and parachute to a reporter for the *Hawaiian Gazette*:

We go up in a balloon which holds 75,000 cubic feet of gas and lifts

An advertisement in the *Honolulu Daily Bulletin* on October 31, 1889, for the first successful balloon flight and parachute drop in Hawaii's history. Library of Congress.

2,800 pounds. Only one goes up for a reason you will understand later on. The parachute is fastened to the side of the balloon with a rope. It has no ribs, like an umbrella, but is perfectly flexible all over. It is made of pongee silk with 36 ropes sewed in it like ribs of an umbrella, and then all brought together at the bottom. Underneath the parachute is an ordinary trapeze. When we get ready to jump, we swing out of the balloon throwing one leg out of the trapeze under the parachute. Then we cut it loose at the same instant pulling a cord that collapses the balloon. We fall the first two hundred feet with terrible rapidity and then comes the most dangerous part of the jump, next to landing, for in falling the two hundred feet the parachute opens and it brings up with a jerk that almost hurls you off the bar. It did hurl that poor fellow off in Texas the other day. Well, again, after the first jerk you fall again quite rapidly and then comes another jerk, after which it is very pleasant until you get close to the ground. Now, if your parachute was to touch the roof of a four-story building say, it would instantly turn sideways, collapse and you would fall the rest of the way like a rock. So far I have been very fortunate, but I have had some narrow escapes.[10]

Given that King Kalākaua's fifty-third birthday fell on November 16, Frost announced that the "Van Tassell Bros." would perform a parachute jump over the city in honor of the king from the foot of the Punchbowl,[11] with a landing near the Government House.[12] Near the end of the grand celebration for King Kalākaua, the twenty-six-year-old Joe climbed aboard the balloon and was launched at 2:19 p.m.[13] On the way up, Joe shouted to Park that he estimated he would land not more than a mile from the park.[14] However, while the surface winds at the launch location weren't all that strong, the trade winds aloft were much stronger. Once at altitude, the balloon was blown rapidly to the southwest, toward the Pacific Ocean. In a short time, the balloon passed over Iolani Palace, where Joe was supposed to cut loose and begin his descent. But as rapidly as he made his preparations, the balloon continued making haste, over the city's opera house and toward the ocean. Just three minutes after launch, he separated from the balloon. The thousands watching from the streets below began to cheer. But as soon as the parachute opened, it began drifting out to sea along with the balloon. Together, the balloon and parachute continued past the lighthouse, past the outer buoy, and into the open ocean. Joseph made his ocean landing roughly ten minutes and eighteen seconds after launch, having drifted about 5 miles from the Punchbowl. Five minutes after, the balloon also landed in the ocean.

Two sailboats, the *Kahihilani* and a cutter belonging to the HBMS *Espeigle*, happened to be in the entrance to Pearl Harbor and noticed the parachutist drifting seaward. Meanwhile, the yacht *Hawaii* was off the coastline of Waikiki with Lorrin Andrews Thurston, minister of the interior of the Kingdom of Hawaii, on board. All three vessels set off immediately for the spot where Joseph had landed. Park Van Tassel, Frank Frost, and Wray Taylor (a reporter for the *Daily Bulletin*) frantically made their way to the harbor and boarded the tug *Eleu*, operated by a Captain Rice. However, twenty-five long minutes elapsed before the steam-powered tug could get under way. Two rescue boats were also immediately launched from the RMS *Zealandia*, which was about a mile away from port, having journeyed from Sydney to Honolulu by way of Auckland. The rescue boats conducted a search from 3:00 to 5:30 p.m. without any success in locating Lawrence. A boat from the Myrtle Club came to help. No trace of Lawrence or his parachute could be found. Floating on the surface of the ocean, the balloon was fished out of the water and brought onboard the *Eleu*, which returned to Honolulu Harbor. Rumors that sharks had devoured Lawrence circulated quickly, as some in the rescue party spotted a group of large sharks nearby. It is also equally probable that the weight of the parachute and its iron ring below simply pulled Joe under to his death. His body was never recovered.[15]

News of "Van Tassell's" tragic death made national and international papers.[16] Frost later attempted to clear the air with a letter to the editor of the *San Francisco Examiner*, detailing that before the launch, Joe had been offered a life preserver but had declined, as he believed himself to be a good swimmer and did not believe he would be landing in the ocean.[17] Nearly two years after the incident, Clarence W. Ashford, attorney general of the Kingdom of Hawaii, recalled to the press in Chicago that as Joe was nearing the water, several local Hawaiians had spotted sharks near the area where Joe would land. He went on to note, "Just before Van Tassel struck the water two of the mammoth man-eaters rolled over on their backs and opened their huge jaws. One of the sharks grabbed Van Tassel almost before he touched the water and in a couple of gulps the man was swallowed." As with many tragic deaths, the rumors and second-hand accounts of Joseph Lawrence's death grew more horrific with time.[18]

Lawrence's background was also embellished in the papers. Some reported that he had studied medicine, that he had made a balloon ascension for Queen Victoria in England, that he had been with a circus, and that he was a man without morals. But those who knew him realized the amazing degree of fiction that can be generated for a better story.[19] Even Queen Lili'uokalani later included Joe Lawrence's tragic flight in her famous book *Hawaii's Story by Hawaii's Queen*:

> As we were all gayly going to lunch . . . attention was attracted to a balloon which was at the moment ascending from the foot of Punch-Bowl Hill. Scarcely had the light globular object reached the upper currents of the atmosphere, when it was whirld [*sic*] away with fearful speed, for it was a very windy day. On watching the car under the balloon, we noticed that the man had cut himself adrift, and

# Journal des Voyages

### ET DES AVENTURES DE TERRE ET DE MER

Nº 658. — Prix : 15 centimes. — JOURNAL HEBDOMADAIRE — Bureaux : 8, rue Saint-Joseph.
Abonnements. — Paris et Seine, 8 fr. — Départements, 10 fr. — Étranges, 12 fr. — Dimanche 16 Février 1890.

LA FIN D'UN AÉRONAUTE. — Il tomba au milieu des requins. (Page 100, col. 1.)

The tragic fate of Joseph Lawrence (performing as Joseph Van Tassell) on February 16, 1890, grabbed worldwide attention, including a cover story in *Journal des Voyages* in France. Personal collection, Gary Fogel.

was descending from mid-air in a parachute. He was coming down bravely; but what was the horror of all of the spectators to observe that instead of landing on the wharf, or even in the port, he was being carried far out to sea, beyond the breakers, where the waters were alive with sharks. Steamers and boats . . . immediately got under way to effect his rescue, but he was never seen again. The balloon from which he had made his fatal leap also disappeared, and no trace of either was discovered. The poor man probably met his fate from the jaws of the monsters of the deep the moment he touched the water.[20]

Reporters failed to realize that there were two "Van Tassells" (Park and Joseph) and immediately assumed that the more experienced balloonist and parachute jumper, Park, was the one who had perished. This confusion continued for some time until Clara noted in an interview with the California press that Park was quite likely alive. She said that while Park was a strong swimmer, Joe Lawrence of Albuquerque was not, and if Park had perished, Joe certainly would have sent immediate word to Clara, but none had been received. She also mentioned that Park "had not taken a leap since the one at the Cliff House."[21] Following this news, some papers corrected their previous stories; in other cases, the correction came years later, if at all.[22] It took until April 1893 for people to propose balloon exhibitions in Hawaii again, with the next successful balloon launch and parachute descent made in February 1896 by the same James Price that Van Tassel had encountered in Salt Lake City earlier in 1889.[23]

Lawrence left a mother, two brothers, and three sisters.[24] His mother resided in Kansas.[25] Following his death, some questioned why he didn't agree to use a life preserver, as it was clear that there were strong trade winds aloft and a high likelihood he could end up in the Pacific. Perhaps the decision was one of pride when going aloft in front of the king. Others wondered why ships weren't stationed in the harbor in the unfortunate likelihood that a landing at sea would be made. However, most were resigned to believe that the simple lesson from such tragedy was that Honolulu was not the proper place for balloon ascensions. A $50 reward was offered for anyone who recovered Joseph's body from the sea, but no one ever collected.

Later it was determined that Lawrence had been engaged to marry Janet Grant of San Francisco and that he had written to her on the morning of his ill-fated flight: "We are supposed to make an ascension this afternoon but things are not ready, and Van is at home in bed, drunk, and if there is anything to be done he will have to do it, as I will not take any chances on my life with a drunken man. If I can get a position here of any kind, I will remain, in preference to going along with the party, all of whom have been on a continuous toot since leaving Frisco."[26]

It is easy to infer that had Lawrence survived, he would have ended his parachuting relationship with Van Tassel and returned to San Francisco. However, Frost was sure to state to reporters from the *San Francisco Examiner*, "As regards to P. A. Van Tassell being drunk, I must say that it is a complete falsehood. He was never more sober in his life on that fatal day."[27] Lawrence's unfortunate death shocked the entire Van Tassell Troupe, which had to decide whether to continue on with the tour or not, now that Park's parachute jumper was gone.

# 13. AUSTRALIA

DESPITE JOSEPH LAWRENCE's tragic death, Park Van Tassel and Frank Frost decided to continue with their tour. The reasons for this remain unclear, although given that shows were likely already booked, canceling them probably meant a considerable loss of income and possible debt. They departed Honolulu on November 25, 1889, aboard the SS *Mariposa* headed for Sydney by way of Auckland.[1] There is no record of any balloon flights in New Zealand by Van Tassel during their transit.[2] And while there is record of only Van Tassel and Frost boarding the *Mariposa* in Honolulu, arriving with them in Sydney on December 12, 1889, was James William Price, the parachutist Van Tassel had encountered earlier that year in Utah.[3]

Price was born in Gentry County, Missouri, on May 15, 1871, but for a time called Cleveland his home.[4] He took balloon instruction from Q. N. Fisk, making his first balloon ascension at Clinton, Missouri, on July 4, 1883. From there it is believed he traveled to England to tour with balloons, although no hard evidence of this tour can be found. He came back to the United States in 1885 and toured through 1887, when he heard of Baldwin's parachute jumps from balloons. From that point, parachute jumps became part of his routine.[5] Working in Australia as Van Tassel's parachutist in place of Lawrence, Price adopted the stage name Professor James Van Tassell—yet another of Park's many famous "brothers." The fortuitous nature of Price happening to be on the same ship was unlikely to be coincidental; it was likely part of a plan from their time together in Utah. It may also be the case that young Australian Millie Viola encouraged their trip to Australia, although there are no records of a Ruby Hawker or a Millie Viola aboard the *Mariposa* on this voyage.

Together, Van Tassel and Price began a lengthy series of balloon ascensions and parachute jumps across Australia. The first of these was originally planned

Illustration of James W.
Price in the *Evening Bulletin*, Honolulu, February 18,
1896. Library of Congress.

PROF. JAMES W. PRICE.
(The man who is going to jump through 5000 feet of space at Remond Grove on Saturday.)

for December 21, 1889, with the "brothers" using a "mammoth balloon" at
Bondi Aquarium near Sydney. Admission was one shilling; half-price for
children.[6] The Executive Committee of Sports at Bendigo, Australia, also
arranged for the "brothers" to give "a double balloon ascent and double parachute falls on terms, and if their performance was not successful there should
be no pay."[7] The ascension was to take place on Boxing Day 1889 from the
Agricultural Show Grounds as a part of a sports and gala event.[8]

On Saturday, December 21, a large crowd gathered at Bondi Aquarium[9]
and its surrounding hillsides to witness a balloon ascension and parachute
jump by J. P. Van Tassell (James Price). Newspapers described the balloon as
being made of gray calico with patches in many places, bearing "the appearance of having done much work." Inflation of the smoke balloon started at
4:00 p.m., but just as that process was about to get under way, a pole supporting the balloon snapped. The balloon came down with an "immense force" but
without damage, narrowly missing several assistants. Another pole was supplied, and the balloon was inflated in roughly thirty-five minutes over an
earthen furnace. Once it was inflated, Price sat on the trapeze bar below the

balloon and shouted, "Let go!" The balloon rose instantly. It floated briefly toward the west and then along the coast in a slight breeze. At a height of about 3,000 to 4,000 feet, the parachute was observed to open and Price was on his way back to Earth. He landed not far from the aquarium in the scrub near the Ocean View Hotel. A large crowd ran to his location, but Price was already walking back to the point of takeoff. The balloon landed shortly after. Word of this successful feat spread quickly throughout Australia,[10] with Frost describing James as "cool as a cucumber."[11] News of the success was also reported back to Hawaii and the States.[12] Although this was not the first parachute jump in Australia, parachuting was still so novel that few had ever witnessed such a daring feat.

Given their success, a second launch and jump was scheduled at Bondi Aquarium for December 26 (Boxing Day).[13] At 1:00 p.m. that day, thousands again began to gather at Bondi Aquarium, awaiting the balloon flight. It remains unclear why a launch wasn't made on Boxing Day at Bendigo as previously considered. As the crowd sweltered in the heat, troubles began with the inflation process. A strong breeze made things difficult, and approximately fifty people were enlisted to help keep the balloon steady. Getting the balloon to remain over the hot air coming from the fire was challenging. The strong winds kept shifting the balloon, and at one time it was in danger of being set aflame when a bucket containing flaming gasoline got very close to the fabric. Park, Frank, and James had differences of opinion about how to handle the inflation. A newspaper reported that "on more than one occasion sharp words were passed, which would have been far better left unsaid." Clearly Van Tassel and Price were still getting to know each other, and having to do so on the job.

At 6:20 p.m. Price and the secretary of the Bondi Aquarium walked to a podium near the aquarium's seal pond to address the crowd. Price said, "My friends, ladies, and gentlemen, my partners want me to go up, but I know there isn't sufficient lifting power yet in the balloon. She won't carry me clear of that ere switchback, and that's all the trouble, but not to disappoint you I'll make the attempt, and that's all about it. If I get clear of the switchback I'm all right. I've been ten years at my business, and I think I ought to know it."[14] Price then proceeded back to the balloon to prepare for launch. When it was clear that the balloon lacked sufficient lift to get over the nearby hillside with the weight of the aeronaut, the balloon was released without a passenger. It floated away and was soon lost to sight, landing about 3 miles away at Coogee. Deposited in the home garden of a Mr. Sandbrook, the balloon ruined a flagpole and all its rigging.[15]

Price once again walked to the rostrum and expressed regret that the inflation had not worked as desired. Sandbrook later sued the Bondi Aquarium for £25 in damages to his house and grounds caused by the balloon's "landing."[16] A Judge Wilkinson consulted with both parties, and in the end the Bondi Aquarium Company paid a settlement of £10 to end the matter.[17]

On December 28, the *Sydney Morning Herald* noted that, weather permitting, another attempt would be made that afternoon.[18] That same day, the *Leader* in Melbourne published the story of "Joseph Van Tassell's" tragic passing in Honolulu.[19] This timing suggests that the Van Tassel troupe had kept the news hidden from view as they began their tour of Australia. As a new balloon was sorely needed, an advertisement was placed in the *Daily Telegraph* in Sydney: "WANTED, 15 GIRLS, to sew on Balloon by week. Apply immediate, Van Tassell Brothers, Peyton's George Hotel, Market St."[20]

Van Tassel, Price, and Frost settled their differences and set forth on building a new large balloon for an ascension on January 11, 1890, at Bondi Aquarium.[21] By January 9, the new balloon was complete and was christened the *Australia*.[22] The balloon had a capacity of 70,000 cubic feet and was designed to be inflated with either gas or hot air. It was billed as the "largest balloon ever inflated in Australia."[23]

The *Australia* was brought to Bondi Aquarium on January 11 as planned, but the weather once again did not cooperate, leaving spectators to be entertained instead by an "electric orchestra," a strong man, and a set of "midgets."[24] Frost informed the media that the "brothers" would make an ascension at Newcastle on Australia Day, January 26.[25] Newspapers billed the "Van Tassell family" as "the leading parachutists in the world."[26]

Rather quickly, the "brothers" became an even larger family. Two new mysterious sisters, Gladys Freitas (performing as Gladys Van Tassell) and Valerie Freitas (performing as Valerie Van Tassell), were added to the troupe. Not much is known about their origin. Both sisters had lived in Sydney since at least July 1885, when they had made their debut at the New Masonic Hall as "American sisters" in a theatrical performance.[27] Performing as the Fraties

Sisters, they continued their trapeze and dance act through the summer of
1885. They took a hiatus for some time before Gladys returned to perform a
trapeze act with a Mr. G. St. Clare on June 1, 1889, at Coogee Palace Aquarium in Sydney as a prelude to a balloon launch and parachute jump by a
Professor Jackson.[28] Soon thereafter, the sisters were performing as a pair
again as part of an "American troupe" at locations in Sydney from June 22 to
late December 1889.[29]

Valerie had a dancing act, while Gladys continued her trapeze work, billed
as the "Aeolian Wonder."[30] After one of the sisters had an unfortunate fall
from the trapeze, for a time they changed their act to a "song and dance"
routine. However, either by plan or good fortune, on December 24, 1889, the
sisters provided a double trapeze act as a part of a show prior to James Price's
jump at Bondi Aquarium. It must have been quite a show, as they became
affiliated with the Van Tassell Troupe quickly, at first to repeat their double
trapeze act to entertain the crowd during the balloon inflation. Likely in
reference to Park, Australian newspapers suggested that "Professor Van Tassell" was from New York State.[31] While Park was not from New York, the Van
Tassel family did trace its roots back to New Amsterdam (which became New
York), and this was likely the source of the confusion.

Balloon ascensions and some parachute jumps had occurred in Australia,
but with a large opportunity for fraud: showmen would charge at the gate and
then devise excuses to not attempt a launch, only to float away in the balloon
with the money. Frank Frost made considerable effort to ensure that the Van
Tassell Troupe was considered genuine. For the Newcastle ascension, Walter
Sidney of the Centennial Hotel held himself responsible for the return of gate
moneys if the ascent did not take place.[32] The event was scheduled for Monday, January 27, the official observance of Australia Day, even though it tradi-
tionally fell on January 26. Between two thousand and three thousand people
arrived at Newcastle Racecourse and paid a shilling for admission, only to
find a strong wind from the northeast. In fact, the wind was so strong that the
Van Tassell Troupe debated whether it was worth inflating the balloon at all.
Before any inflation began, the Van Tassell Sisters entertained the crowd with
their double trapeze act. This was followed by music from the Fourth Regiment Band. At 7:00 p.m., the balloon still sat in a less-than-full state. Many
in the crowd went to recover their money and leave, only to find that the man

with the gate money had already left. Hundreds left in disgust, and shortly thereafter either Park or James made a short speech to explain that the wind had made the launch impossible. But the crowd clamored for an ascent, and Price said he would try. The balloon was eventually released unpiloted, but it turned upside down and came back to Earth after being relieved of its buoyancy. The disappointed crowd left, while the Van Tassell Troupe reassured them that an ascent would be made at 9:00 the following morning (January 28) and that admission would be free of charge.[33]

As promised, on the morning of January 28, James Price (performing as James Van Tassell) made an ascent in the *Australia* from Newcastle Racecourse. However, at such an early time, and after the troubles of the previous day, only two hundred to eight hundred spectators were present, with more on Shepherds Hill. The morning was clear and bright, and it took only twenty minutes to get the balloon prepped for launch. After Park made all preparations, James "threw off his coat and said, 'Now I will show you an ascension.'" At 9:25 a.m. he held onto the trapeze bar and shouted, "Let her go." The balloon raced to 500 feet with James hanging by his hands, something that amazed the crowd almost as much as his daring parachute jump. At a height of 4,000 to 6,000 feet, Price pulled a rope and dropped "like a meteor" for hundreds of feet before the parachute finally opened. He landed near the A. A. Company's Hamilton coal pit near the Cronin farm, a short way from the colliery. The balloon landed a quarter of a mile farther downwind in a tree. Its recovery that afternoon required additional effort. As most of the people of Newcastle could see the event from all over town, there was great excitement.[34] Ironically, some newspapers noted that "Professor Van Tassell [Price] made a most successful balloon ascent and parachute jump, a la Baldwin, to-day," without any realization that it was Park Van Tassel who, together with Thomas Baldwin, had first tried jumping with a flexible parachute in San Francisco.[35]

Another ascent was arranged for Saturday, February 1, 1890, at the Albion Ground in West Maitland. Special trains were arranged to bring people to Maitland at 3:00 p.m.[36] Continuing with the tradition of recent ascensions, the Van Tassell Sisters provided a trapeze exhibition prior to the launch. The event also included a cricket match and a band. The launch was scheduled for 5:00 p.m.[37] But once again, Mother Nature threw a wrench in the works.

While five hundred people assembled at the cricket ground on Saturday afternoon, the weather was windy and showery. The balloon launch was scrubbed, and those who had paid admission were given tickets for Monday. On that day, the sisters performed to much delight,[38] but the balloon launch was again postponed due to weather. On Wednesday, one thousand spectators gathered at the cricket ground to watch Van Tassel's balloon launch and jump. There was difficulty in inflating the balloon, and an error with the detaching hook for the parachute left James Price on the ground while the balloon was launched. Needless to say, the crowd was not amused by the unpiloted balloon sailing aloft.[39] The launch was moved yet again, to Saturday, to coincide with the Wallsend Races, an amateur handicap horse race. The troubles that haunted the Van Tassell Troupe needed to be remedied quickly if the remainder of the tour was to be a success.

# 14. QUEENS OF THE AIR

MARKETING MATERIALS FOR Saturday, February 8, 1890, announced that one of the Van Tassell Sisters (billed as "Miss Val. Van Tassell") would make the balloon launch and descend by parachute at the Newcastle Racecourse. It remains unclear how Valerie was chosen for the task, or if she volunteered, but what was clear is that no woman had ever performed anything like this before in Australia. A newspaper noted, "As she is a first class athlete, no particular danger is apprehended."[1] Newspapers continued to suggest that the Van Tassell Sisters were in fact sisters of both Park and James, or daughters of one of them.[2] The balloon was scheduled to launch at 4:00 p.m. However, as with previous trials at Newcastle, there was great difficulty during inflation due to a strong breeze. While waiting for the wind to ebb, the band of the Fourth Regiment played a selection of songs while the Van Tassell Sisters performed their trapeze act. Inflation did not finish until 7:00 p.m., and at one time during inflation, the balloon was scorched by the fire used to generate the hot air. A few repairs were made and shortly after 7:00 p.m. everything was ready. Two thousand spectators watched as Val affixed herself to the trapeze under the great balloon, gave a kiss to her sister, and was launched skyward. In her "fancy costume," she waved one disengaged hand to the onlookers below. The balloon was released at the sound of a pistol fired by Park on the ground. Hovering briefly at apogee, the courageous Valerie jumped and began her rapid descent. The parachute opened, and she made a safe landing in a paddock near a brick kiln at Merewether (near Hamilton Pit, where a well-known disaster in June 1889 led to the death of eleven miners). Throngs of onlookers rushed in her direction to verify that she had survived. Meanwhile, the balloon landed in a paddock near Burwood. After the success, Valerie appeared with Frank Frost in front of the crowd, who regaled her and the rest of the Van Tassell Troupe as heroes. At the Centennial Hotel, where they were staying, owner Walter Sidney spent considerable time managing the many people who wanted to see the adventurous Valerie. The effort was a success and made national news as the first female parachute jump in Australia's history.[3] The citizens of Newcastle came together to provide Val with a gold medal in recognition of her daring parachute jump.[4]

After this tremendous success, the Van Tassell Sisters offered to make a paired balloon ascension and jump at 6:00 p.m. on Thursday, February 13, 1890, at the Newcastle Cricket Ground. However, no drop was made on that day. Instead, Gladys made a solo parachute jump on Saturday, February 15 from the Newcastle Racecourse. Following her launch at 6:05 p.m., she performed several acrobatic stunts on a trapeze bar before throwing both legs over the bar, coming to rest in a seated position for the rest of the ascension. The crowd loved the antics. At an altitude of about 3,000 feet, Park Van Tassel fired a starter pistol, indicating that it was time for Gladys to jump. She quickly did so and descended very rapidly for the first 300 feet, at which point the parachute opened nicely. With about 400 feet of altitude remaining before touching down, she proceeded to make another set of acrobatic feats on the trapeze bar, such as hanging on by one leg. The crowd of onlookers was amazed by these feats, and when Gladys landed in the very center of the racecourse, there was much elation.

Gladys noted to newspaper reporters that "the sight [from up above] was something lovely."[5] The local citizens were so taken with her efforts that they presented her with an additional £11. The *Australian Star* recognized the ascension as "the most daring ever witnessed in the colonies."[6] Meanwhile, the balloon landed behind Cameron's Hotel at Hamilton, and a large crowd gathered there to assist with its collection. When Gladys made an appearance that evening at the Centennial Hotel, a large crowd cheered her for a considerable time.[7] Local reporters felt the name Gladys Van Tassell was a "sweetly romantic and aristocratic name."[8] The Van Tassell Troupe headed off for Sydney to provide another ascension at Bondi on February 22.[9]

News of Gladys's fantastic acrobatic feats spread quickly. More than three thousand spectators showed up at the Bondi Aquarium on February 22. A roughly equal number gathered in and around the area, unwilling to pay a shilling to see the activity up close. Despite a strong northwest wind, James

Studio portrait of Gladys Freitas
(labeled "Gladys Mantasso" instead of
"Gladys Van Tassell") from the Elite
Studio in Sydney, circa 1890. Photographer Bradley & Rulofson. State Library
of Victoria (H24476).

Price, Park Van Tassel, and Frank Frost began inflating the *Australia* at
5:30 p.m. Twenty minutes later, everything was ready for launch. Valerie
Freitas (Val Van Tassell) arrived on scene, shaking hands on the way to the
balloon. She was launched at 6:30 p.m. to a tremendous cheer: "The crowd
cheered her till its collective throat seemed too hoarse for it to even speak."[10]
She pulled herself up and onto the trapeze and then turned over and hung
upside down, blowing kisses to the crowd below. Righting herself on the
trapeze, she continued to rise above 2,000 feet, at which point Park Van Tassel went to fire the starter pistol to signal her release. However, this time the
pistol wouldn't fire. Valerie continued to drift toward Coogee Bay at an
increasing pace, wondering when she should leap. Just as she was disappearing
from the crowd's view, it was clear that she had jumped, as the parachute
became visible on its way back to Earth. The lighter balloon continued to rise
higher and flew away toward Botany Bay. Meanwhile, Valerie descended to a
perfect landing next to a beautiful garden owned by a Mrs. Dennett on Arden
Street in Little Coogee. Valerie had to steer the parachute as best she could
in order to narrowly miss the house and a set of people playing cricket

nearby.[11] After securing her parachute, she borrowed a cloak from Dennett, hailed a horse-drawn cab, and made her way back to Bondi Aquarium. Upon arrival, roughly thirty-five minutes after her launch, she was met with a tremendous ovation. The spectators continued clapping until Valerie appeared on stage to take bows for their applause. News of this amazing feat traveled quickly across Australia.[12] A reporter from the *Australian Star* later interviewed Valerie and noted,

> She was afraid she would be blown out to sea, and felt very qualmish when she saw the raging sea beneath her. She did not know whether to cut loose and chance getting safely down on the rocks or take the more perilous alternative of being drowned, for that she would be as she couldn't swim a stroke, though she intended to learn some day . . . when she did not hear the expected pistol shot telling her to cut away she thought she would use her own judgment, as at this time she had passed over the Waverley Cemetery, and the wind had changed, she knew she was safe, and that fact, though she had never been afraid, restored a certain amount of nerve.[13]

Park Van Tassel was quoted as saying,

> We are going to show a sensation the world has never yet seen. We are going to build a balloon—a coal-gas one—that will carry the whole family, and we are all going up together and coming down in separate parachutes; but, you know, we can't do this at once, owing to the stinginess of those people who won't give us any encouragement, but for the sake of a shilling will remain outside and have a cheap show, and, therefore it takes a long time to rake up enough to enter into a big enterprise such as I contemplate.[14]

The reporter for the *Australian Star* wrote, "Everyone was loud in praise of the daring young lady who risked her life to prove that the apparently improbable theories of air-flyers were not such impossible achievements as our grandfathers thought."[15] Given that Valerie and Gladys had agreed to take turns with parachute jumps, Gladys noted to reporters, "We leave for Melbourne by steamer and I suppose we shall be giving the people down there a trial. They've not seen a woman come down in a parachute yet. Well it will be my work to introduce them to the novelty."[16]

News of their success in New South Wales preceded the Van Tassell Troupe to Melbourne, Victoria. On March 5, 1890, a crowd of roughly ten thousand spectators packed the Friendly Societies' Grounds.[17] In addition to those who paid their shillings to be on the grounds themselves, others waited on footbridges over railway lines, on balconies of the Government House, and at homes in the surrounding area, waiting to catch a glimpse for free. The Princes Bridge was jammed with spectators, and by 4:30 p.m. it was difficult to find any view of the dry Yarra River bed, where the *Australia* was being prepared. Pamphlets spread to the crowd discouraged "dodgers"—those who dodged their duty to pay a shilling to see the young lady who would soon risk her life in the sky.[18]

As was the case at Sydney, a strong breeze made it impossible to inflate and launch the balloon at the scheduled time of 4:30 p.m. This provided additional time for people to pay their shillings but also additional time to inspect the hot-air furnace and piping required for balloon inflation. By 6:00 p.m. the wind subsided (a fortunate occurrence, as it was not clear how it would be possible to repay everyone should the launch not take place). Frank Frost fired up the furnace and the inflation was under way. Gladys made her appearance to the crowd. A reporter noted, "Most people found it difficult to imagine that a young lady could possess the courage to essay a feat from which 99 percent of the so-called sterner and more courageous sex would turn away in dread."[19] Gladys prepared for launch, and upon her word of "I am right," a cry was heard to "Let go all." The twenty or so people who had been holding the balloon steady released their control. As the balloon rose to the south, Gladys performed her acrobatics on the trapeze bar and then returned to a seated position. Park Van Tassel fired the starter pistol when the balloon reached approximately 4,000 feet, and Gladys pulled the catch rope to the parachute and leaped into space. Free-falling for about 50 or 60 feet, the parachute opened gracefully, but the descent was reported to be faster than previous parachute jumps. Gladys steered the parachute to a landing near the barracks on St. Kilda Road.

Melbournite and event organizer James MacMahon rode on horseback in the direction of the balloon, arriving on the scene just shortly after Gladys's landing. A prearranged cab carried Gladys back to the launch grounds; she arrived about twenty minutes after launch. She mentioned to reporters that she "found the aerial currents of the most tantalizing nature, for although they had the same general direction, she found that they had different and greatly varying forces in the different strata of air."[20] Meanwhile, the balloon had been blown away to the south, landing in the bay near the anchored HMS *Nelson*. The crew of the *Nelson* took good care of the balloon before its return to Van Tassel. Later that evening, Gladys attended a performance of *Nemesis* at the Melbourne Opera House, sitting in a private box arranged by the management. Upon recognizing that she was in attendance, the audience regaled her with an ovation.[21] Calling her Australia's new "Queen of the Air," the Melbourne *Herald* noted, "Yesterday afternoon, the most daring action which has been attempted in Victoria was achieved by a woman."[22] An ascension for Valerie was arranged for Sunday, March 9, 1890.

It is of interest to note that although news of these jumps spread throughout the rest of Australia, the delay was in fact rather pronounced. For instance, when the Van Tassell Troupe was entertaining crowds at Melbourne, readers in Queensland were just learning of their activities in Newcastle and Sydney. News of the ascents and descents by the Van Tassell Sisters continued into late April.[23] Adelaide learned about the activities in Melbourne after March 14.[24] Out in Western Australia, Perth only began hearing of the events in Sydney in late March.[25]

On March 8, the *Herald* in Sydney carried a fascinating and detailed story of the mysterious and brave Van Tassell Sisters, noting that Valerie was the younger of the two by two years and making reference to their "mother," Clara Van Tassel, who had "made the first parachute jump by a woman in the world."[26] Meanwhile, Gladys (age twenty-one) was supposedly born in Boston in 1869 and had "made previous descents from giddy altitudes, but she was always accompanied by her father."[27] Note that there are no records of Park Van Tassel being Gladys's father or providing any balloon flights to Gladys or Valerie before their time together in Australia. Valerie was younger than Gladys by two years, so it is believed she was nineteen at the time of these jumps. And given that the name Freitas has a Portuguese anthroponymy, and the city of Boston, Massachusetts, had a large Portuguese population, the

A detailed illustration in the *Melbourne Punch* of March 13, 1890, showing all phases of a balloon ascension and parachute jump by the Van Tassell Sisters. National Library of Australia.

relation of the sisters to Boston is certainly possible. However, no records of their migration to Australia can be found. Be that as it may, the "family" was now the talk of Victoria. That same evening, the Van Tassell Sisters completed trapeze work for the audience from the stage of Victoria Hall. They were slightly out of practice, as Gladys fell during the trapeze act. She was "partially stunned" and largely unhurt but unable to continue the performance.[28]

On Saturday, March 9, it was Valerie's turn to descend by parachute over Melbourne. Advertisements told the public that the balloon would be launched at 4:00 p.m. However, once again, high winds were not in their favor. An attempt to inflate the balloon caused a large tear. Fixing the rent required a patch measuring 6 square feet, which took time to apply. At roughly 6:30 p.m., word spread through the massive crowd that Valerie would be

PEOPLE WHO ARE TALKED ABOUT.

TWO FEMALE ÆRONAUTS.

MISS VALERIE VAN TASSELL,
Who is to make a balloon ascent, and drop with a parachute to-day.

MISS GLADYS VAN TASSELL,
Who made the balloon ascent, and drop with a parachute on Wednesday last.

THE DEFEAT OF SAMPSON
THE "STRONGEST MAN ON EARTH"

On March 8, 1890, the front page of the *Herald* in Melbourne described the Van Tassell Sisters as the talk of the nation. National Library of Australia.

launching soon. Ten thousand people were reported to have paid their admission to witness the event.[29] Later reports put the number of paying spectators at twenty thousand.[30] As the sun set and the winds ebbed, the sky was left in the "pearly light" of twilight for the launch. Valerie made her way to the balloon at the Friendly Societies' Grounds and was greeted with applause, partially because the event was about to unfold, partially out of growing impatience. She was released to the sky quickly, and it was a more spectacular sight than Gladys's previous launch simply because of the clearness and beauty of the dusk sky above. As the balloon arrived to a height of about 5,000 feet, Van Tassel fired his starter pistol and Valerie jumped, falling rapidly for about 100 feet before the parachute unfurled. She landed safely behind a boat shed on the south bank of the Yarra River near the barracks on St. Kilda Road.[31] The balloon either came to rest near the city's gasworks[32] or flew over Albert Park and landed in the sea; reports were unclear.[33] It was collected later by the Van Tassell Troupe.

The press noted that Park Van Tassel would soon construct a new balloon to help avoid the delays associated with previous inflations.[34] It was also noted that several members of Australia's government were on hand to witness Valerie's jump. They included "Dr. Dobson [member of the legislative council] and Messrs Zox, Hall, W. T. Carter, and Shackell [members of the legislative assembly]. The Secretary of Defence was there; so was Dr. St. John Clarke. Of the dramatic profession, Mr. G. Musgrove, Messrs Vincent and Grattan Riggs arrived. Many leading gentlemen of the Civil Service were sure to make an appearance."[35]

# 15. ON TO ADELAIDE

ON MARCH 10, 1890, it was announced that the Van Tassell Troupe would soon be visiting the city of Geelong, to the southwest of Melbourne.[1] However, not everyone believed the troupe was acting rationally with its death-defying stunts. The *Australian Star* noted that the Western Australian attorney general Charles Warton, was reviewing acts of parliament in search of precedent to "prevent the darling young foreigner [either Valerie or Gladys] from sailing over Melbourne on her balloon and tumbling gracefully on a well-controlled parachute. The Justice Department wishes to indict her on the criminal charge of attempted suicide. But the Justice Department will fail."[2] A gossip columnist from a newspaper in Melbourne wrote:

> I suppose that all this sort of thing is very thrilling to many folk, but for myself if feats of daring are to be performed for my delectation, I prefer their happening where I can observe them without a telescope. Moreover I am too callous to experience the full charm of these descents. If Miss Van Tassell had been killed the circumstance would have seemed to me of no consequence at all, and interesting only as an item of news to be duly chronicled. Better women die every day in the discharge of duties for performing which they receive not a tithe of the money lavished on these adventurous females for their useless pranks.

James MacMahon visited the nearby mining town of Ballarat on March 10, 1890, to arrange for a Van Tassel performance.[3] The Ballarat ascension was confirmed to the public on March 12: the launch would take place on Saturday, March 15, at the Eastern Oval between 2 p.m. and 4 p.m. On March 15, roughly sixteen hundred spectators paid at the oval, but a far larger number, roughly ten thousand people, viewed for free from the nearby railway embankment and surrounding heights.[4] While it was thought that Gladys Van Tassell was to leap, James Price leaped instead. The wind and gusts were noted as the reason for this change.[5] However, given that this was the test flight of their new balloon, perhaps it was determined that someone with greater experience should make the flight.

The ascent was delayed until 5:30 p.m., and hot smoke was used rather than gas for inflation. With James on the trapeze, the balloon made a rapid ascension to several thousand feet, drifting to the south roughly three-quarters of a mile in a strong north wind over the center of the city. He successfully released and descended, landing in a garden near the intersection of Humffray and Grant Streets near the Redan mines.[6]

An ascension for Sandhurst (also called Bendigo) was in preparation,[7] and Joe MacMahon (James's brother) completed the arrangements on March 20, with an ascension and jump scheduled for Wednesday, March 26. However, on the day of the event at the Agricultural Society Show Grounds, once again the weather failed to cooperate. Gusty winds blew from the southeast. Despite the winds, at 3:15 p.m. Van Tassel (either Park or James; it is not clear which) addressed the fifteen hundred spectators to say that he would try to inflate the balloon. When it was about one-quarter full, two large rents appeared and the gas escaped. The balloon was emptied while the rents were sewn, this effort taking more than an hour. It seemed to many that they were just buying time, but Park and James knew that such issues occurring aloft would be disastrous, and likely fatal. Another inflation was attempted, but with the wind still blowing and the time now past 6:00 p.m., Van Tassel announced that there would be no performance. He promised that they would attempt the ascension again at 5:00 p.m. on Thursday, March 27.[8] However, Thursday was worse than Wednesday. Just as the balloon was being inflated, it caught fire in several places, and the holes caused by the fires were large enough to make any chance for an exhibition impossible. The restless crowd, once again tested by their patience, began expressing their displeasure. The Sandhurst attempts were considered a "fiasco" in the papers. Park Van Tassel suggested that the troupe had made eighteen descents in Australia by this time, twelve with this balloon, but this is unlikely given its history. Balloons of this nature were expected to last twenty-five flights, but it was clear that by Sandhurst, this balloon was finished.[9] A new balloon was ordered from Melbourne. The Van Tassell Troupe would try again on Wednesday, April 2. However, the local populous remained eager for a refund of their shillings. To quell the uprising, MacMahon announced that another performance would be made on April 2 for free and that all proceeds received at the March 26–27 events would be donated to the Easter Fair.[10]

The new balloon was ready for action by April 1.[11] Meanwhile it was also announced that the Van Tassell Troupe would soon visit Hobart, Tasmania, to give an exhibition.[12] A newspaper on April 2 noted that the ascension at Sandhurst would be made by "Mr. Van Tassell," with proceeds in aid of the Bendigo Hospital and Benevolent Asylum.[13] Those who received coupons from the March 26–27 events would be admitted for free.

The Van Tassell Troupe took extra care to make sure the ascension of April 2 went smoothly. To ease public concerns, members of the Easter Fair Committee were put in charge of the gates. MacMahon also announced that if the ascension did not take place as promised, all receipts, including those from March 26–27, would be returned on presentation of coupons at the Evans music warehouse in town. This act restored a good deal of public confidence.[14] The public was specifically prevented from being near the balloon and the tools for its inflation. An estimated five thousand people were in attendance.[15] Shortly before 4:00 p.m., inflation began despite a gusty wind from the south. A set of volunteers helped control the balloon, and in about twenty minutes it was ready to be airborne. James Price took his place on the trapeze, but the volunteers released before he was ready, causing the balloon to jump several feet and to lose some hot air before it could be stabilized again. The balloon was refilled slightly and at 5:00 p.m. everything was back to being ready. At the signal, the release was made and James rode into the air, carried in a northerly direction. At an altitude of about 5,000 to 6,000 feet, the balloon settled on its own, causing the parachute to open out. James saw his chance and jumped without having to endure the usual fall. The descent was as advertised, but Price had to dodge a tall iron-spiked fence near the point of landing, choosing instead to fall through a eucalyptus tree roughly 200 yards from Sydenham Gardens. Onlookers applauded him and helped him return to the show grounds, where he was met with further rounds of applause. He and Frost thanked the public for their patience. The balloon was recovered near Whipstick, roughly 7 miles from Sandhurst.[16]

On April 7 it was announced that the Van Tassell Troupe would make another ascension at Sandhurst as part of the Easter Fair festivities on April 10, with half the proceeds going to charity.[17] Once again, James Price served as the aeronaut. The weather that day was beautiful, the balloon was filled in record time, and the event was made with a certain degree of perfection. James ascended in a south breeze to a height of about 5,000 feet before jumping, descending quickly, and landing perfectly near a camp of Chinese workers at Ironbark. The large assembly of people who had followed him on horseback and in vehicles brought him back to the show grounds, cheering and with great enthusiasm. Price addressed the crowd to say that "he hoped that they were satisfied that the failures on the first two occasions . . . were not due to any fault of his."[18] Price took considerable personal pride in his work and noted for the newspapers that he would return to repeat his performance at Sandhurst in the near future "before leaving for India."[19] The gate receipts amounted to £82, which was split evenly.

Arrangements were made for the Van Tassell Troupe to visit Adelaide and make a parachute jump in the new balloon on Saturday, April 26, 1890, at the Adelaide Oval.[20] They arrived in Adelaide on Wednesday, April 23. A reporter from Adelaide's *Evening Journal* interviewed the now-famous Park, "father" of the amazing Van Tassell Sisters:

> First of all I asked Mr. Van Tassell for some particulars concerning the parachute, to which he answered—"I am the inventor. For a long time I saw what resisting power an ordinary umbrella had and it occurred to me that if I could only construct a large umbrella, which the parachute really is, without any ribs, and so made as to open freely with the pressure of the atmosphere, it would be possible for such a thing to bear a man's weight." "And you were the first to make use of your invention?" "No, I tossed up with Tom Baldwin to decide whether I or he should go up and come down under the wings of the parachute. He cried 'Head!' and had to do the trick. Of course you have heard of his wonderful performance in California and England? Why, he was paid $20,000 for four performances at Golden Gate Park in

San Francisco. The first parachute leap was performed by him on
January 30, 1887, and I guess it made a big sensation." "It is needless
to ask if you are an American?" "Oh, yes, I am proud of being that.
I belong to San Francisco, and for the last fourteen years have been
engaged in building balloons and making ascensions in them." "What
is the greatest height you have attained?" "Well, I have often been up
pretty high, but the furthest point that I ever reached was at a distance
of 15,600 feet from mother earth." "How many parachute descents have
I made? Well, let me see, the last one was about six months ago, when
I descended in a parachute for the sixty-second time. I started experiments directly after Baldwin, and all my performances were crowned
with success." "For next Saturday's performance I am building a new
balloon, having just cut it out, and I am anxious to have a successful
afternoon's work on Saturday." The report went on with details about
the parachutes, that they were made of linen and measured 51 feet from
the lower end of the ropes to the top of the parachute.[21]

A reporter interviewed both Valerie and Gladys, describing Valerie as "of
medium height, good figure and face, a wealth of auburn hair, and genial style
about her that is very taking."[22] The sisters were in the process of making (or
perhaps mending) Gladys's parachute at their Adelaide hotel during the
interview. The reporter asked Gladys, "What is the sensation like when you
cut yourself adrift from the balloon?" She replied, "Well, in the first place you
dive through the air at such a speed that you can hardly think. It is like falling
from a steeple, and as the balloon soars away you experience a feeling of lone-
liness—like having an old friend taken away from you. You fall, as a rule, from
50 to 100 feet before the parachute expands, and then as you gradually descend
the feeling is a very pleasant one."[23]

J. Colton & Company in Adelaide began work on the troupe's latest balloon on Monday, April 20, and completed it by Friday, April 25. A reporter for
the Adelaide *Evening Journal* noted, "Twelve hundred and fifty square yards
of calico has been used and the balloon is composed of 365 pieces . . . fifty-two
of which are 75 feet long. The circumference of the balloon is 140 ft.,[24] and its
capacity is about 77,000 ft., which is a guarantee that it will ascend comfort-
ably with two persons."[25]

Newspaper advertisements for the April 26 balloon ascension hailed "Gladdys" as "America's Greatest Aeronaut, and the Only Lady who has ever made successful Parachute Jumps" and estimated the size of the March 5 crowd in Melbourne at "over 100,000 people."[26] As with previous jumps by the Freitas sisters, not everyone was pleased. In an editorial in the local paper, James Robertson, councillor for the town of North Unley, wrote that the Adelaide Council had not approved the forthcoming ascension and that if any accident were to happen, responsibility would fall to the cricketing association.[27] Others expressed outrage at the risqué garments worn by the Van Tassell Sisters for their ascensions, denouncing the stunts as "immoral."[28]

The exhibition scheduled for April 26 was apparently delayed to May 3, 1890, when several thousand people gathered at the Old Exhibition Grounds of Adelaide. After watching a fencing match between a Captain Jennings and W. V. Virgo, which Jennings won 15–14, preparations were made to launch the large new Van Tassel balloon, now christened the *City of Adelaide*.[29] Within roughly thirty minutes, the balloon took shape, and the very interested crowd burst into the enclosure where the balloon was being prepared. Meanwhile, the local police were pulling members of the public who wished to see the launch for free out of trees in the botanical park. Apparently, an insufficient number of police were available to keep control of the situation near the balloon itself. At roughly 5:05 p.m., Gladys appeared in light blue tights and was received with a warm round of applause. During launch preparations, someone in the crowd yelled "Let go!" and those holding the balloon released their grips, much to Park Van Tassel's concern and a danger to Gladys. One person holding the ropes properly refused to let go, was carried about 6 feet into the air, and finally did let go, without report of injury after the resulting fall. Up Gladys went on her flight anyway, performing trapeze work until the balloon became rather stationary over North Adelaide. According to a barometer taken with her to measure pressure and then later to back-calculate an altitude estimate, she rose to 7,640 feet. The balloon began to descend slightly, opening the parachute, and she jumped, descending to Earth. On the way down she performed more trapeze work, dangling by her calves and doing other feats. She landed at Wellington Square in North Adelaide. The balloon came to rest about a half mile away. A cab brought Gladys back to the grounds, and the large crowd let out a tremendous cheer.[30] A band at the

Advertising material for a parachute jump
by Valerie Freitas (billed as "Miss Val. Van
Tassell") at Kensington Oval in Adelaide, South
Australia, on May 10, 1890. National Library of
Australia (nla.obj-39339460).

nearby Wellington Hotel played Handel's "See the Conquering Hero
Comes."[31] While seven thousand to eight thousand people had assembled on
the exhibition grounds and paid their shillings, newspapers estimated that
twenty thousand people had witnessed the event.[32] Word quickly made it to
other cities, including Perth, Brisbane, and Sydney.[33]

The Van Tassell Troupe made plans to leave Adelaide for Brisbane by train,
with rumors that they would be leaving on Monday afternoon, May 5, 1890.
However, that morning, Park Van Tassel was arrested. It seems that Madame
Cora du Lamond of Melbourne had advanced Van Tassel £126 to cover costs
in the city, on the stipulation that she would receive half of any gate receipts
if exhibitions were held in Adelaide. Madame Cora was a well-known

entertainer and magician in Australia and believed she was to help the Van Tassell Troupe arrange exhibitions in Adelaide. However, a third party, Edwin Thorne, was used instead of Madame Cora, without her knowledge or consent. She filed a grievance for £80 in damages. On payment of £60 to the court, Van Tassel was released from custody.[34]

Another balloon ascent was made on Saturday, May 10, this time at the Kensington Oval and by Valerie. The weather could not have been more perfect, with clear skies and only a slight breeze. The *City of Adelaide* was filled at 5:00 p.m., and as an equal to Gladys, Val performed perilous trapeze work even at very high altitudes. The launch was essentially vertical, until the very top, when the balloon drifted slightly. Valerie jumped toward Magill Road. There, she came to Earth "in the neatest manner possible"[35] but in a field of stinkwort, not more than a mile from the Kensington Oval. Two prominent cyclists, W. Cox and W. Kuhnel, had tracked her progress and stood in the field as Valerie made her descent. Before landing she called out, "Don't get underneath." She was returned to the oval by cab and was presented to the crowd of eight thousand by L. M. Tier, much to the excitement of the many spectators. Newspapers reported that the ascent and descent were so perfectly achieved that the task was "robbed . . . of half of its terrors."[36] That evening the Van Tassell Troupe attended the theater to watch a performance of *Ruling Passion*, a play that included a balloon scene.[37]

# 16. DIVISION

ON MAY 13, 1890, newspapers in Geelong, Victoria, advertised that the Van Tassell Troupe would finally be coming to their town. However, these same advertisements also noted a conspicuous change: the troupe was "formally Van Tassell, but now [operated under] original names."[1] A rift between James and Park about the antics in Sandhurst and Adelaide, including Park's arrest and settlement with Madame Cora, left Price to exhibit in Geelong while Park continued on with Valerie and Gladys Freitas to Brisbane. At the same time, Price's former colleague Ruby Hawker (performing as Millie Viola) joined up with Price and was featured as the one to jump in Geelong. Interestingly enough, Millie had traveled to Australia to make a jump with James Price on April 25, 1890, before Price met with the Van Tassell Troupe in Adelaide. It seems that Price's growing frustration with Park built over a period of time, as it would have taken Millie weeks to make the voyage from the United States to Australia. Frank Frost also departed from the Van Tassell Troupe, choosing to continue on with Price and Viola instead.

This division was largely lost on the public. The *Geelong Advertiser* noted incorrectly that Viola "is perhaps more generally known in these colonies as Miss Van Tassell" and mentioned "her brother J. W. Price."[2] While Price wished to distance himself from Van Tassel, having just spent months following the progress of the Van Tassell Troupe, it was hard for the public to understand Millie's stage name. Similarly, Park Van Tassel wanted to distance himself from Price, as it seemed for a time that more than one Van Tassell was jumping simultaneously at different locations in Australia.

On May 13, 1890, at Geelong, it took more than an hour to inflate the balloon with hot air at the Agricultural Society's grounds in front of thousands of spectators. Millie Viola's launch was made in haste due to winds, and

Illustration of Millie Viola in the *San Francisco Call*, January 20, 1896. Library of Congress.

Millie Viola.
[*From a photograph.*]

there was no record of any trapeze work on the way up in the style of the Van Tassell Sisters. However, the descent that resulted was considered amazing: "Suddenly, to the relief of every one, the parachute expanded and the sight was pretty beyond expression. The descent was so slow, so graceful, that the feeling was one of regret that the sight could not be prolonged, and that the graceful Viola was only a beautiful meteor to flash across the sky at the interval beyond our calculation."[3]

The entire performance, from launch to landing, lasted roughly seven minutes. The balloon continued on its way in the direction of Breakwater, landing on the opposite side of the river, where it was later recovered. Viola was brought back to the starting location to the many accolades that were now common at these events. The local paper elaborated on her considerable experience in the United States—that she had made "37 different flights in balloons," even parachuting in 1888 near the shores of Lake Michigan, with her brother Price making sure she wore a life preserver.[4] Viola was just the third woman to parachute in Australia.

Price and Viola arranged for a double ascent at Geelong for Saturday, May 17. Viola was supposed to descend by parachute while Price remained with the balloon to bring it back down in a controlled fashion.[5] If this was the plan, it must have been with a gas balloon in mind rather than an uncontrolled smoke balloon. However, for unknown reasons, Price and Viola traveled to Maryborough, Victoria, instead, providing a parachute exhibition there on Wednesday, May 22. The balloon ascension was made from Princess Park with one thousand spectators, who each paid a shilling. A flight to 6,000 feet was made, with a perfect release and descent with a landing near Maryborough and Talbot Roads. The balloon was recovered about 1 mile south of that location. Very quickly, they returned to Geelong, with the hope of making their dual balloon flight as previously promised.[6] While no record of the dual ascension can be found, Millie did make another jump on Saturday, May 24, from the show grounds at Geelong in front of one thousand spectators. She landed with her parachute near Carlo Street while the balloon floated out to sea. It was recovered near Hutton's Wharf at North Geelong.[7]

Meanwhile, at Brisbane on May 14, announcements heralded that the now nationally famous "sisters Van Tassel" would be performing at the exhibition grounds on May 17.[8] However, inclement weather forced a cancellation. Those who had paid the entrance fee were provided with a card for return entrance for the next event, scheduled for Thursday, May 22.[9] During their time at Brisbane, the troupe stayed at the Shakespeare Hotel.[10] As promised, on May 22 they set up the balloon at the exhibition grounds. And as with many of their previous flights, the number of paying spectators and those who attempted to view from the surrounding area for free was roughly an equal. At 6:00 p.m., Valerie appeared, "in the ordinary attire of female athletes."[11] As she ascended, she performed her usual trapeze work. At a lower-than-usual altitude of about 1,600 to 1,700 feet above the Acclimatisation Society Gardens, she jumped and returned to Earth via parachute. She landed on the hospital grounds uninjured, on the lawn opposite the residence of the hospital's doctor.[12] Meanwhile, the balloon eventually landed in an old manure paddock at Kelvin Grove. Valerie once again returned by cab to the awaiting crowds. Capitalizing on the success, the troupe announced another balloon ascension for Monday, May 26.[13]

Back in Victoria, the May 24 issue of the *Bendigo Advertiser* noted that James Price "intends to fulfill a half promise he made at the time of the last Easter Fair. It is to give in conjunction with Mdlle [Millie] Viola, a double balloon ascent and parachute drop, and this sensational event will take place from the Agricultural Show Grounds on Saturday next. Mr. Price informs us that he is not the balloonist who was in trouble recently in Adelaide."[14] The Bendigo City Council approved Price's launch for the show grounds, to be held on Saturday, May 31, on "usual terms" of 10 percent of gate receipts and a preliminary deposit of £10. Price made his parachute jump at Bendigo.[15] However, it seems that on another attempt, the balloon was released skyward with both Millie Viola and James Price still on the ground, leading to complaints and groans from the crowd.[16]

Meanwhile, back in Queensland, preparations were made for the last appearance of the Van Tassell Troupe in Brisbane with an ascension by Gladys on Monday, May 26, from the Breakfast Creek Grounds.[17] However, tragedy was about to unfold. During preparation of the balloon, and while the balloon still lay on the ground prior to inflation, the crowd rushed in to the enclosure near the balloon as inflation began at 4:15 p.m. Park Van Tassel shouted loudly to the crowd to move back, but they paid no attention. Just as Van Tassel was about to light the furnace, one of the large wooden poles that retained the ropes for the balloon gave way and fell inward towards the balloon. It came down directly on a twelve-year-old boy named Thomas Reid, striking him in the back of his head. Two doctors who happened to be in attendance rushed into service, but it was for naught. Reid was pronounced dead at the scene, and there was nothing more that could be done. Gladys fainted and, upon regaining consciousness in a rather unnerved state, declined to make her ascension.[18] In light of the tragedy, J. A. Grant, manager of the Breakfast Creek Grounds, officially canceled the performance. He told onlookers that another balloon attempt would be made on the following Saturday.[19]

Some spectators who had witnessed the event placed blame directly on Van Tassel for not properly securing the pole to the ground in the first place. However, Van Tassel was positive that everything would have been safe had the crowds not rushed into the enclosure and put additional pressure on the guy ropes. It was clear to all that an insufficient number of policemen were on-site to control the crowd adequately. News of the tragedy spread quickly across Australia.[20] It is likely that even James Price and Millie Viola were made aware of the accident back in Victoria.

On Wednesday, May 28, a formal inquiry commenced at City Police Court in Brisbane to determine the cause of young Thomas Reid's death. Testimony was heard before P. Pinnock, with a Subinspector White conducting the inquiry. Providing a description of the events was "Mark [Park] Albert Van Tassel"[21] While Van Tassel complained that the crowd had put pressure on the guy ropes, the police claimed that insufficient caution had been taken to block spectators from the area in the first place. Assistant Under-Colonial Secretary William H. Ryder had been standing a mere 5 or 6 feet from the pole that fell. He testified that the pole fell simply by the weight of the balloon, with stakes holding the ropes in place being driven an insufficient depth to secure the pole properly.[22] The inquiry continued on Friday, but given that there is no record of Van Tassel's arrest, it is believed that in the end, Pinnock considered the matter to be an accident. For the exhibition scheduled for May 31, he required that the Van Tassell Troupe adhere to stricter safety procedures and required the police to cordon off the portion of grounds nearest the balloon, with all guys and stakes properly examined.[23]

At the exhibition on May 31, three thousand people entered the Breakfast Creek Grounds to witness the balloon ascension and parachute jump. An almost equivalent number watched from outside the gate without paying. A prearranged fencing match took place, with the balloon ascension following. Inflation began at about 5:00 p.m. Despite all efforts and a large staff that Van Tassel had arranged to help secure the area near the balloon, the public would not stay out of the balloon enclosure. Without sufficient police support, several citizens literally laughed at any effort to remove them from the enclosure. When Van Tassel made it clear that there would be no ascension if they remained, people finally began to clear the area. While the balloon could have been filled in thirty minutes, these delays pushed things back to 5:45 p.m. Both Gladys and Valerie appeared on the scene at 5:30 p.m. and were greeted with warm cheers. Both showed the clear nervousness that comes with making an attempt after a tragedy, and Valerie consoled Gladys as she prepared for the trip. Park also felt a certain unease. He made it clear to Gladys that no unnecessary risks should be taken—there would be no trapeze work on the way up with the balloon. He mentioned later to the press that he would have moved the exhibition to coincide with a more auspicious occasion, but both sisters had urged him to go on with the act as planned.[24]

Prior to launch, there was some debate as to whether or not Gladys should wear a life preserver, as the launch was near the ocean and Gladys was unable to swim. She consented to use one on this flight, as safety was preeminent. At 5:45 p.m. she called out a meager "Let go," which was restated by Van Tassel in a louder voice, more audible to the team holding the balloon in place. She rose rapidly to 300 or 400 feet, with the crowd cheering below. Either forgetting or ignoring Van Tassel's instruction, she rather quickly commenced with trapeze work, dangling by the backs of her knees. The balloon rose and crossed a river and then was caught in a strong easterly breeze toward Lutwyche. In the moonlit dusk, only the river and the city behind her were visible from her altitude of 4,800 feet. The balloon began to slowly descend, opening her parachute—her cue to jump. On the descent over Lutwyche, she avoided a large house by swinging the trapeze bar, landing instead, on her knees, just to the left of the house on "lumpy ground," opposite a home belonging to a Mrs. Collings. The parachute continued on slightly, coming to rest near another house. Once again, a return was made to the starting location in a cab, to an enthusiastic ovation. The balloon was eventually recovered 6 miles away from the grounds.[25]

Having succeeded in getting past the tragedy, the troupe announced that they would head west to Maryborough, Queensland, for an ascent there and then perhaps come back to Brisbane in three weeks.[26] Meanwhile, depositions on the part of the defense and prosecution continued in the inquiry into Thomas Reid's death.[27] Most testified that they heard Van Tassel urge the crowd to get back from the area where the balloon was being prepared on that fateful day and that some in the crowd obeyed but then rather quickly came back and pulled on the guy wires associated with the poles.[28]

The Van Tassell Troupe prepared for an exhibition at the Maryborough Show Grounds on June 5, with the Van Tassell Sisters first giving an exhibition on the double trapeze at the Albert Rink. At the balloon ascension, "Miss Gladdy" was to provide the jump.[29] However, on the day of the event, the winds were quite strong and no launch was made, despite the large audience that had assembled. The event was postponed to Saturday, June 7, and management refused to take any admission fees.[30] On Saturday, Gladys did not

disappoint the citizens of Maryborough. Despite some puffy rain clouds in
the area, only a slight southerly breeze was found, and it was a fine day for a
launch. The silk balloon came to life and by 5:00 p.m. all was ready.[31] When
Gladys and Valerie appeared, they received a round of applause. Val helped
Gladys remove her overcoat, "and she stood revealed in her charming athletic
costume."[32] She performed her trapeze act during the ascension as the balloon
drifted to the north. The balloon rose and entered into a cumulus cloud. For
twenty to thirty seconds, Gladys and the balloon completely disappeared
from view, climbing to an estimated 7,500 feet. Then, in amazement to the
spectators, Gladys appeared, descending with the parachute as if falling like
rain from the cloud. Val rode in a cab to help fetch Gladys at her landing near
a hospital near Walker Street. They returned together, escorted by twenty
horsemen, and were hailed with a hero's welcome at the grounds. They were
taken into the exhibition hall, and the crowd followed with another great
ovation. Inside the exhibition hall, the show grounds manager, N. Tooth,
made a few remarks on Gladys's courage and skill. Gladys noted:

> The trees looked like vegetables, and I could not tell at first whether
> they were large or small. Then I saw someone on horseback waving
> a handkerchief to me near an open spot. I steered for that, and as I
> came down I caught on the top of a tree, breaking off two branches
> and alighted in a swamp, splashing myself with mud. The man who
> had waved to me was Constable Amies, who had arranged to be on
> the lookout for me. I was not hurt, and after waiting a little while my
> sister came up in a cab, and we drove back to the grounds.[33]

The Van Tassell Sisters noted to the press that they "proposed to make a tour
through the oriental countries before returning to America."[34] The troupe left
for Rockhampton by the steamer SS *Eurimbla* on Sunday, June 8.[35] They were
scheduled to perform on Saturday, June 14, at the Cremorne Gardens in
North Rockhampton[36] and were likely accompanied by Edwin Thorne, who
by then had left the Bland Holt Company to assist the troupe with their
travels.[37]

The town of Rockhampton was especially pleased to have the Van Tassell
Troupe, as it was the first time any aeronaut had performed there. A large

crowd arrived at the gardens and an even larger crowd watched from all parts
of town, especially from the roof of the new Criterion Hotel. Valerie was
launched at around 5:00 p.m. and made a perfect ascension in nice weather,
followed by a rapid but good descent to a landing in a prickly pear plantation,
a few yards outside the gardens. She was scratched but otherwise uninjured.
The balloon came to rest only about 200 yards from the gardens in a paddock
owned by a Mr. Hadgraft.[38] That same evening the Van Tassell Sisters performed their double trapeze work at the Theatre Royal on the southwest
corner of East and Williams Streets and were received with considerable
enthusiasm by the crowd. The Van Tassell Troupe left Rockhampton on Sunday, June 15, on a tender to connect with a steamer for Townsville.[39]

Despite the success, there was always a percentage of the community who
voiced their concern that ascensions such as these were merely "foolhardy
exhibitions."[40] A local reporter wrote:

> Plucky indeed must be that girl be who could fearlessly place herself
> upon a crossbar attached to a balloon, permit herself to be borne
> hundreds of feet in air, and while this was being done, execute some
> most intricate and difficult acrobatic feats, with the certain assurance
> that one slip and she would be dashed into a thousand pieces below;
> and finally cut herself loose so as to descend to earth, with again the
> chance of being killed should the parachute fail to open, or of being
> drowned should it perchance be blown to sea. . . . Does the ascent
> on Saturday afternoon assist us in any one particular either of moral
> principle or ethical rules of conduct, to be one whit better men and
> women than before? The answer, we fear, must be in the negative . . .
> to the performance on Saturday, however much we may admire the
> young lady's pluck, yet the conclusion cannot be avoided that only the
> "almighty dollar" was the inspiring element, and that no other princi-
> ple, save to excite wonder in order to pilot up the profits, was behind
> the fact of the ascent.[41]

At 2:30 p.m. on Sunday, June 22, in Townsville, members of the Australian
Defence Force turned out for a routine march, headed by staff. They marched
along Eyre Street, into the center of Townsville by Denham Street, and then

along Flinders and Charters Towers Road to Acacia Vale Gardens, where the
Van Tassel ascension was to take place.[42] With two thousand spectators at
Acacia Vale Gardens, Gladys prepared for her ascension. However, given the
event was occurring on a Sunday, a group of ministers, including the Reverend James Stewart, made their way into the enclosure where the balloon was
being prepared. Attempting to delay the proceedings, Stewart began reciting
a speech by Sir Henry Norman, but groans and jeers soon cut short his
address. An Inspector Isley asked Stewart to remove himself from the enclosure and the reverend complied, but not without continuing with his admon-
ishment of the crowd as "wrongdoers" who were "breaking a law, which gave
him pain." He said that "in the name of his Maker, and in the name of all that
was good and pure, he would protest against such a desecration of the day of
rest."[43] But before the reverend could conclude his remarks, a Colonel French
entered the enclosure, with his six hundred cadets nearby. The reverend then
admonished French: "On behalf of Christians I protest against the Defence
Force, which costs the colony £40,000 per annum, assisting to desecrate the
Sabbath." The groans from the audience now became a chorus. Finally, the
ministers retreated from the scene. Cadets were ordered into the enclosure to
hold the balloon in position while others took to the task of setting the fire
that would heat the balloon. The headquarters band played at intervals to keep
the public amused.

Gladys prepared for the flight, and just when the command to let go was
given, a Major Des Vœux presented her with a bouquet of flowers, reportedly
from his knees. At an altitude of 200 feet, Gladys dropped the flowers back
to the major. The balloon drifted, and about a quarter of a mile from the gardens, she released and descended to a perfect landing in a Mr. West's garden,
carefully avoiding a bed of pineapples.[44] Once again, she was retrieved by cab
and lauded with cheers. The band played "See the Conquering Hero Comes,"[45]
and the troops did not return to their camp until after 7:00 p.m.[46]

Despite the very successful ascension and parachute jump, the press wondered how it could be that taxpayer dollars were spent to march troops to a
parachute jump, to have the cadets pay one shilling to witness the event, and
to do so on a Sunday while ignoring the complaints of a reverend, and on top
of that, to have an officer *go to his knees* in front of thousands of spectators to
present flowers to a scantily clad female acrobat. To the media, this was the

"true story" of the event. The *Brisbane Courier* commented, "If the private adventure which seeks the people's money by balloon and parachute is to be permitted on Sunday as well as week day, what form of profit-seeking by amusement can be arrested? On what ground can we shut out theatres on Sunday, prohibit the fixing of sporting events—from horse-racing to pugilism—for that day, and generally prevent the people's heritage of a seventh-day rest descending to the degraded place it holds in Europe?"[47]

The Reverend Stewart complained to the press that "he never was so insulted, even in the slums of Brisbane, as he was on Sunday by the Government officials at Acacia Vale Gardens."[48] After it became absolutely clear that Major Des Vœux had actually been standing at the time he handed the bouquet to Gladys, newspapers were forced to print retractions, with one reporter writing, "We trust that he will accept this expression of our regret."[49] But the damage was done, as the division in the community was now obvious and obviously not going away any time soon. Some questioned whether the cadets were soldiers or showmen's assistants. Some expressed concern for the major's wife and what she must be feeling given that the bouquet had an obvious "sweetly romantic" effect.[50] Later reports noted that Colonel French was simply acting on the request of his local officers and men to witness the ascension and because of this chose the destination of Acacia Vale for the march, giving them a rest at that position so they could see the flight.[51] After an inquiry, the chief secretary of the Australian Defence Force flatly denied that the commandant had marched along with the men to Acacia Vale, that the men had no choice in the matter, that Colonel French had forced cadets to assist in the exhibition, and that Major Des Vœux had gone to his knees when presenting the bouquet to Gladys.[52] The public discord continued to July 11, when a meeting was held at Protestant Hall so that members of the Lord's Day Observance Society, led by Richard Edwards, could discuss the matter with the public. The Reverend Stewart provided his rationale for the importance of the day of rest, with several motions carried in favor of the reverend's actions at the balloon ascension. The matter had become far more a debate about the importance of the Sabbath than anything having to do with balloons, parachutes, or scantily clad women aviators. Despite the debate, Vantassel Street in Townsville was later dedicated in honor of Gladys's flight of June 22, 1890.[53]

On Sunday, June 29, the Van Tassell Troupe was scheduled to make an ascension at Charters Towers. However, in light of all the controversy, an order from the colonial secretary canceled the ascension.[54] One does wonder, after so much fuss in Townsville, why the Van Tassell Troupe would dare arrange for another Sunday ascension so quickly in Queensland. Acrobatic feats were no match for the public discord. The Republican Association in Charters Towers protested the cancellation, but it was impossible to change the order from the colonial secretary.[55] A "farewell exhibition" was arranged at the Charters Towers Racetrack for Thursday, July 3, 1890. Some storekeepers in town gave their employees a half-day holiday so they could attend. A large force of police stood guard around the enclosure near the base of the balloon. At 5:30 p.m., the balloon sailed aloft, drifting slowly to the east, carrying Valerie into the sky. As was typical, she worked the trapeze on the way up. The balloon came to its stationary period and began to descend. With the parachute already slightly inflated, Val jumped, making her descent in roughly half the time it took for the balloon to also come to rest. According to reports, within about 5 feet of landing, she leaped from the trapeze bar, making a perfect landing on her feet. This caused cheers from the crowd that had gathered near where she was expected to land. Escorted back to the racetrack, a distance of 1 mile, she was again hailed as a hero.[56] Perhaps as a retort to the article suggesting that nothing good came of such exhibitions, one reporter wrote, "The exhibition is only an example of how men, after studying nature and natural sciences, can apply those sciences for the benefit of mankind, and after witnessing such a scientific exhibition as yesterday's, one's mind will more readily revert to the Power who rules the Universe and marks the sparrow's fall, than if he sat listening to a sky-pilot hashing up the Queen's English, and keeping one's mind morbid and melancholy by the everlasting parading in our eyes the fact that we shall some day be returned to (h)ashes and dust."[57] The Van Tassell Troupe was scheduled to make a series of balloon ascensions from the Cooktown Turf Club. However, when the club refused to

(*Opposite page*) Inflation for the first balloon ascension ever held at Charters Towers, Queensland, on July 3, 1890. It was also the last balloon ascension and parachute jump in Australia by the Van Tassell Troupe. Local History Collection, CityLibraries Townsville.

reduce the costs for renting the racecourse for the exhibition, the troupe canceled their stop in Cooktown.[58]

Meanwhile, during this same period, James Price continued to make sporadic parachute jumps in Australia. These were made without Millie Viola, as she had by that time departed Victoria aboard the *Albany I* for West Australia. On July 15, Price attempted an ascension at Broken Hill, New South Wales, but was forced to postpone.[59] On July 17, he succeeded in launching in "red woolen tights" at about 4:00 p.m. from an area opposite the Theatre Royal.[60] He rose for a good five minutes, drifting roughly a quarter of a mile over about four thousand spectators below. He jumped, at a high rate of speed, and the parachute finally opened. On the way down he was observed waving his hand to the crowd. He descended to the southwest and landed three-quarters of a mile from his launch location.[61]

Having toured the major cities on the east coast of Australia, the Van Tassell Troupe departed, heading for Java. Edwin Thorne, who had traveled with the Van Tassell Troupe throughout Queensland as their new promoter, returned to Sydney via the SS *Jumna* in October 1890, having reportedly "had his fill of ballooning."[62] In October 1890, there were reports of "Prof. P. A. Van Tassell" making parachute jumps yet again in New South Wales. This mysterious professor supposedly made an ascent from the Wagga Wagga Show Grounds at roughly 4:00 p.m. on October 17, making a graceful descent by parachute to a landing near Agricultural Hall, about 150 yards from his starting point.[63] He arrived in Bathurst, New South Wales, on October 20, 1890, escorted from the train station with his balloon in a four-in-hand horse-drawn carriage.[64] On October 22, high winds prevented this Van Tassell's ascension at Bathurst. Instead. he provided free tickets for another attempt on Thursday, October 23.[65] On that day the winds were still strong, yet he continued to inflate his balloon at the Bathurst Show Ground. A strong east wind put a rent in the canvas and that was the end of the day's performance. The one thousand spectators were disappointed, but the aeronaut "announced his determination to make an ascent before he left Bathurst."[66] Even the public began to suspect something sneaky was going on. One anonymous author wrote on October 25:

I will make a few suggestions as to Van Tassell and his balloon, and

they are these:—(1) That Van Tassell (is he here) never meant an
ascent on Wednesday last. (2) That a majority of the public on Van
Tassell's own asking decided that he was able to carry out his contract on the day mentioned, but Van decided otherwise. (3) That the
balloonist was not in costume according to his bandstand speech, to
fight the clouds. (4) That he said he could fill his balloon with hot
air in 17 minutes, and it wasn't filled! (5) That on Thursday evening
the balloon was ripped by some *person or persons unknown*, just as the
monster was going half-mast high. (6) That the 10's to 1 and 3's to 1
wagers that it went up would have been lost. (7) That we all hope to
see the *original* Van Tassell "up in a balloon" this afternoon, and if
he goes 8000ft. in ascent and then descends in his parachute, we will
forgive him and bless him![67]

It seems that by Friday, October 31, this particular Van Tassell had departed
Bathurst without making an exhibition. Local papers noted that "Bathurst
witnessed recently one of the most representative 'sells' that it was ever given
to a people to behold."[68] It is possible that upon arriving back in Australia,
Edwin Thorne figured he could make some extra money posing as Van Tassel,
as it is unlikely that the very proud James Price would ever stoop to leaving a
location in such a way or staging himself as if he were Van Tassel. However,
between late September and late October 1890, Millie Viola and James Price
continued to make parachute jumps largely at Bondi in Sydney.[69] While the
folks in Bathurst were puzzled, and while the folks in Sydney remained in
awe, the real Van Tassell Troupe set sail from Queensland for Java.

# 17. COMPETITION

AFTER SPLITTING FROM Thorpe, the Van Tassell Troupe headed for Batavia (at the time, the capital of the Dutch East Indies; today central Jakarta, Indonesia), arriving on August 4, 1890, to make ascensions for large crowds of spectators.[1] However, the troupe now consisted of just Park Van Tassel, Gladys Freitas, and a man by the name of Lawrence. It is not clear why Valerie departed, or where she went, but she would rejoin the troupe at a later date.

On either August 18 or August 25, the Van Tassell Troupe made an ascension with a smoke balloon from the estate of a local prince at Solo (now called Surakarta), where the emperor of Java resided with his grand Vizier and court. At the height of the ascension, Gladys descended via parachute. Everything went fine except that Gladys nearly went through the roof of a house on her landing, but she managed to avoid injury.[2] The *Singapore Free Press* eloquently described Gladys as "a Tassel that will form an interesting pendant to a parachute."[3]

On September 7, the troupe arrived in Singapore, a part of the Straits Settlements, which were ruled by the United Kingdom, aboard the *Giang Ann* from Semarang. They were on their way to Shanghai, China.[3] British balloonist Percival Spencer had already supplied the first balloon and parachute jump in Singapore's history, on May 10, 1890, and there is no record of the Van Tassell Troupe attempting an ascension during their brief stay.[4] Instead, they continued on, arriving in Shanghai on September 17 via the *Peshawur*, eager to make the first balloon ascension and parachute jump in Shanghai's history.[5]

Gladys's ascension at Shanghai took place from the Chinese Garden "near the point" on September 27, with a Mr. Woods and a locally well-known lion tamer named Frame helping with the arrangements. Throngs of people crowded the road to the point prior to the balloon being filled at 4:00 p.m. Another large gathering of spectators waited at the garden. A bamboo enclosure kept people and wind away from the balloon as it was being filled. The wind was strong, and there was some doubt whether the launch would take place, but after a period of thirty-five minutes, the balloon was ready. There was concern that the parachute might end up in a nearby river in the Hongkew (now Hongkou) district, so Gladys wore a life preserver on the ascension. She launched and rose to a height of about 1,700 feet while doing trapeze work along the way. Carried by a westerly breeze, the parachute made a successful landing about a half mile from the launch location near Point Road.[6] Reporters noted,

> When all was ready, Miss Van Tassell took hold of the trapeze bar suspended from the parachute, the balloon was let go, and the young lady kissing her hand to the spectators as she went, was swung rapidly across the lawn and upwards, fortunately striking in her sudden flight nothing more solid than a much-startled coolie,[7] who was staring open-mouthed at the rising monster. As she floated slowly westward in the glory of the setting sun, Miss Van Tassell calmly went through three or four exciting evolutions on her trapeze, and when the balloon was about 1,700 feet above the earth, as it seemed, the parachute detached itself and came slowly earthwards the lady falling lightly to the ground, near the Point Road, and being taken in a carriage to the gardens, where she was enthusiastically welcomed. It was a delightful exhibition, and the gracefulness of it took away the expected sense of its danger; for danger there must be, even with the most careful preparations.[8]

Van Tassel's balloon, however, continued on its own adventure, landing outside the Hongkew boundary line and then bumping along the ground for a period of time. Locals secured the balloon and took possession of it, claiming that it had destroyed a part of a roof upon landing. However, inspection of the roof showed that the damage was clearly not recent, as there was grass growing through the bricks and tiles that were strewn on the ground—indications that the roof was damaged long before the balloon fell from the sky. But the locals refused to return the balloon without payment of $12 for the damages, a sum that was finally reduced to $6 through bargaining. Despite an agreement on the amount, when Van Tassel returned to obtain the balloon on September 30, the locals wouldn't release it even after being paid. This led Van Tassel to forcibly repossess the balloon, despite efforts by the locals to prevent his carriage from leaving the scene.[9]

Another ascension was planned for Chan-su-ho Garden on Bubbling Wells Road for October 4, 1890. Thousands of spectators flocked to the garden to watch the spectacle, which was captured well by the local press: "Parachuting is another of the inventions of the western barbarian which come as a shock to the Celestial notions. Of balloons the natives know something; but the spectacle of a woman flying through the air and descending for nearly a mile apparently with only the aid of an umbrella was certainly enough to excite 'hi-yahs'[10] without number."[11]

Gladys was launched at sunset from the gardens and performed several "blood-curdling feats" of trapeze work in her five-minute ascension to 4,000 feet. At that point she jumped, coming steadily down to a landing in a cotton field near a well-known English pub named Oliver's Bungalow. The balloon fell about 3 miles away and was rescued, faster this time, but not before locals "wantonly cut off nearly the whole of the top sections."[12] Given the many issues, the Van Tassell Troupe left Shanghai for Manila, capital of the Philippines.

On November 20, 1890, Gladys made a successful ascension and parachute descent over Manila. However, the crowds were unusually small.[13] According to Park Van Tassel years later, in 1901, the portion of his journey through Manila was his greatest financial debacle:

I had to have all of my programmes stamped by the Government and was charged well for it. Besides the license there was a tax on everything. The first day it rained, and I had to go post haste to the Governor to get a permit to postpone my exhibition. After I had stood on the porch in the wet half an hour, he rebuked me for not coming sooner. I was forced to hire a band, and then was taxed for every tune that it played. This money, they said, was to go to the man who invented the tune. When they played "Auld Lang Syne" I thought "Well, this composer's dead, and I've got a rebate coming," but they charged me for it just the same. They took 15 percent of the gate money and charged me so much a head for every policeman on the grounds and at the gate. They rung in thirty-five policemen on me, some of them the toughest you ever saw, dressed in overall stuff and looking like monkeys. . . . Well, I gave three exhibitions in Manila and took in $3000. The Government taxed me out of all of that and some more that I brought to town, and I had to pawn a ring worth $1000 for $500 to get away.[14]

The Van Tassell Troupe very happily escaped the Philippines to the Straits Settlements to provide an exhibition in the vicinity of George Town, on the north portion of Penang Island (in modern-day Malaysia). Gladys made a balloon ascension in December 1890 or early January 1891. As with flights in Australia, she did trapeze work during the ascension. After reaching an altitude of 4,000 feet, she made a safe parachute descent.[15] According to Park, two ascensions were made in Penang,[16] but a detailed description of only one can be found in the reports of the time. From Penang, the troupe traveled to Rangoon, Burma (modern-day Yangon, Myanmar), making three ascensions in front of "immense, gaping crowds"[17] as they watched human flight for the first time. Children in Burma, taken by Gladys's leaps, made mud dolls, attached them to paper parachutes, sent them up on paper kites, and pulled release strings to mimic her descent.[18] Meanwhile, by the end of January 1891, back in Oakland, California, Clara Van Tassel was finally granted a divorce on the basis of desertion. Clara, the first woman in the western United States to make a parachute jump, resumed her maiden name, Clara Coykendall.[19]

As the Van Tassell Troupe continued its journey, other aeronauts were also traveling Asia and providing balloon and parachute exhibitions. For instance, Fitzherbert Kight made a balloon ascension in December 1853,[20] and on December 29, 1877, at Calcutta, J. Symmons Lynn made a successful balloon ascension.[21] India's first parachute jump came when Percival Spencer traveled from London to Bombay (now Mumbai) and leaped in front of an estimated one hundred thousand spectators on January 26, 1889.[22] He ascended to a height of 1,760 feet in the *Empress of India* and made a successful return by parachute, earning Rs 25,000 for the flight (a value of about £1666 in 1890 or about $240,000 in 2020 dollars).[23] In early 1889, Spencer provided parachute exhibitions at various locations, including Calcutta. There he had a perilous launch that voided any opportunity of using his parachute; instead he came down with the *Empress of India* a considerable distance from town. It took several days for him to return, uninjured, from the jungle.[24] On April 10 of that year, for a price of Rs 500, Spencer introduced Indian acrobat and trapeze artist Ram Chandra Chatterjie to ballooning in the *Viceroy*. They launched at Narkeldanga with a landing near Barasat, with Chatterjie becoming the first Indian aeronaut in history.[25] Chatterjie eventually purchased the *Viceroy* from Spencer and renamed it the *City of Calcutta*. With this balloon, in May 1889 Chatterjie made the first solo balloon ascensions by an Indian. He made the first balloon ascension and parachute descent by an Indian on March 22, 1890, in the *Empress of India* with Spencer in attendance. Unfortunately, Chatterjie died on August 9, 1892, as the result of a ballooning accident.[26]

After introducing parachuting to various locations across India, Spencer then traveled to Singapore, making a balloon ascension and the first parachute drop there on May 10, 1890.[27] Spencer made at least two balloon ascensions in Yokohama, Japan, and another from Ueno Park in Tokyo in October 1890.[28] He continued with a balloon flight and parachute jump in Kobe, Japan, on November 3, 1890. His unfortunate landing in the ocean required a boat rescue, and while he and his parachute were recovered, the balloon was lost.[29] However, Spencer continued unabated with an ascent and parachute drop in November 1890 and another for Emperor Meiji in Ueno Park.[30] Spencer's exhibitions caused quite a stir in Japan, and he quickly became the subject of a Kabuki play titled *Riding the Famous Hot-Air Balloon*, with famed Kabuki artist Onoe Kikugoto playing the role of Spencer. Although the Japanese had experimented with lighter-than-air balloons as early as 1877, Spencer's parachute jumps were probably the first in the nation.

Meanwhile, as Spencer was introducing ballooning and parachuting to India in 1889, Thomas Baldwin made the first balloon ascension and the first parachute jump in New Zealand's history with a flight on January 21, 1889, at Dunedin.[31] Like Spencer, Thomas Baldwin and his "brother" Ivy Baldwin toured Asia as well. On Monday, January 15, 1890, Thomas and Ivy arranged for a balloon ascension and parachute jump at Ueno Park. While Spencer had use of a beautiful silk balloon with an elaborate inflation mechanism involving pipes and gas, in true American fashion, the Baldwins used a cloth balloon, a pile of firewood, and some kerosene. A very hot fire and a short flue system had the balloon inflated in just fifteen minutes. Ivy Baldwin ascended in the balloon, completing a series of acrobatic maneuvers on the way up. At about 5,000 feet, he jumped. After a free fall of about four and a half seconds, he came to a perfect landing. The balloon collapsed and provided a trail of gray smoke over the sky of Tokyo until landing. Local writers noted, "The cream of Tokyo's curiosity about balloons has now been skimmed, and if Spencer and the Baldwins have successors, the financial results will probably be very different."[32] These and other daredevils traveled from city to city, eager to be the first to exhibit ballooning and/or parachute jumping. It was a very real financial race; whoever was first would surely derive more income than all who followed.

Millie Viola continued with a series of parachute jumps with James Price in Western Australia in 1891. Later that year at Perth, Viola's parachute collapsed halfway down after unexpectedly encountering strong thermal turbulence in midair. She came down at a very high rate of speed, with the parachute saving her life by becoming tangled in a dead tree. Viola escaped the situation with just a few bruises.[33] James Price continued providing parachute exhibitions at Hobart, Perth, and other locations in Australia[34] as well as New Zealand before moving on to South Africa. In December 1891, Price also dealt with an unfortunate set of circumstances. He ascended, and at about 2,000 feet, the balloon burst. Price jumped for his life via parachute. His safe landing was, ironically, in a cemetery. A second ascension at the same location resulted in precisely the same bursting effect, and once again he descended safely to Earth.[35] But the safety issues were a very real concern. A similar event occurred at Bombay in December 1891 at the Garden of Parel, where a Lieutenant Mansfield ascended in his balloon. High winds caused the balloon to break apart at altitude, and before he could get his parachute to work properly, he plummeted to the ground, dying on impact.[36] Unfazed, another aeronaut, billed as Professor Lawrence,[37] began making balloon ascensions and parachute descents in India in early 1892.[38] It is possible that Lawrence was now assisting the Van Tassell Troupe.

Against this backdrop, the Van Tassell Troupe found themselves in a race with other performers, traveling from major city to major city on shipping

lines, trying to be the first to jump to maximize crowds and rewards. Newspapers commonly compared their status, so it was quite likely that each team
was keeping tabs on the others. For instance, in December 1890, the *North-
China Herald and Supreme Court & Consular Gazette* noted, "The Baldwin
Brothers have been giving successful balloon ascents at Tokio [*sic*] and Yokohama, their *modus operandi* being the same as Mr. Van Tassell's as regards the
inflation of their balloon."[39] The same paper failed to realize that it was precisely these three individuals who had (re)introduced parachuting to the
United States at San Francisco.

During the summer of 1890, while others were exhibiting in Asia, William
Ivy (performing as Ivy Baldwin) returned to California, making two balloon
ascensions and parachute jumps at the San Jose Fair Grounds, both on August
15, 1890.[40] The Southern Pacific Railroad hired him to provide a balloon
ascension at Santa Monica on September 4. Up in the clouds, he leaped from
the balloon, descending in spectacular fashion.[41] With Van Tassel and Thomas
Baldwin in Asia, Ivy Baldwin quickly took their place as the main showman
on the parachute descent circuit in California. A few months later, Ivy
returned to Asia. On January 3, 1891, Thomas and Ivy made the first balloon
ascent in Hong Kong, followed by the first parachute descent in Hong Kong.
The flight was made at Happy Valley Racetrack, and the exhibition was
repeated in Macau.

With Spencer and the Baldwins traveling from place to place in Southeast
Asia, and with the difficulties encountered in Shanghai and Manila, the Van
Tassell Troupe headed for greener pastures in India. Some reports suggest
that they first traveled to Japan, but it is likely that these reports confused Van
Tassel with Baldwin or Spencer.[42] Their busy schedule would have allowed
minimal time for such a trip, and ship passenger logs do not verify the claim.
Further, it is likely that if the Van Tassell Troupe did perform in Japan, they
would have received considerable mention in the press, unless the performance was a private demonstration for Emperor Meiji.

In India, Valerie Freitas rejoined the troupe on tour. She made a successful
balloon ascension and parachute descent at Hyderabad on February 20, 1891,
for Asaf Jah VI Mir Mahboob Ali Khan Siddiqi Bayafandi, the sixth nizam
of Hyderabad. While it remains unconfirmed, this was likely also the first
parachute jump by a woman in India. On March 13, one of the Van Tassell

Sisters made a balloon ascent and parachute descent at Poona from the grounds of the Empress Garden in front of several thousand spectators. She once again performed trapeze acts when going skyward. When the balloon reached its maximum height of about 3,500 feet, she jumped with a partially inflated parachute and landed on the east side of the Southern Mahratta Railway, about 3 miles from the garden. The villagers in the field where she landed were rather shocked to see a woman falling from the sky. The Van Tassell Troupe left that evening for Mysore (now Mysuru), scheduled to return to Poona to entertain the citizens with a balloon race on their way to Bombay (modern-day Mumbai).[43]

Moving on to Mysore, they provided an exhibition on March 18, 1891, for Chamarajendra Wadiyar X, the twenty-third maharaja of the Kingdom of Mysore, Britain's Sir Oliver St. John, and an estimated ten thousand spectators. The maharaja was quite interested in seeing this exhibition and rewarded Van Tassel with a considerable sum of money.[44] Valerie was prepared for launch, but just as the balloon started on its ascent, it split in two at an approximate altitude of 300 feet, allowing all the hot air and smoke to rapidly escape. Valerie's parachute opened immediately, and she leaped to safety only 150 yards from her point of launch. Her descent was rapid, and she was shaken by the landing but otherwise uninjured. The maharaja and a Dr. Benson were the first to attend to her at the scene. News of the incident spread throughout English-language papers in Southeast Asia.[45]

This near disaster, coupled with the accident in Queensland, was perhaps too much for the Freitas sisters to endure. Gladys fell in love with the manager of the Helvetia Estate at Delhi. They married in July 1891 at Penang in the Straits Settlements.[46] Valerie also fell in love and married during this period. Reporters later noted, "Traveling with him [Park Van Tassel] at this time were two female parachute jumpers, both of whom laid some claim to beauty. Their charms ensnared two Hindostanese of high degree and both women accepted the offers of marriage which were made to them."[47] The Freitas sisters had made their mark for women's parachuting throughout Australia, Southeast Asia, China, and India. However, with their service as a part of the troupe now lost, and uneager to jump from balloons himself, Van Tassel was once again left adrift.

# 18. REDIRECTION

NOW AGE THIRTY-EIGHT, and with sufficient income from his recent successes in India, Van Tassel decided to travel to London and develop a new strategy for exhibitions. He left India on July 31, 1891, having worked with the Freitas sisters to perform in front of eight rajas in both Burma and India.[1] While in London, he reportedly made several ascents and parachute descents in mid-August at a naval exhibition there, although yet again it seems that reporters may have confused Van Tassel with Percival Spencer, who is known to have performed at the same exhibition.[2] However, one thing is certain: while in London, Van Tassel made arrangements to return to India and provide a sponsored balloon ascension for the *Graphic*, a London-based weekly illustrated newspaper. He planned to make use of a very large new balloon for a spectacular cross-country journey from Calcutta to Bombay, a distance of 1,400 miles.[3] It would be the first flight of its kind in India. Van Tassel left London for Paris, to secure this new balloon, which was reportedly made of silk and had a capacity of 100,000 cubic feet.[4] He was accompanied by a reporter from the *Graphic*, who was to provide an accounting of the journey and flight for the newspaper.[5] After purchasing the balloon, they traveled to Turin, Italy, and from there to the coastal port of Brindisi, Italy, before departing in early September for a return to Southeast Asia.[6]

His return to India is mysterious. It seems he first visited Sumatra to continue his daredevil ways before heading to Bombay.[7] And things did not go well in Sumatra. He was reported to have died, having "fallen 500 feet from his balloon."[8] Details of the near disaster are difficult to obtain, but the stories suggested that he parachuted through the hatch on a ship, fracturing his skull.[9] It seems that Van Tassel traveled rather quickly from Sumatra to

*What a life am I right?!*

Calcutta, where once again, for a third time in his life, he was reported in newspapers as having met a "shocking death":

> It was in India that he had one thrilling escape. On the banks of the sacred Ganges he ascended in the presence of the Majarajah [*sic*] of Boad. Boats had been provided to use in case of a mishap, and when the aeronaut and his parachute dropped into the rain-swollen torrent, the native boatmen stood by in wondering helplessness. The life-preserver that he had strapped around him saved Van Tassel from sinking, but the current sent him swiftly down the river, so swiftly that when the boatmen recovered from their surprise and set out after him they could not overtake him. For seven miles he swam and drifted down stream, and finally the sacred river threw him, weary and chilled upon its sodden banks.[10]

*~the*

However, the very much still alive Park Van Tassel responded to the international press, indicating that the repeated reports of his death were premature. It remains unclear if the real Park Van Tassel was making the jumps or if some imposter was doing this in his name.

As further evidence that all of the above was likely the result of a different Park Van Tassel, it is known from passenger lists that the real Park Van Tassel arrived at Bombay from London on October 4, 1891, aboard the *Peshawur*.[11] Thus it is either that the real Van Tassel traveled back and forth to London a second time after his mishap in Calcutta in September 1891 or he never did make it to Sumatra and Calcutta, and the stories were the result of an imposter.

Despite this confusion, it became increasingly clear that Park wasn't going to be attempting further parachute jumps on his own, because the manifest from the *Peshawur* indicates that Park arrived with a woman, Jeanette "Jenny" Rumary.[12] Jeanette was born in 1865 to George John Rumary and Jane Tingley. At times Jeanette claimed to be either Park's wife, daughter, or another relation. Whatever the actual relationship, with quite a difference in age, they came to India calling themselves "Mr. and Mrs. Van Tassell," with Jeanette eager to take the place of the Freitas sisters in jumps with parachutes as a part of a revised Van Tassell Troupe. Nothing is known of Jeanette's background or her prior experience in ballooning, but it is clear that they met in London during his trip. The previously arranged cross-country flight from Calcutta to Bombay was pushed to early 1892, when prevailing winds were thought to be more appropriate.

A balloon ascension and parachute descent by Jeanette, performing as Jeanette Van Tassel, at Victoria Gardens in Byculla (a suburb of Bombay), was postponed from October 16 to October 18 due to an inability to get the gas balloon inflated in time, likely because of issues with piping. The large gathering of people who assembled on October 16 were disappointed, having already waited three and a half hours.[13] Arrangements were made for Jeanette to carry one thousand small printed advertisement cards to be dropped from 1,000 feet during her ascent.[14] Four of these certificates would be promissory notes for Rs 500, also entitling the holder to receive a discount of 25 percent on goods purchased at Southwell & Austin, Limited, a dressmaker on Hornby Row in Bombay.[15] The commissioner of police made sure that those who were turned away on October 16 were given access on October 18. For unknown reasons, he also prevented Jeanette from carrying the tissue paper certificates aloft. The issues with the gas piping were fixed, and the balloon was filled rapidly, well before the scheduled ascent at 4:30 p.m. The gardens, roads, and rooftops all became filled with people as Jeannette appeared at 4:45 p.m. in a satin, yellow-gold robe designed by a prominent costumer by the name of Wörth.[16] She took her position on the trapeze bar and at 4:50 p.m. she was released to the sky. Just in case the balloon headed to sea, she went aloft with a life buoy attached to the parachute ring. At about 3,000 feet, Park Van Tassel ordered for a gun to be fired. Jeannette jumped, and after a rapid fall of about 100 feet, the parachute slowly expanded. She floated down to a landing on the roof of Elias David Sassoon's bungalow near Victoria Road. A ladder was required to get Jeanette and the parachute down from the roof. Twenty minutes later she was driven back into the gardens with Park and a man named Southwell Piper, who was likely their booking agent. Those in the exhibition area applauded Jeannette as she went back to her tent.

However, it seemed that one of the sailors who helped with the launch forgot to tie the escape valve in an open position to allow gas to slowly escape from the balloon, limiting the height of its flight. Free of Jeanette, the balloon shot higher in the sky. At about 5:30 p.m., it either burst or released its gas. It came down in rapid fashion in the direction of Butcher's Island, landing either on the island or in the sea.[17]

Van Tassel continued to express his interest in a balloon journey from Calcutta to Bombay, perhaps to remove himself from the perils of parachute jumping or simply to be heard in the newspapers over the din of other daredevil parachute jumpers. A reporter noted:

> When Mr. Spencer was performing on the balloon in Calcutta, it will be remembered that he thought at one time of trying a trip through the air to Bombay, and wished some gentleman to accompany him, but somehow or other the trip never came off. I see that Mr. Van Tassell is now thinking of carrying out the same idea, and of doing through the air what Lieutenant Varges lately did on horseback. The trip might be a very pleasant one if the wind currents could be dependent on, but that is the difficulty. A month spent in a balloon like Jules Verne's intrepid explorers of Africa, looking down upon smiling villages, toiling ryots,[18] grazing herds and flocks, as well as upon the haunts of the elephant and the tiger, with an occasional thunderstorm sending flashes of lightning round one's head, all this would be pleasant indeed. But against this would have to be set the chance of getting drowned in the sea, or landing among the snows of the Himalayas. Landing in any part of India would be safe enough. If the wind currents can be relied on to blow steadily from the north-east at this time of the year, the journey might be accomplished, and would be a highly adventurous one. It is not, perhaps, generally known that balloons can travel very much quicker than railway trains. The highest recorded speed, I believe, is over two hundred miles an hour; so that with a strong breeze, and the advantage of a direct route and no stations to stop at, a balloonist might get from [sic] Bombay in a few hours."[19]

In November, newspapers noted that Park was accompanied by "Miss Jeanette" rather than "Miss Valerie" or "Miss Gladys."[20] However, confusion remained about their marital status. For instance, in late 1891, "Mr. and Mrs. Van Tassell" provided two parachute exhibitions in Bombay—one by Park, the other by Jeanette—which were both successful. However, during Jeanette's flight, the parachute did not open immediately, causing great concern.[21] Their exhibitions in Bombay were honored by the presence of Colonel George Robert Canning Harris, the fourth Baron Harris, more generally known as Lord Harris, a British colonial administrator and governor of Bombay.[22]

On December 21, 1891, a telegram from Bombay to the press in San Francisco announced that Park Van Tassel would be traveling to Mysore to assist in rainmaking for the maharaja. The concept was simple enough, but it remains unknown if it was actually ever tried:

> The parachutist Van Tassell, who visited Shanghai last year, has lately returned from England to India and will proceed under special agreement to Mysore, where the Maharajah, who has taken up the idea of rain-making operations, wishes to utilize his experience. Mr. Van Tassell believes he will not have the slightest difficulty in producing rain by the methods so successfully employed in America; namely, by explosions of dynamite, etc., at altitudes varying from 3,000 to 4,000 feet by means of balloons. Should these experiments succeed, and Mr. Van Tassell receive sufficient inducement and assistance from Government, he will at once erect a balloon manufactory to meet requirements. Mr. Van Tassell's next idea is, some time in December, to make a trip in one of his large gas balloons across India, from Calcutta to Bombay. . . . The aeronaut proposes to take with him a photographer, and he is said to have also reserved a seat in the car for an artist from one of the London illustrated papers, and in this way hopes to make the trip as full of interest to himself as to the public at large, by a publication of his experiences in cloudland, with sketches and photos of the various scenes passed over during the long aerial voyage.[23]

Park and Jeanette continued to Benares (now Varanasi), Allahabad (now Prayagraj), Delhi, Lucknow, Calcutta, and many other cities in India, performing parachute acts.[24] In Calcutta they visited the portrait studios of F. Kapp & Co., which produced a set of cabinet cards that showed them in their aeronaut attire. Given that air currents for the Calcutta-to-Bombay flight would be best near the end of December, the journeys were generally in the north of India, making travel to Calcutta easier.[25] However, as time went on and they still awaited delivery of their large cross-country balloon, Jeanette made additional parachute jumps at other locations in India. At Madras (modern-day Chennai), on Saturday, January 16, 1892, huge crowds gathered near the Elphinstone Hotel, on the roads, on the rooftops, everywhere—"the people who did not witness the ascent might almost be counted on the fingers of one's hand."[26] Even the governor was a witness. At 5:15 p.m. the inflation began, but a high wind caused Park to be concerned. Despite the wind, Jeanette launched at 5:40 p.m. At first the balloon flew from Black Town (now Muthialpet) toward St. Thomas Cathedral Basilica, but at an altitude of about 7,500 feet, Jeanette encountered a new current and started for Kodumbaukum (now Kodambakkam) instead. She released to a successful parachute jump and landed in a set of paddy fields. Jeanette returned to the hotel to a hero's ovation. A reporter quipped, "In the way of aerial 'shows,' Miss Van Tassell's ascent and descent is unique and is the most graceful performance that can be imagined."[27] They left Madras on January 25 with their business manager, a Mr. Colville, headed for Calcutta to complete Park's arrangements for his voyage across India.

Park noted to the press that "[India] was the only country in the world where such a trip could be made, there being no high mountains to disturb the currents of air which run steadily across the continent."[28] He felt it would be possible to travel as fast as 35 to 100 miles per hour at altitude, making the 1,400 miles in about fourteen to twenty-four hours. His balloon was being finished in Bombay in February 1892, and he expected it to be delivered to him in Calcutta by the end of the month. Two passengers for the flight were already chosen, a special correspondent of the *Graphic* and a friend, "Mr. Mears."[29] The balloon was suggested to be capable of lifting 5,000 pounds of total weight. Van Tassel noted, "When a short distance from terra firma, I take some tissue paper cut into small squares out of my pocket and regulate myself accordingly as they float by my side, and land with their force. As soon as the car touches the ground, I tell my visitors to step out. Then I get out, and as soon as the car is clear I burst my balloon with one rip, and up she goes for a quarter of a mile and collapses."[30]

On February 13, 1892, Park and Jeanette made arrangements for a balloon ascension and parachute descent at Calcutta as a part of a large flower show at the Agri-Horticultural Society Gardens.[31] As it turned out, the large barracks and parade grounds occupied by the Seventeenth Bengal Infantry were directly opposite the gardens. As the balloon launch neared, at about 4:45 p.m., the soldiers began to clear away the crowd that was assembling on their parade grounds to avoid paying the fee to be closer to the balloon. These spectators did not leave as quickly as the soldiers desired. When the troops forced the issue, the spectators rushed en masse across the road in front of the garden gate. An Inspector Creagan and several European constables attempted to clear the massive crowd from the gateway. In the confusion, a noncommissioned military officer got in the way and was arrested by the police and taken away. Several key individuals tried to pacify the soldiers by suggesting that the local police would control the rest of the scene and that the soldiers could return to their barracks. However, when the soldiers realized that their officer had been arrested, they requested his release and police officers refused. This sent the soldiers into a rage. They began "upsetting stalls, breaking bottles, and assaulting people . . . then commenced a fusillade of bottles, stones, pieces of bricks, anything that came handy, against the gate and anybody inside the gardens." A European by the name of Constable Donahue was caught up in the melee outside the gardens and was injured, requiring rescue. Meanwhile, the honorary secretary of the gardens, a Mr. Blechynden, was badly cut above one of his eyes after trying to come to the assistance of a Superintendent Hogg.

All this confusion happened shortly after the inflation of the balloon. While those inside the garden and its balloon enclosure were mindful of events happening just outside, Park continued filling the balloon with hot air and smoke, "engendered by burning box-wood saturated with kerosine oil in a flu, through which it passed into the balloon."[32] Dressed in "a suit of tight-fitting clothes," Jeanette took her seat on the trapeze and assistant Slade Murray gave the signal to let go by firing a rifle. Jeanette ascended to about 2,500 feet and waited for the balloon to cool and slowly begin its descent. As it did so, the parachute expanded and she jumped, floating to Earth gracefully in roughly two minutes. Jeanette did her best to steer away from a grove of trees but just grazed one, which snagged the parachute. She remained suspended in a branch and then managed to get back safely to the ground, suffering a tear in her skirt. She returned to the enclosure to applause and the promise of another jump.

With the parachute jump complete, the crowds began to disperse without further incident as a strengthened police force of ten European constables, ten mounted sergeants, four European inspectors, six local officers, and sixty local constables kept the peace. An inquiry began shortly thereafter to better understand the cause of the initial riot.[33] Park and Jeanette fled to Madras to wait for things to calm down. They had returned to Calcutta by early March 1892 to make preparations for the cross-country balloon trip.[34] Their preparations made international news, even as far as Scotland, France, and Spain.[35] An exhibition was planned for the Tivoli Gardens. Park was using only smoke balloons, as gas was not conveniently available. A newspaper reported, "By some chemical process of his own discovery he can readily fill his large hot air balloons, of which he has several."[36]

While in Calcutta, Jeanette made a parachute jump dressed in a yellow and crimson silk costume. The ascent was fine, but her descent ended in a "green slimy tank at Entally." Four locals rescued her and brought her back to the starting point to a grand applause.[37] Still waiting for the proper currents, from Calcutta they moved to Dacca (modern-day Dhaka), where another parachute jump was made on March 16, 1892. The launch location was just opposite the Ahsan Manzil, the palace of the nawab of Dacca, along the banks of the Buriganga River. At 6:20 p.m. Jeanette launched with the balloon, climbing to more than 6,000 feet.[38] She jumped and the parachute opened perfectly, but at the end of her flight, a large *Casuarina* tree in Ramna Park snagged her parachute, leaving her about 20 feet up in the tree, dangling from the parachute. Several locals attempted a quick rescue with a makeshift bamboo pole for her to climb down. However, just as she put her weight on the pole, the bamboo broke and she fell the remaining 20 feet, severely injuring her spine.[39] For the next two days she became increasingly ill, and on the morning of March 18, 1892, Jeanette Rumary died from complications of the injury. News of her death was carried internationally.[40] Some reports noted that Jeanette was believed to be eighteen at the time.[41] Descriptions of the event itself suggest that the rescue went awry:     *EW wasn't she "married" to him*

The vast crowd assembled on the occasion on the fetes given by the Nawabs of Dacca watched the parachute as it detached itself from the balloon at a great height, and it was observed that it opened out and began to descend as evenly and gently as could be wished, but, unfortunately, when approaching the ground, the machine caught in the bows of a casuarinas tree. Even the Miss Van Tassel retained her presence of mind, and quietly disentangling herself from the cords and trapeze, secured a firm hold of the tree at a height of about 20ft. Here some spectators hastened to her assistance, and tried to help her down with the aid of bamboo rods lashed together. It was while endeavoring to slide down these that the frail bamboos unfortunately broke, precipitating the unfortunate young lady to the ground, and causing a shock to the spine producing paralysis, from which she died on the following day.[42]

On March 17, a correspondent for the Calcutta *Englishman* wrote,

The Nawabs of Dacca, ever anxious to entertain their friends, arranged with the aeronaut Mr. Van Tassel that he should exhibit at Dacca, and the 16th instant at 5 p.m. was the time fixed for the ascent. Accordingly all Dacca mustered on the bund and in all the riverside houses to witness the performance. The ascent was to take place from the opposite bank of the river, facing the Nawab's Palace, the Ahsan Munzul [*sic*]. Mr. Geo. Garth invited his personal friends to his house, from which an excellent view was available, and soon after 4:30 all his guests had assembled. An hour passed without any visible sign of the balloon. The many thousands on the bund exhibited some impatience, every now and then a murmur arising like that of the sea. At 6:20, a gun was fired, and a mighty roar from the multitude announced that the balloon was free. Quickly it mounted high into the air- so quickly that by the time it reached the opposite bank of the river the aeronaut was scarcely distinguishable, and the balloon itself, which is 78 feet high by 8 [*sic*] feet diameter, looked a comparatively small object. Within some five minutes of the time it left the ground we saw the parachute open out and become detached from the balloon. There was no sudden drop or fall of any kind, and Miss Van Tassel was descending as gently and apparently as easily as could be desired. The wind took the parachute in a north-westerly direction, and it fell eventually near the race course, catching on a casuarina tree in its descent.

Miss Van Tassel was able to extricate herself from the trapeze and to secure a hold of the tree at a height of from ten to twenty feet. Some spectators ran to her assistance, and tried to help her down by means of bamboos, but one of the bamboos broke and the lady fell to the ground, striking her head. Dr. Nicholson was sent promptly to the spot in the Nawab's barouche, which conveyed the lady to her quarters at the Dak Bungalow, where she still lies. Her injuries are pronounced not to be dangerous, but concussion of the brain is feared. Of course we are all saying that it is a pity she attempted to descend from the tree until proper means could be obtained. But such regrets are vain, and we can only hope for the best. As for the exhibition it was most successful, the balloon ascending 6,000 feet. It is possible that Mr. Van Tassel himself may make an ascent before he leaves this district, as this accident may prevent his keeping an appointment with Kapurthala Raja for the 21st instant.

Since writing the above, I have been to enquire regarding Miss Van Tassel, who, it appears is not so well to-day."[43] *understatement*

The same correspondent continued on the following day, March 18:

As I have telegraphed to you, Miss Van Tassel died from the effect of her injuries this morning. The event has come upon us with a shock, and a most painful feeling prevails throughout the community. It was generally believed that the lady's injuries were slight, and the doctor's reports tended to encourage the hope that she would be better in a few days. But it would seem that her fall, which was upon the face and breast, resulted in some injury to the spine, high up. She suffered great pain, but her sufferings were of short duration. The day after the accident, the patient became feverish, but it was not till yesterday that paralysis was seriously apprehended. In the latter stage of her illness, Miss Van Tassel was unconscious, her husband [sic], was by her side, attending to her night and day, and one of the Dacca ladies rendered all the service in her power during part of the time. More as a matter

of form than anything else, an inquest was held, the inevitable verdict
being accidental death. The interment took place in the Dacca cemetery at 4:45 p.m. and an affecting scent took place at the grave. During
the Burial Service, the sorrowing husband [*sic*] broke down and gave
way to his grief. Mr. Colville, the Manager, was also overcome by his
feelings, and after the Burial Service burst forth in a eulogium on the
deceased. A native of California [*sic*], the late Miss Van Tassel was
about eighteen years of age."[44]

While it is quite likely that Jeanette Rumary was from the United Kingdom
and not California, it is almost assuredly the case that she was twenty-seven
at the time of her death. "Mrs. Van Tassell" was interred in the Christian
Cemetery at Wari (now Narinda) in Dhaka. There are also no known records
of a marriage to Park Van Tassel during their time together, although that
was certainly possible. In Sydney, the *Evening News* confused Jeanette's
death considerably, suggesting that she had died "while giving an exhibition
of her skill in Austria" and that she was the same "Miss Van Tassell" that had
visited Sydney "not long ago"—an obvious confusion with the Freitas sisters.[45] Similar misconceptions that Jeanette was the same as either Val or
Gladys came from London,[46] and the incorrect news reports were further
propagated throughout Australia and likely other British colonies. The *Evening News* even published a photo of Gladys, suggesting that it was one of
the last photos of the "unfortunate lady parachutist, who died on the morning of March 18."[47] Additional confusion spread, with some reporters absolutely convinced that the "Miss Van Tassel" associated with the death in
Dacca was Valerie Freitas. This confusion was challenged by a reader of the
Allahabad *Morning Post* on April 20, 1892:

> I note in the *Morning Post* of the 21st an article on Miss Jeannette Van
> Tassell's death, wherein you state that *another* Miss Van Tassell is now
> *trying* her hand at aerial navigation at Ahmedabad. Allow me to state
> that the young lady who has just lost her life has only made six balloon
> ascents and parachute descents in her life, but that Miss Valerie Van
> Tassell, who is now here [Ahmedabad], has made successful ascents
> and descents all through Australia, Java, China, Japan, Manila, the

Straits Settlements, Burma, and the following places in India: Hyderabad, Poona, Mysore, Jeypore, Bhavanagar, Junagad, Indore, Jamnagar,
Ahmedabad, etc. This statement I am prepared to prove at any time, and
I defy Professor P. A. Van Tassell to contradict it. Miss Gladys Van Tas-
sell, who is now in Germany making ascents and parachute descents,
is the sister of Miss Valerie, who joined the Professor of that name in
Australia two-and-a-half years ago, but left him in July last in Bombay.
Professor P. A. Van Tassell then went to Europe and brought out the
lady whom he called Jeannette, and she made her first balloon ascent in
Bombay.[48]

Indeed, after parting ways with Park Van Tassel, Valerie Freitas (now married
to J. C. Owen) had continued making balloon ascensions and on the evening
of Sunday, March 20, 1892, had made a successful balloon ascension and parachute descent at Ahmedabad, performing trapeze acts on the way up. She
landed on the roof of a hut near the Parsi Fire Temple and received only
bruises to her right eye and hands. While many crowds watched from the
banks of the river, few paid the entry fee to be closer to the balloon enclosure.
She was cheered loudly upon her return to the point of launch at Gaekwad
Haveli.[49]

It is likely that Park Van Tassel was unaware of the continued exhibition
by the Freitas sisters. But utterly distraught by Jeanette's death, Park abandoned his attempt at a balloon voyage across India "owing to serious illness,"
likely in the form of depression.[50] He took a hiatus from exhibitions for the
remainder of spring and into summer 1892, drifting throughout India.

# 19. THE LONG ROAD HOME

RETURNING TO THE air in August 1892, Park Van Tassel made a balloon ascension at Queen's Garden in Delhi in the presence of the deputy commissioner of Delhi and a large crowd. The balloon ascended and drifted slowly to the east, with "the aeronaut" making a parachute descent from 3,000 feet to a landing at the Lahori gate of the fort, with the balloon landing inside the fort.[1] Never far from the comfort of companionship, at some time between the summer and fall of 1892, Park (age thirty-nine) fell in love with Edith Ann Nowlan (age eighteen). They were married on November 28, 1892, at Dinapur (now Danapur).[2]

In Vietnam, an exhibitionist named Victor Valazie provided a balloon ascension and parachute drop at Saigon (now Ho Chi Minh City) on Christmas Day 1892. However, owing to considerable difficulty with the balloon inflation, the parachute drop was made in the dark of night and not well observed. Valazie attempted another jump on January 8, 1893, in front of a large crowd at an altitude of 2,000 feet. His parachute failed to open for the first 800 feet of his fall and then opened so suddenly that he was left barely holding on with one arm. Without control, he went through the roof of a brewery with such impact that he died when hitting the floor.[3] While it is believed that Van Tassel was not associated with this tragedy, others have reported that Van Tassel was the one who made the jump on January 8, 1893.[4] However, there are no reports of any flights by Van Tassel in 1893, as he was likely in India with Nowlan at this time.

It should be noted that during the mid-1860s and into the 1890s, the increased daring of aeronauts led to an increasing rate of accidents and fatalities. Those who were engaged in a careful and rather safe use of balloons in the first half of the nineteenth century were replaced by exhibitionists who raced to make increasingly difficult stunts. Whether through the use of older equipment that would fail at altitude, balloons that would catch on fire during an improper inflation, or issues with parachutes, the risks were real and life-threatening. As historian Tom Crouch noted, "The smoke balloonists, who were already plummeting out of the sky at an alarming rate, began to perform an even more dangerous stunt after Thomas S. Baldwin reintroduced the parachute in 1887. . . . Suddenly, during the late 1880s and early 1890s, semisuicidal daredevils seems to be leaping over every small town in America, often with disastrous results."[5] The same was true for aeronauts around the world.

Additionally, the economies of the world began to suffer in the economic depression of 1893. British investment abroad decreased considerably, and the economy of the United States would take several years to recover. However, by the summer of 1894, Van Tassel was off once again, making balloon ascensions and parachute descents for new crowds. It is likely that his bourgeoning relationship with Nowlan had soured, although no records of divorce can be found. On August 6, 1894, near Tower Hall at Colombo, Ceylon (now Sri Lanka), Van Tassel ascended to 7,000 feet in front of a large crowd and descended with a successful parachute jump. This flight is credited as the first balloon flight and first parachute jump in Sri Lanka's history.[6]

Park continued on from Sri Lanka to Africa. In East Africa he providing an exhibition for Sayyid Ali bin Said Al-Busaid, the fourth sultan of Zanzibar, "while 200 Mrs. Sultans looked on through grated windows."[7] He traveled to South Africa, stopping in Durban, Pietermaritzburg, Port Elizabeth, and East London for exhibitions. Details of these events are quite sketchy, but it is clear that former acquaintance James Price had already spent considerable time giving balloon ascensions and parachute jumps in South Africa, so it is likely that the crowds were thin.

Leaving Africa, he continued to Persia (now Iran), stopping in Shiraz, Isfahan, and Tehran. According to Park's own accounting in 1901, "We had to travel by horseback and muleback. There are only four miles of railway track in the whole country. After the Shah came back from England, filled with ideas of civilization, he started to build a railroad, but after the track had been laid for four miles the people objected, and as many of them camped on the right of way, blocking the work of the builders, the line went no farther."[8]

On June 7, 1895, Park Van Tassel provided an ascension and parachute jump in the presence of Naser al-Din Shah Qajar, the shah of Persia. The shah was so pleased with the exhibition that he decorated Van Tassel with the five-pointed star of the Third Order of the Lion and the Sun. This was the highest honor possible without making the recipient a prince. The recognition also carried the honorary rank of general in the Persian army. The shah also provided "General Van Tassel" with a gem-studded sword. Van Tassel departed Tehran for Tabriz with an American passport made out by Minister Resident Alexander McDonald and bearing the name General Park Albert Van Tassel.[9] While at Tabriz he provided an exhibition for the governor of Tabriz, but during the exhibition, someone stole the gem-laden sword. No trace of the sword was ever found. After forty-five days on horseback in Persia, Van Tassel left for Russia. He first gave an exhibition at Tiflis (now Tbilisi) and then at Odessa. Traveling on to Europe, he is believed to have made ascensions at Warsaw, then Berlin, Aachen, Paris, and finally London.

While Park was quite capable of coloring the truth, as part of his recollections in 1901, he noted that after his first arrival in India in 1891, he traveled eight times back and forth between London and India, but the details of only one or two of these trips can be confirmed. What is known, however, is that having taken the better part of a year between 1894 and 1895 to travel from India and Sri Lanka to Africa, Persia, Russia, and then London, Park rather quickly returned yet again to India.

On Saturday, December 7, 1895, Van Tassel arranged for a balloon ascension and parachute jump at the Government House at Parel, a neighborhood in Bombay. This was a difficult arrangement to make, as only four years previously, an exhibitionist called Lieutenant Mansfield had died at the nearby Victoria Gardens making a similar attempt, and the local police were steadfastly against another performance of this type. Newspaper reporters began questioning the value of parachute exhibitions except for their possible use by the military.[10] The commissioner of police, R. H. Vincent, remained vigilant in not providing the permission required to Van Tassel. However, when Van Tassel went directly to the governor, he approved, overruled the local commissioner, and offered the use of the Government House and its grounds.

A portion of the large grounds were roped off as a paid spectator area. And by the time the day arrived for the event, these grounds were full of three thousand to four thousand people. However, many more thousands of local citizens arrived hours before the event along the main roads leading to Parel, crowding the roads, climbing trees, hills, walls, and the roofs of houses to obtain their vantage points for free. The railway stations were packed, beyond what anyone had expected, but the local authorities made sure there were no incidents.

Inflation of the balloon was to begin at 4:15 p.m., but in light of a strong northerly breeze, Van Tassel delayed the inflation as long as possible. But the longer he waited, the stronger the winds became. At 4:45 p.m. the process of inflation started; it lasted for thirty minutes. The large *City of London*[11] measured 78 feet high, with a diameter of 58 feet, and was a "dirty vermillion color."[12] Roughly seventy soldiers, sailors, and laborers helped maintain the balloon during its inflation. Just as the balloon was nearly completely inflated, one of the guide poles fell in an unexpected direction toward the spectators, who had just enough time to get out of the way before it landed. The scene was eerily similar to the unfortunate incident in Queensland. Adding to the chaos, during the last parts of the inflation, the large crowd outside the enclosure rushed in to get a better view, easily mixing with those who had paid for the opportunity. It seemed that on this one attempted flight, in his return to India, all the different problems that had at one time or another been issues were conspiring make the flight as difficult as possible.

With increasing winds and sunset approaching, and before any other calamities could take place, Van Tassel took his place on the trapeze and yelled "Let go!" The balloon immediately rose quickly, with the large crowd cheering it higher. Van Tassel's hat fell off at an altitude of about 300 feet, landing near a refreshment stand in the grounds. He climbed to 3,600 feet in a strong breeze, which took him south toward the sea. Rather than climb any higher, he pulled the collapsing cord on the balloon and jumped, falling about 150 feet before the parachute opened. In the strong winds, the parachute rocked back and forth and without much control. He came to a hard landing near Lowjee Castle, about half a mile from the Government House. The parachute became entangled in the leaves of a nearby palm tree but without much damage. Meanwhile, the balloon came to Earth near the town of Ohinohpoogley, about another half mile farther downwind from where Van Tassel had landed. Van Tassel returned to the Government House grounds at about 7:00 p.m., trying to make his way back through the crowds. Those who remained near the enclosure received him with loud cheers.[13]

At one point during his Indian travels, Van Tassel made an exhibition for Sayyid Hamid Ali Khan Bahadur, the nawab of Rampur. Van Tassel later recalled,

> I was going to give an ascension and parachute drop before thousands of the Nawah's [sic] people, and the Nawah made me promise that I wouldn't come down inside the harem. I always had to promise that, but this time—well, I promised but the parachute didn't open until I was too far down to steer well, and in spite of all I could do I sailed over the palace and dropped right into a mulberry tree in the middle of the harem. I could hear the ladies inside shrieking as I came down. They all ran in out of sight. If the Nawah had not come into the inner court of the harem himself, together with the British resident, I guess the guards would have chopped me up when I came down out of that tree.[14]

In late February or early March 1897, a female parachutist by the name of Beaumont provided a balloon ascension and parachute jump during a horse show at Jacobabad in Beluchistan, in what is now Pakistan. It was reported that Park Van Tassel provided direction and assistance for her exhibition. She rose perfectly to an altitude of 7,000 feet and parachuted down to a perfect landing. A newspaper reported, "The [locals] scampered on horses, camels, and on foot to the spot where the parachutist landed, and cheered her lustily. At the conclusion of the exhibition Miss Beaumont was called to the Collector's bungalow, where she was presented with a gold medal from the Sirdars as a token of their appreciation of the wonderful feat."[15]

At least one "Miss Van Tassell" (likely Valerie, but perhaps either Gladys Freitas or Beaumont) continued making balloon ascensions in India into 1898. At Jacobabad on January 13, 1898, William Mansfield, first Viscount Sandhurst (Lord Sandhurst), was afforded a special exhibition of horse and camel races at the local racecourse. Between the races, "Miss Van Tassell" made a successful balloon ascension to about 5,000 feet. It is assumed that she descended with a parachute, and given there was hardly any wind, "the descent

PROF. VAN TASSELL AND HIS BALLOON.
Ready for an Ascent, in India. Before Lord and Lady Curzon.

*Deseret Evening News* coverage of a balloon ascension in India by Park Van Tassel (date unknown) for George Nathaniel Curzon (Lord Curzon) and his wife, Mary Victoria Leiter (Lady Curzon). Lord Curzon later served as viceroy of India. Library of Congress.

was a point not more than a hundred yards or so from the point of ascension."[16]

Van Tassel kept providing his own exhibitions but at a decreasing pace. At Darjeeling, his efforts provided inspiration to youngsters, who began to fashion balloons of their own as toys.[17] On March 14, 1900, Van Tassel arranged for a balloon ascension and parachute jump at Jhind (now Jind). The filling of the balloon was aided by sepoys[18] from Jhind State, who helped stabilize the balloon with ropes. But at the time of launch, three of the men became entangled with the ropes of the balloon and parachute and were carried up into the air. One of the three fell right away, but the other two were tangled so tightly that they could not easily free themselves. As the balloon rose higher, one of these men fell but miraculously was caught once again in the ropes that dangled below the balloon. Van Tassel could have released himself by parachute but did not. He instead told the two men to hold on tightly. The balloon ascended to its maximum height, began to cool, and descended. During the descent, the parachute opened, and the ever-relaxing balloon formed its own parachute. The three men descended safely to Earth, much to the thrill of the large crowd that had assembled to watch the ascent.[19]

In October 1900, it was reported that in Lucknow, Park Van Tassel suffered a stroke, causing paralysis on his left side. He underwent initial treatment in Lucknow but in early 1901 decided to return to California, without young Edith Ann.

# 20. OTHER AERONAUTS

*Lirt of those he worked with*

WHILE VAN TASSEL was traveling all corners of the Eastern Hemisphere from 1894 to 1900, those with prior association to Van Tassel also continued their exhibitions. Following the economic depression of the 1890s, many of these aeronauts returned to San Francisco at about the same time as Van Tassel, eager to continue to make their living as the United States recovered.

## The Viola Sisters

Ruby Hawker (performing as Millie Viola) was one of three sisters who began jumping from balloons with parachutes. Lillian Mary Hawker[1] made balloon ascensions and parachute jumps as Leila Adair in New Zealand at Takapuna (near Auckland), Hamilton, Cambridge, and New Plymouth in March and April 1894.[2] A newspaper described her as having a "pale face, with dark restless grey eyes, short brown hair clustering in thick little curls all over a shapely head."[3] At times she also was known as Leila Rayward. She suggested to the papers that she hailed from Texas and reportedly made her first balloon ascent at the age of thirteen with Park Van Tassel at Los Angeles in roughly 1885. However, research suggests that like her sister Ruby, she was born in Australia and somehow came to the United States at a young age. Adair confirmed in the *Sydney Evening News* in 1895 that Viola had made her first successful parachute descent from a balloon at Chicago in 1888.[4] Adair also said she made her first parachute jump from a balloon with Van Tassel's assistance in the Black Hills of South Dakota, although there are no known reports of Van Tassel ever traveling to South Dakota. A reporters recalled her story:

It was very windy, and a first experiment at making their own gas.
Everything went wrong, and when 6 o'clock came there was no sign
of the balloon ascending. The crowd comprising [of] miners and
cowboys, grew more and more impatient, and would listen to no
explanation, though Van Tassel promised a free show [the] next day.
They gathered round shouting "Imposters! Let us lynch the man,
and duck the woman in the nearest sluicing-pond! Let us tear their
balloon to pieces!" The latter was made of silk and worth 3000dol.
I suggested to Van Tassel to get right away—a woman alone might
stand some chance. All the afternoon I had been waiting in my little
American buggy, the bag with the takings between my feet. Out
west they are a wild, lawless lot. I had two loaded revolvers in the
buggy, and knew how to use them. So I just stood up with one in
each hand and explained that "I meant to have twelve lives before
any man touched me or my balloon. . . . I am an American woman,
utterly alone [a]mong American men, and instead of threatening
you or to take the horses out and drag my buggy along, because
of my pluck in risking my neck for your amusement, as I will do
to-morrow." This seems to have touched them in the right place, and
the end was that the mob almost fought for the honor of dragging
her buggy to the inn. And the following day, when she landed with
her balloon in an ash tree, the very men who had been ready for any
violence cut down the big limb where she caught, and insisted on
carrying her along seated on it, making a fresh collection for her as
they went amounting to 3000dol.[5]

Prior to her jumps in New Zealand, Adair reportedly toured through California, Australia, and China and made a parachute descent at Hong Kong.
On May 24, 1892, she returned to the profession at Bendigo, Australia, while
her manager ran off with the gate receipts. At Dubbo in New South Wales
she made an attempt, but the balloon caught fire on the way up and she
descended unharmed. After the passing of her husband, in 1894 she made an
extensive tour of New Zealand and for ten months made descents at Te
Aroha, Cambridge, Wellington, and many other locations. At Christchurch
she nearly met with disaster: during liftoff of the balloon, her parachute

caught a guide wire and pulled her back to Earth, causing a fall of 40 feet. She remained unconscious for a week but survived.

Adair's background was made even less clear when in 1895 she noted to the *Sydney Evening News*, "Though my professional name is Adair, I am Prof. Price's sister, not his wife as has been stated, so I reckon it's just as well to set that right."[6] While there is no known direct familial relation to James Price, it is indeed unusual that Price had performed previously in Utah with Millie Viola but that Leila Adair had apparently learned the art of ballooning from Park Van Tassel, despite Millie Viola and Leila Adair actually being Hawker sisters from Australia.

To add even further confusion, a third Hawker sister, Ethel Harriet Hawker,[7] also born in Australia, eventually followed her sisters into the profession, performing as Essie Viola. In May 1895, Essie ascended in her balloon at Gympie, Queensland, only to have both the balloon and the parachute catch fire at 1,000 feet. She jumped anyway and made it back to Earth without serious injury.[8] A reporter noted,

> Just at the instant that the balloon was let go it swayed heavily about, and displacing the damper used for regulating the flame, caught fire as it shot into the air. Miss Millie, her sister, tried to seize her, but the intrepid young aeronaut would not be stayed, and she went up like a rocket. But she did not come down like a stick. Hanging by her feet, she went nearly half a mile and then commenced to drift away from the river, where she started. At this stage the balloon, which at the start was noticed to be on fire, became a blazing mass, extending towards the parachute. Seeing the situation of affairs, there was intense excitement among the spectators. The huge balloon descended [in] literally one mass of flames, with the frail girl waving her handkerchief in the most fearless manner. No help was possible until the earth was reached. Down the balloon came, and was etched with intense anxiety, until the intervening trees hid the spirited young lady and her blazing chariot from view. Long before the numbers of people were following her, to give all of the assistance possible, and she was extricated from the burning mass as soon as she touched the ground. On regaining a footing on the solid earth in a most nonchalant

manner she requested the bystanders try to save her parachute. The balloon was utterly destroyed, and the parachute badly damaged.[9]

Later in 1895, Essie traveled from Australia to San Francisco and announced to the press that she would ride over Niagara Falls in a barrel, well before anyone had accomplished the feat. To make things even more dangerous, it was proposed that the barrel be dropped by balloon into the river before going over the falls.[10]

    With no protective equipment, Sam Patch had survived a plunge after jumping from a platform into the Niagara River near the base of Horseshoe Falls in 1829. Later in 1829, Patch died after jumping into the icy waters of the Genesee River in upstate New York. In 1886 Carlisle Graham made two successful rides through the rapids at the base of Niagara Falls in a barrel, but a planned trip over the falls was never actually made. Graham's journey generated considerable publicity. For Essie to propose doing this in 1895 was considered rather preposterous. Reporters from the *San Francisco Call* quoted Essie as saying,

> I have been just crazy to go over the falls . . . ever since I heard four years ago that man Graham had done it. He was knocked senseless, you know, and otherwise injured, and I almost hoped he would die, so that I might be the first to do it successfully. But I'll be the first woman to do it, anyway, and I'm going to bet every cent I've got that I don't get hurt a bit. You don't think betting is wrong, do you? Yes, four years is a long time to wait for the chance, but until now something always prevented. We had engagements ahead for balloon ascensions, and . . . I wanted to see everything since I have had enough of the colonies and want to stay in America for the rest of my life.[11]

She continued to describe her time in New Zealand: "We, my sister and I, made several ascensions there. One time she came down among the Maoris. They thought her the angel from heaven which, they say, will come to help them drive the British from their land and they hurried her away into the interior. We had to get the mounted police and call out the volunteers before we could get her back."[12]

For her Niagara attempt, she planned to team up with Robert Earlston, who would be in charge of the balloon that dropped the barrel into the Niagara River, with the event managed by a man named Major Clemens. But no records of any attempts by Viola at Niagara can be found. Perhaps she learned at a later date that Graham had not actually gone over the falls as she had supposed. It wasn't until 1901 that the first person went over the falls in a barrel. That was Annie Edson Taylor, who survived the trip on her birthday, October 24, in 1901. In 1911 Bobby Leach was the second person to make it successfully over the falls in a barrel.

By January 1896, both Essie and Millie Viola were living in San Francisco and making regularly scheduled balloon ascensions and parachute drops very near where the "Baldwin brothers" and Van Tassel had made the first leap. For instance, in late January 1896, several thousand spectators gathered at the Haight Street Grounds in the afternoon, with some assisting with balloon inflation. But when the balloon was half-inflated, rains came and most spectators left. Undeterred, the Viola sisters continued with the balloon inflation and at 4:30 p.m. the balloon was ready to go. Essie appeared on the scene "accompanied by her sister and a curly-haired little boy."[3] She kissed the boy and her sister and took her position on the trapeze. At the order of "Let go," all the ropes were released and the balloon slowly rose northward. At just about 15 feet of elevation, Essie leaned backward to turn on the bar, and all of a sudden the parachute unexpectedly released from the balloon. Essie hit the ground and was covered by the parachute while the balloon continued to rise skyward. She complained of pain in her back and her head.[14]

During Essie's recovery, Millie planned a balloon launch for February 2, 1896, but the balloon caught fire before it could be released.[15] In April 1896, Essie returned to the spotlight, performing once again with a balloon ascension and parachute drop at Chutes Park south of San Francisco.[16] She also made an ascension at the Haight Street Grounds in late April, coming down via parachute on a street near the end of the panhandle of what is now Golden Gate Park. Similar jumps continued sporadically into July 1896.[17]

## James Price

After parting ways with the Van Tassell Troupe, James Price continued touring Western Australia. He moved to Johannesburg, South Africa, for a period of four years, ending in November 1895.[18] He noted,

> I was born . . . in Springfield, Illinois, about 185 miles from Chicago, and I showed in America for seven years before I went abroad. About six years ago I decided to have a spin round the world, and in November, 1889, I struck my first port, Honolulu. It was on November 16 of that year that King Kalakaua's birthday was being celebrated, and in honour of the event I went up in the balloon and came down in the parachute. I made several ascents in the capital of Hawaii, and there I met with a great misfortune in the loss of my partner, Joe Van Tassel, who was blown out to sea, and eaten up by sharks before he could be reached. I have a mortal horror of sharks since then. Leaving there I came to Australia, and Van Tassel (a brother) and I, together with Miss Viola, Miss Leila Adair and the Freties [*sic*] Sisters, known as the Van Tassels, made several ascents. From Australia I went through the Straits settlements, and showed at Java, Sourabaya [*sic*], Batavia, Singapore, where I gave an exhibition before the Sultan of Jahore. At Siam I appeared before the King. Through India I had a successful career and then went on to Ceylon, where I appeared before Sir Arthur Havelock at Colombo. I then visited the Mauritius and after Madagascar. At the latter place Queen Ranavalona II sent the natives 250 miles to bring me before her, and she was delightfully pleased. From there I went to South Africa, and stopped there nearly four years.[19]
>
> My experiences in South Africa were very favourable. I made my first ascent in October, 1891, when I went aloft from Pietermaritzburg. From there I went to Durban, in Natal, and from there to Johannesburg, in the Transvaal. I had great difficulty in making an ascent in Johannesburg, as the altitude is so great, something like 6000ft. above sea-level. The air is so light that the balloon would not go higher than 500ft. . . . Altogether I made over 32 ascents in the town, and was presented with a gold clasp imitation of a balloon as a memento of my 32nd ascent. In Pretoria . . . I was introduced to President Kruger, General Joubert, and some members of the Volksraad.[20]

Back in Australia, on Boxing Day 1895, Price made a balloon ascension and
parachute jump from an altitude of 8,000 feet at Clifton Gardens in Sydney.
He was hailed in the papers as an American hero, an aeronaut with more than
five hundred successful balloon ascents to his name.[21] Returning once again
to Hawaii, Price made a balloon ascension and parachute jump at Remond
Grove on George Washington's Birthday, February 22, 1896.[22] On the previous evening, at 7:00 p.m., Price had sent aloft a paper balloon from the corner
of Fort and Beretania Streets to test the winds aloft.[23] While two trains were
arranged to carry spectators to the location, "neither train was crowded due,
possibly, from the fact that people who take an interest in aerostatics had not
recovered from the shock experience at Van Tassell's death a half dozen years
ago."[24] Inflation of the smoke balloon began under the direction of Price and
a man named Willifred Burns. There was a light southerly breeze that day and
no danger of Price being carried out to sea. Despite this, Price indicated that
if there was a trajectory that took him toward the sea, he would release at
500 feet and come down by parachute right away. At 4:20 p.m. the balloon
was ready. Price sat on the trapeze bar and gave word to let go. "It was a fascinating sight but to those who had seen [Joe] Van Tassell go to his death
there was a certain unconquerable awe about it all that was appalling."[25] At
an elevation of 3,000 feet, Price released and made a graceful descent back to
Earth. The balloon gradually collapsed and soon followed. A Pearl City pine-
apple farmer reached Price about the time he landed.[26]

In March 1896, a newspaper announced that James Price had joined with
the Wirth Circus Company and would leave Hawaii for a tour of Japan to
provide balloon and parachute exhibitions.[27] He returned to the Hawaiian
Islands later that summer. On August 29, 1896, at Wailuku, Maui, he filled his
balloon and at 6:00 p.m. was launched. At an altitude of about 130 feet, the
balloon burst, collapsing nearly instantaneously. Whether this was planned to
avoid a trajectory to the ocean or was accidental, Price immediately cut away
with the parachute. However, the damp parachute did not open and Price
"shot like an arrow" to the ground.[28] Very fortunately, he landed in a large
mango tree in the yard of tax collector W. M. Robinson. The branches broke
his fall, and with the exception of a swollen eye and facial bruises, he survived
the event without other physical harm. He returned to Honolulu aboard the
steamer *Hall* on September 1.[29]

## Thomas Baldwin

After he jumped from Van Tassel's balloon with a parachute in 1887 at San
Francisco, Thomas Baldwin went to Quincy, Illinois, to make additional
jumps and from there embarked on a whirlwind tour of England from July
through September 1888. He made more than ten jumps in London alone,
with wide publicity across England, even performing for Parliament and
Prince Albert Edward of Wales. While in England, he proceeded to patent
the flexible parachute design that he had coinvented with Van Tassel. The
application for "Improvements in Parachutes" was made on July 28, 1888, and
the specification was accepted on October 19, 1888. British patent no. 10,937
was coauthored by Guillermo Antonio Farini and Baldwin. While Farini had
many patents to his name, none of his other patents had anything to do with
parachutes. So it is likely that without Van Tassel's knowledge, Baldwin found
someone in London familiar with the patent process and paid him to develop
the patent as a "coinventor" so that Baldwin could protect his position while
providing lucrative demonstrations throughout the British colonies. It
remains unknown if or when Park Van Tassel became aware of this patent.

From England, Baldwin traveled to other parts of Europe, making additional jumps and then touring South Africa, Australia, and New Zealand
before returning to Quincy, Illinois in December 1888. Within this short
span, Baldwin became an international sensation. In the summer and fall of
1889, he was joined by William Ivy.[30] They made a tour of the American
West, including the 1889 New Mexico Territorial Fair at Albuquerque. "Professor" Baldwin planned smoke balloon ascents with parachute drops. Taking
advantage of the special exhibition, Albuquerque saloonkeepers hiked the
price of a glass of beer from five to ten cents. His first ascent was scheduled
for October 2.[31] Unfortunately, Baldwin could not get his balloon inflated
properly and so could not launch. He explained that he had forgotten to take
into consideration Albuquerque's rarified air and promised to do better the
next day. On his next attempt, Baldwin managed a proper inflation. Several
hundred men held down the balloon until he arrived. He looked at his balloon and exclaimed, "Oh, ain't she a dandy. Who says we ain't going high this
time?" He then attached himself to the balloon with ropes and shouted, "Let
her go!" As the balloon began to rise, the ropes broke and Baldwin dropped
to the ground, landing unceremoniously on his posterior. The balloon went

Drawing for "Improvements in Parachutes" from British patent no. 10,397, submitted by Thomas Baldwin and Guillermo Farini, accepted on October 19, 1888. British Library Business and Intellectual Property Reference Service.

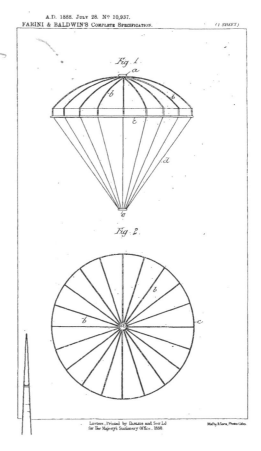

off without him. Things went better during his third attempt. On the final day of the fair, he soared to 3,000 feet and redeemed himself in the eyes of the public.[32]

After their American West tour, the "Baldwin brothers" went on to Japan, performing in large cities through the spring of 1890. From there they performed in Shanghai and Hong Kong, then Singapore, the Straits Settlements, Java, Burma, and India. In late spring 1891, Thomas returned back to Quincy with his wife for the birth of their first child, while Ivy continued making exhibitions in India. Ivy too returned to Quincy in September 1891. By 1897, both Ivy and Baldwin had returned to California, making exhibitions in the Bay Area.[33]

## Professor Lawrence

Professor Lawrence also continued his exhibitions in India and Southeast Asia. In Singapore, on January 6, 1894, he made a balloon ascension from the grounds of the Chinese Club and descended by parachute. The crowd was somewhat smaller than expected, and the balloon rose to a height of only 20 feet. He tried again the following day but a large hole burst on the side of the balloon. But he did manage to make an ascension and parachute jump on the third day, without much of a crowd in attendance.[34] In 1897 Lawrence made a parachute jump at Naini Tal in India, rising to 7,000 feet into a heavy downpour with the balloon disappearing in the rain and clouds. He returned to Earth safely via parachute, but the balloon was ruined.[35]

## Fannie Van Tassell

In Unionville, Ontario, at central Canada's Great Fair, another "Van Tassell" was at work. On September 18, 1895, a Fannie Van Tassell gave a balloon ascension and parachute jump for the crowd.[36] There is also a record of Fannie providing a balloon ascension and jump at the North Adams Fair during the same time period.[37] Any relation between Fannie and Park Van Tassel remains unknown.

The method of parachuting from balloons popularized by Baldwin and Van Tassel in San Francisco had spread worldwide, bringing considerable fame and imitation. Yet, as more and more aeronauts attempted daring acts, the financial rewards decreased and the novelty of the approach waned. However, San Francisco remained a central hub of technology and innovation. It was not by chance that many returned to the Bay Area, eager to be part of the next gold rush in the sky.

# 21. CALIFORNIA, HERE I COME . . .

FOLLOWING HIS STROKE, Park Van Tassel returned to San Francisco aboard the *Nippon Maru* in early July 1901, at the age of forty-eight, after a period of nearly twelve years, having lost a friend to a parachute accident, his wife Clara in divorce, two "girlfriends" to marriage, and another "wife" to a parachute accident—and having married again and likely divorced again before leaving India.[1] Upon his arrival, Bay Area newspapers recalled his early activities with ballooning in the region and also noted, "Van Tassell has seen the royalty of almost every realm worth mentioning since his departure twelve years ago. Australia, Java, the Philippines, the whole of India, Persia, Russia, Germany, France, England, were all visited in turn."[2] Newspapers focused on his celebrity in these foreign lands. He had flown before hundreds of thousands of spectators, with some believing that Park must have been reincarnated, as "no man can have power over the air except he die and come back."[3] Park was eager to recuperate and "take another expedition to cloudland."[4]

Van Tassel returned to a very different California than he had left years before. Societal attitudes toward the concept of piloted flight had changed. Lighter-than-air balloons were now more common, and the antics of the Viola sisters and others at the Haight Street Grounds, Chutes Park, and other locations made parachute jumping from balloons more a regular occurrence than a true novelty. However, heavier-than-air flying machines still appeared distant, despite the progress being made. Even one of the brightest minds at the time, William Thomson (Lord Kelvin) in Scotland, noted in 1896 that he had "not the smallest molecule of faith in aerial navigation other than ballooning,"[5] and in 1902 he more famously predicted that "no balloon and no aeroplane will ever be practically successful."[6] California's own Joseph LeConte, a noted professor at the University of California at Berkeley, stated

in 1888 that heavier-than-air flying machines were impossible.[7] But early successes with heavier-than-air gliders by Otto Lilienthal in Germany, Octave
Chanute in Illinois, and John J. Montgomery in southern California suggested to some that powered, controlled, heavier-than-air flight might be on
the horizon.

In July 1869, at Shellmound Park near the current site of San Francisco
International Airport, Frederick Marriott demonstrated the first powered,
unpiloted dirigible flight in the United States with an untethered flight of his
*Avitor Hermes, Jr.*[8] A native of England, Marriott had previously worked with
William Henson and John Stringfellow in the development of the Henson
Aerial Steam Carriage. Marriott came to California as a part of the gold rush
in 1850, making a living as a journalist and publisher. His success with *Avitor
Hermes, Jr.* as part of the Aerial Steam Navigation Company was intended to
lead to a larger human-carrying dirigible. However, due to economic trouble
and his untimely passing, the full-size dirigible was never produced. Early
tests for his *Avitor Hermes, Jr.* were made in the same Mechanics' Pavilion in
San Francisco where Van Tassel and Baldwin later experimented with parachutes.

Similarly, in roughly 1884, Dr. August Greth began experimenting with
dirigibles. A native of the Alsace region of France, he became interested in
aviation while serving in the French army. Greth immigrated to California in
1882 and became a physician in San Francisco. Struggling to make ends meet
but still with knowledge of French efforts in ballooning, Greth set out to
build America's first dirigible. In 1897 he established the American Aerial
Navigation Company, which built the dirigible *California Eagle*, on a lot just
off Market Street.[9] When fully inflated, the *California Eagle* had a length of
roughly 75 feet and a diameter of 25 feet, with a small steel tube frame supporting the motor and operator, and netting over the balloon to keep it from
buckling and to support the weight of the frame beneath. Greth was familiar
with the Brazilian aviation pioneer Alberto Santos-Dumont's efforts with
dirigibles in France. However, Greth's concept differed in that his craft had
multiple, steerable propellers, all connected to a single motor, rather than
controlling pitch via weight shift, which was common to Santos-Dumont's
series.[10] The large hydrogen gas bag also did not make use of the automatic
expansion valves that were common to the dirigibles of Santos-Dumont.

The dirigible was evaluated through a series of captive tests and was ready for flight in the fall of 1903. On Sunday, October 18, 1903, Greth set up the *California Eagle* at the corner of Market and Eleventh Streets in San Francisco.[11] Launched under its own buoyancy, it ascended to a height of 2,000 feet, at which point Greth started the 10-horsepower motor and began his journey. Initially descending several hundred feet, Greth steered the dirigible to the north and then to the south in a semicircle. Over the Presidio, the fog began to dissipate and the hydrogen gas in the dirigible began to expand quickly. Greth worked to let gas escape from the balloon, which was so expanded that the bag was in danger of bursting. During that confusion, Greth was unable to keep the motor functioning properly and the wind caused him to drift out over the Bay. The dirigible lost power and began to descend, eventually landing and then floating on the surface of the Bay about 200 feet from shore. Picked up by boat and towed to shore, Greth suggested to reporters that "the balloon was entirely under his control for the greater part of the time that he was in the air, and would have been completely so except for the certain defects in the motor and the balloon."[12] Despite his not being able to land properly, the flight showed that Greth was on the right track and also brought a new form of aviation to the citizens of San Francisco, who gazed skyward at the very unusual floating sausage.

At roughly this time, and probably reading about the events in the local papers, Thomas Baldwin connected with Greth in pursuit of a stronger motor and with interest in using dirigibles for exhibition. Baldwin was brought on as Greth's aeronaut. It is likely that in Baldwin, Greth saw an aeronaut with considerable time and experience aloft, while in Greth, Baldwin saw increased opportunity for fame and fortune. A larger 20-horsepower motor was secured and a larger aluminum carriage was constructed in late 1903/early 1904, with a test flight in the *California Eagle* made by Baldwin on April 23, 1904.[13] Taking off just after 8:00 a.m. on a windless morning, Baldwin climbed higher and higher, making circles and heading west toward the Pacific, with an American flag flying at the stern of Greth's dirigible. Everything was running perfectly when all of a sudden the motor stopped, reportedly owing to Baldwin's inability to keep the "mixture of air and gasoline at the right proportion."[14] Baldwin tried to restart the motor but to no avail. He let gas slowly escape from the bag, coming to a landing on a marshy area near San Bruno

Road, with minor damage to the aluminum frame. Children watching nearby
ran to grab the long ropes and keep the dirigible in place. Baldwin released
more gas, and ten minutes later, the large yellow silk balloon and net were
ready to be rolled up and returned to San Francisco.

As the dirigible was encountering its difficulties in the air, young engineer
F. W. Belcher, who had helped install the motor in the *California Eagle*, noted
to reporters,

> The engine has stopped working. Captain Baldwin does not under-
> stand the manipulation of the motor machine, and does not know
> how to keep the mixture proper. He will not be able to start it again,
> because he does not know how to do it. I am sure that this is the cause
> of it. The engine is all right, and if I had gone up with it I am positive
> it still would be working. I am perfectly familiar with all the details
> of this machine, and know it is in first-class shape. I am terribly dis-
> appointed that Captain Baldwin forced me to get out of the ship just
> at the instant that she was about to ascend. I have never been up in
> a balloon, but I know that my engine was in such absolutely perfect
> shape that had I been in charge of it the results would have been suc-
> cessful. At any rate, the ship shows she will be a success.[15]

In another newspaper account, Belcher said, "Oh why did I not go myself?
He said that the engineer would make it too heavy, which I can see now was
not so, else he would not now be sailing up to such an altitude. To go so high
was not necessary. We did not expect him to go but just above the house-tops.
Had I known what he was about, I certainly would have prevented it."[16]
Baldwin was later quoted as saying, "I confess I was not familiar with the
motor, and was unable to start it going again. This is the reason why I could
not further continue on the trip I had anticipated."[17]

The total cost of the dirigible was estimated at $12,000, with funding by
investors in Greth's American Aerial Navigation Company. This particular

(*Opposite page*) Clipping from the *San Francisco Call* on April 24, 1904, showing
Thomas Baldwin (upper left) and August Greth (lower left), as well as Greth's dirigible *California Eagle* in flight. Library of Congress.

# GRETH'S DIRIGIBLE BALLOON SOARS ON HIGH AND PARTIAL SUCCESS MARKS ITS FLIGHT

*AIRSHIP STARTING ON ITS FLIGHT*

THE "CALIFORNIA EAGLE," ITS IN-
VENTOR. AND MAN WHO MADE AN
ASCENT IN IT YESTERDAY.

## Machine Easily Managed in Midair.

## Trip Cut Short by Accident to Motor.

The new Greth airship ascended into
the heavens yesterday morning and
demonstrated the fact that under the
existing favorable weather conditions
she could be controlled at will by her

dirigible was 105 feet in length and 25 feet in diameter, with a gross weight of 2,200 pounds. It required 40,000 cubic feet of gas for inflation. The motor was a De Dion Douton, imported from France, providing power to the two propellers. Greth was quoted as saying,

> In a large way, I was pleased and confirmed in my belief that my scheme of navigating the air is practicable. Even the present machine, in unpracticed hands and with more weight than it should have carried, proved dirigible, which is the main problem to be solved in aerial navigation. The motor we had was to have been directed by a man trained to its use. At the last minute he was displeased by an employe [*sic*] of the company, who claimed the right to make the ascension under a contract he has as aeronaut for the organization. He may have been capable of handling the steering apparatus with which I have equipped the machine, but the motor evidently bothered him. When he reached a certain altitude he found a lower temperature and pressure than is present on the earth. Students of aerial navigation could have found a remedy for such conditions, but an untrained man facing a fall of 1,000 feet is likely to lose his head. As a result the cold air and the pressure generated by the motor caused what is called a "freeze" in the machinery, which made the craft a victim of the shifting currents. The apparatus is not all I wish for in the way of equipment, but I am satisfied that even with the present craft I can sail in the air wherever I choose to go and descend at pleasure.[18]

The papers immediately suggested that Greth's contraption was now the international front-runner for the upcoming competition at the 1904 Louisiana Purchase Exposition (also known as the St. Louis World's Fair) for the longest flight by a dirigible. The $100,000 prize was of considerable interest to investors in the American Aerial Navigation Company and, quite clearly, Thomas Baldwin. Greth parted ways with Baldwin, with Baldwin having become rapidly educated in the latest developments and issues with dirigibles.

A longer flight was made by Greth in the *California Eagle* on May 2, 1904, from San Francisco to South San Francisco, a distance of 8 miles.[19] Greth and his engineer launched at 8:30 a.m. with the intent of flying to San Jose, a distance of 52 miles. However, over the Five Mile House on San Bruno Road, the propellers paused and the operators could be seen making adjustments. Finally the propellers started up again, but the dirigible began a descent, coming to a gentle landing despite strong winds.[20] The thrust provided by the small propellers and motor was simply inadequate for making much progress into a strong headwind, but the equipment did help with steering and control.

Prior to his interaction with Greth, Baldwin already had an interest in dirigibles and possibly an interest in building his own.[21] Realizing that the propellers designed for dirigibles lacked considerable thrust, Baldwin sought out expertise in the Bay Area for the design of improved propellers. He became aware of aeronautics work done by John J. Montgomery at Santa Clara College. Montgomery had been experimenting with gliders since the early 1880s, having made America's first successful gliding flight in 1884.[22] Following these early successes, Montgomery developed his own theories for the circulation of flow over curved surfaces and the generation of lift.[23] Baldwin met with Montgomery over a period of several months in 1903 to learn as much as possible about aeronautics, despite Baldwin's lack of a formal education. Together they attempted to optimize thrust from propellers in a crude wind tunnel constructed on campus. Baldwin also came up with a new concept for Montgomery—the launching of manned gliders from balloons at high altitudes in a manner similar to parachute jumps. If people would pay to see parachute jumpers, they would surely pay more to see gliders released from balloons. Baldwin and Montgomery formed a contract: Baldwin would supply the balloons while Montgomery would supply the gliders. Together they would tour and share the income, with Baldwin supplying $1,000 for the construction of a series of gliders, the hiring of an aeronaut, and experiments with balloon launches. Their contract was signed on April 28, 1904, just five days after Baldwin's flight in Greth's dirigible. With this contract in hand, Montgomery immediately reentered the field of gliding, designing and testing a new series of tandem-wing gliders.[24] Montgomery and Baldwin continued their experiments in April and May of 1904 at Santa Clara College. Baldwin later recalled,

> We experimented for weeks in the placing of the blades on the shaft, that they might work on a column of air equal to the periphery of

the propeller. We found to do this we must bend the blades back
5 degrees. At less than this angle the air rushing around them buckled
back and set up a current of resistance in again coming in contact
with the blades. At a greater angle the air slipped from the blades
without their attaining a full clutch upon it. We figured out the proper
velocity of our propeller. It must go forty-seven miles an hour in its
circular traveling. This is 200 revolutions a minute. To go beyond that
was to lose power. In the solid aluminum propeller, curved true to
an eighth of an inch, and with smooth metallic surface, we are near
perfection in this important feature of the driving mechanism of the
airship.[25]

In another article of the period, Baldwin recalled,

At first we had five or six screws [blades] on the propeller, but we
finally got it down to only two blades, and the curve of those represented the most important point in the whole proposition. To have
this parabolic curve so as to have each screw absolutely clear and
utilize the "air-wake," or air disturbed, at the same time avoiding all
possible resistance, was the important question we had to consider.
We found by a series of experiments that the air in striking a blade
of parabolic curve at a certain angle—say forty five degrees—goes up
over the blade instead of down as commonly believed.[26]

Montgomery immediately initiated construction on a series of tandem-
wing gliders, with experiments at various locations in the Bay Area. Yet,
armed with Montgomery's knowledge of propellers and Greth's dirigible
design, Baldwin traveled to Los Angeles and initiated construction on his
own dirigible, named the *California Arrow*.[27] Initial components of this dirigible were built in Los Angeles, but Baldwin shipped the product to San Jose
for final completion of the gas bag in a yard behind Randall's Cyclery.[28]
Montgomery happened to find Baldwin at the cyclery and was shown the
*California Arrow*. Montgomery departed in stunned silence, perplexed by
Baldwin and his focus on using Montgomery's propeller design, along with
the *California Arrow*, in pursuit of the $100,000 purse at the St. Louis World's

Fair. While working on the dirigible, Baldwin noticed a motorcyclist riding a Curtiss motorcycle. Its two-cylinder, 7-horsepower lightweight motor would be perfect for the *California Arrow*. Baldwin ordered one from the Curtiss Manufacturing Company in Hammondsport, New York. This motor completed the design, leaving Baldwin on a path to success. The propeller was originally described as "having two metallic blades, and nearly six feet in diameter."[29] Baldwin even confirmed later that "in the construction of the *Arrow*, we utilized all of the information obtained by these experiments [with Montgomery], and we were careful about selecting materials."[30]

Baldwin made a series of tests with the completed *California Arrow* at Idora Park in Oakland, and on August 3, 1904, he made a flight that for the first time in US history had a dirigible launching and landing from the same location. The dirigible was now ready for St. Louis. He shipped the *California Arrow* to St. Louis in October, met a balloonist named Augustus Roy Knabenshue, and convinced the lighter-weight Knabenshue to pilot the *Arrow*. At the fair, Knabenshue flew the dirigible for 11 miles, easily securing first place and the $100,000 prize. From there, Baldwin engaged in a promotional tour of the Northeast, including a stop at the Curtiss factory in Hammondsport. His US patent application for his "Air-ship" on November 21, 1904, included several improvements to dirigible design but very curiously neglected any novelty associated with the propeller or rudder.[31]

Montgomery, and likely Greth as well, read of Baldwin's achievements in the Bay Area newspapers. An exchange of letters between Montgomery and Baldwin led to a heated face-to-face meeting at Santa Clara and then public vitriol in the local newspapers, with Montgomery being critical of Baldwin's deceit and Baldwin no longer mentioning Montgomery's assistance in the development of his dirigible whatsoever. Having reached an impasse, Montgomery pursued the concept of balloon-launched gliders on his own.

During the summer of 1904, a now recuperated Park Van Tassel asked the superior court in San Francisco to assist with the repossession of two balloons, a parachute, and other items from a man named Hagawara. Van Tassel felt that the equipment, valued at $500, was being wrongfully held by Hagawara, and as Van Tassel wished to reenter the profession of ballooning, he needed the return of his equipment.[32] The court seemed to agree.

Meanwhile, having flown gliders only from low altitudes, Montgomery sought after an aeronaut with experience at high altitudes. He found a young Daniel Maloney, who had worked at San Francisco's Glen Park making parachute jumps from tethered balloons. Through a training process, Maloney became Montgomery's aeronaut glider pilot. Having little if any experience in ballooning, Montgomery contracted the balloon work to Frank Hamilton,[33] a well-known balloonist who routinely performed at the Santa Cruz boardwalk. Initial success in March 1905 at Aptos, California, with the balloon-launch glider method using Hamilton's balloon and Maloney's piloting skills, led rather quickly to the first public disclosure of the method in April 1905 on the campus of Santa Clara College. This success placed Montgomery, Maloney, and Hamilton in an international spotlight. Having shown the world for the first time in a public manner that heavier-than-air flight was possible,[34] Montgomery refocused his attention on Baldwin, filing two lawsuits. The first lawsuit precluded Baldwin from further display of the *California Arrow*, and the second asked for damages in the form of $100,000, the amount Baldwin was awarded in St. Louis. Montgomery was countersued by Baldwin for liable. Montgomery also filed a patent on his "aeroplane" on April 22, 1905.

In light of the considerable press coverage of his association with Montgomery's activities, Frank Hamilton returned to balloon ascensions and parachute jumps at Idora Park. His wife, Carrie Clifford Hamilton, also made parachute jumps. However, with crowds now accustomed to parachute jumps, Montgomery's antics with gliders generated considerably more press, angering Hamilton. A planned demonstration of the Montgomery glider at San Jose's Agricultural Park on May 21, 1905, was arranged, with Hamilton in charge of the balloon. However, as the grounds soon swelled with spectators, Hamilton demanded a large advance payment. During the ensuing argument, the crowd continued to grow, with spectators now streaming in for free through an unlocked rear gate. Given the need to get under way, Hamilton was given all the gate receipts, but the encounter created ill will between Montgomery and Hamilton; it was clear this would be his last time working with Montgomery. The balloon was inflated, and up rose the glider, the *Santa Clara*, under the balloon. But at an altitude of only 150 to 200 feet, a rope connecting the glider to the balloon broke. The glider and its pilot, Maloney, made a quick landing near the point of takeoff. The rope was to have been secured by Hamilton, but obviously this was done poorly. The spectators

John Montgomery's glider
the *Santa Clara*, piloted by
Daniel Maloney, ascends
under a smoke balloon for
eventual release over Santa
Clara, California, in 1905.
San Diego Air and Space
Museum (Montgomery
020).

booed and demanded a flight, and a second glider was hooked up with the
reinflated balloon and launched. On this flight, the glider became entangled
with two guide ropes, making it unsafe to release. Maloney, still in the glider,
drifted with the balloon to a landing 3 miles away from the scene. Oddly, it
seemed that someone had tampered with this glider, the *California*, before
flight. If he had released, there was a significant chance Maloney would have
been killed.

After the chaos, Montgomery pondered who would have sufficient knowledge to sabotage the glider in such a skilled way. Only a handful of people knew
the mechanics of the glider well enough. They included John Montgomery, his
brother Richard, a Father Bell from Santa Clara University, Hamilton and his
wife, and Thomas Baldwin. As it turned out, Baldwin had been spotted at the
flight, leading Montgomery to immediately assume that Baldwin or one of his

associates was the culprit. The banter between Montgomery and Baldwin in the press now escalated considerably, with Montgomery calling out Baldwin specifically for his sabotage and Baldwin claiming that Montgomery had nothing to do with the invention of the *California Arrow*, despite his previous acknowledgment to the opposite. Greth finally joined in the now very public discourse in the papers, suggesting that "the best that can be said of Baldwin is that he would shine as a circus clown or tightrope dancer."[35]

Montgomery was now forced to find a new balloonist to continue his glider demonstrations. He was introduced to Park Van Tassel, and in June 1905 they completed arrangements for additional flights at San Jose as a part of Fourth of July celebrations. Van Tassel specifically contracted with the Fourth of July Committee to make the ascensions.[36] On July 1, Van Tassel began filling his balloon with "manufactured hydrogen gas." When July 4 arrived, Van Tassel gave a balloon ascension and parachute jump for the crowd. He then refilled the balloon, and the glider was prepared for ascension. However, oddly, while the balloon should have had ample lifting capacity, the same balloon that had just lifted Van Tassel could not lift the combined 188 pounds of the glider and Maloney. The glider launch was canceled.[37] The ten thousand spectators expressed their displeasure. Van Tassel and Montgomery were left perplexed. Initially, Maloney was convinced that Van Tassel had shortchanged Montgomery with an insufficient amount of hydrogen gas for the journey. However, both Montgomery and Van Tassel came to a different conclusion: someone had tampered with either the gas, the inflation tube, or the balloon itself during reinflation. They once again assumed this was Baldwin, or a Baldwin associate, as he was in town at the time and had reason to make sure that Montgomery's aeroplane did not launch as planned.[38]

Montgomery continued to make glider attempts. During a glider exhibition on July 18, 1905, a guide rope hit the cabane of the glider's rear wing during its ascension, knocking the cabane loose. Because of this, when the glider released from the balloon, forces on the rear wing caused it to collapse. Still in the glider, Maloney plunged 4,000 feet to his death. The glider fatality made international news, causing some in the press to wonder if gliders and heavier-than-air flying machines should be avoided altogether as "man-killers." While Montgomery's experiments continued past this tragedy, they no longer included Baldwin or Van Tassel.

# 22. AFTERSHOCK

ON THE EARLY morning of April 18, 1906, a low rumble grew throughout the Bay Area. With an epicenter just 2 miles off the coast of San Francisco, the resulting 7.8-magnitude earthquake lasted from forty-five to sixty seconds, killing approximately three thousand, destroying more than twenty-eight thousand buildings, and leaving 225,000 people suddenly homeless. The Great Quake of 1906 remains one of the worst natural disasters in the history of the United States. At the time, Park Van Tassel lived at 1212 Twenty-Third Avenue in East Oakland. He was in the process of securing a set of supplies from Chicago, including fresh silk for a balloon, but the quake ceased all his operations.[1] The same was true for Baldwin, as his dirigible storage facility on Market Street was destroyed, along with all his dirigibles with the exception of the *California Arrow II*, which had very fortunately been shipped to Hammondsport, New York, just prior. Baldwin abandoned the Bay Area, moving to New York to continue his aerial experiments with Glenn Curtiss and others. Montgomery's glider experiments were also curtailed; he instead focused on the rebuilding of Santa Clara College. In just one minute, technological innovation in the Bay Area came to a halt. Aviation was an afterthought.

But those who had made their careers in aerial exhibition still had to pursue their lines of income. In late 1906, Van Tassel embarked on the construction of a new "mammoth" hydrogen balloon, made of silk and to be used for captive ascensions for weddings, tourism, and photography up to a maximum altitude of 3,000 feet. Newspapers noted that the initial ascent of the balloon, scheduled for October 14, 1906, was to be filmed by the Miles brothers, who during 1906 had filmed activities in the Bay Area relative to the earthquake. Their film *A Trip Down Market Street* remains one of the most important series of images of pre- and post-quake San Francisco.

Park continued to search for income. In early 1907, managers of the Salt Palace in Salt Lake City made arrangements with Van Tassel for the showing of his large captive balloon with a 1,000-foot cable. Van Tassel's display would last from May 30 to September 15, 1907.[2] A special gas house was constructed for these ascensions at the "old baseball ground" at the Salt Palace, so that hydrogen gas could be fed directly to the balloon.[3] Papers in Salt Lake City billed Van Tassel as a local hero for his 1883 ascensions, as well as being the "first of many to make a success of taking photographs from a balloon."[4] Upon his arrival in May 1907, newspapers reported, "Since leaving here 24 years ago Prof. Van Tassell has grown from a young to an old man, while the number of his ascensions has increased from 19 to many hundreds. His balloon has hung above the palaces of almost every kind on the globe, and he has collected a large package of letters from princes, potentates, rajah mudas, poo-bahs, sultans, dattos, nabobs, mikados, and shahs."[5] His grand balloon consisted of 2,000 yards of silk made from 961 panels sewn together into a perfect sphere, at a total cost of roughly $3,000. A reporter noted,

When asked to tell of his experiences while ballooning around the world, Prof. Van Tassell produced a scrap book, on page one of which is a clipping from the Deseret News of July 5, 1883, giving an account of his first Utah appearance. After that in 1889 he took the first pictures ever snapped from a balloon, while his gas bag was floating over San Francisco. This trip was for the "Examiner" in the early days of Hearst's career as a sensational editor. Editors in Kansas City, Portland, and many other cities have been his guests, and "star" reporters have written up many a city as it looked from the edge of his basket while his balloon hovered from 6,000 to 20,000 feet above it.[6]

But just as Van Tassel was making arrangements in Salt Lake City for his first captive balloon ascensions of the season, in the early morning of June 17, 1907, someone broke into the balloon house at the Salt Palace and cut eleven slits into the silk balloon, varying between 4 and 10 inches long. Acid of some type was dumped in six or so places, such that the slightest pull on the balloon would make the silk tear further. Van Tassel and his business partner E. D. Wenban claimed the vandals had caused roughly $6,000 in damages and ruined a year's effort in planning. Prior to this, the balloon had been test-inflated at the Salt Works and a single small slit of 2 inches had been discovered. They were not sure it was vandalism at the time, but when eleven slits were added later, each carefully made along a seam in the most difficult place to patch, it was clear that the vandalism was made with specific ill intent. Upon this financial disaster, Van Tassel noted:

> I shall not attempt to bring another balloon to Salt Lake, for it is evident that someone wishes to prevent my operating here. . . . While I could probably keep them from breaking into the balloon house and cutting another bag, any fellow who knows his business could stand 200 or 300 feet away from the balloon some afternoon while it was near the ground ready for a trip with passengers, and cut it by sailing a piece of glass swiftly against it. It is a trick that has been done hundreds of times and every balloon man knows that the best thing he can do when someone is trying to keep him from operating is to quit because there are twenty ways they can "get you." The fellow that cut my balloon last night knew what he was doing, for he knew just how and where to cut the bag so that it would be hardest for me to repair it. If I was foolish enough to try to patch it up.[7]

Still eager to make a demonstration in Salt Lake City, Van Tassel sent word to Oakland for a new, smaller balloon to be sent to the Salt Palace for parachute jumps.[8] The citizens of Salt Lake arranged for all the proceeds of Van Tassel's parachute jumps to help cover his expenses from the lost balloon.[9] However, there are no reports of successful parachute jumps by Park in Salt Lake City in 1907, and it is assumed he returned to Oakland, far poorer than when he left.

Interestingly, James Price had returned to the West after completing his ballooning tour of Asia, and while it is unknown if Price was in Salt Lake City at the same time as Van Tassel, it is clear that by August 1907 at San Jose, Price was building "the largest balloon in the world," with a height of 94 feet, a circumference of 186 feet, and a carrying capacity of 1,200 pounds. Price envisioned entering the balloon in the Gordon Bennett Cup race in St. Louis, scheduled for October 1907.[10] In September, Price made two ascensions at the

Autumn Festival and Street Fair in Palo Alto.[11] He developed a new system for aerial exhibition: two men and a cannon were carried aloft by balloon, with one man being "fired" from the cannon at 5,000 feet, to descend by parachute.[12]

With competitors at every turn, and now accepting the role of elder statesman, Van Tassel looked to simply enjoy ballooning with the company of others and to encourage others to learn the art of ballooning. While the public now appreciated that heavier-than-air flight was possible, the easiest way to enjoy flight was still via lighter-than-air balloons. And as more and more citizens became interested in taking to the air, it was appropriate that clubs and associations of like-minded individuals would soon form. For instance, the Aero Club of America formed in 1905 to help promote aviation in the United States. A state chapter, the Aero Club of California, formed in Los Angeles on May 26, 1908. Many of the clubs were interested in both lighter-than-air and heavier-than-air flight, with members mainly focused on balloons and gliders.[13] In response to the formation of the Aero Club of California, the Pacific Aero Club and Oakland Aero Club formed in the Bay Area in 1909, with members including Park Van Tassel, Cleve T. Shaffer, and Geneve L. A. Shaffer. The Aero Club of America also began licensing aviators, with Glenn Curtiss receiving license no. 1 in the airplane division and Thomas Baldwin receiving license no. 9 in the balloon division and license no. 1 in the dirigible division.

In late 1908/early 1909, Van Tassel began working on the development of another large balloon. This one was 53 feet in diameter and could hold about 60,000 cubic feet of hydrogen, with a lifting capacity of 3,600 pounds. Twelve hundred yards of fabric were used in its construction. The balloon, christened *Berkeley*, was constructed by five people working for ninety days at the Globe Manufacturing Company at 720 Adeline Street in Oakland.[14]

According to newspapers, Van Tassel had not flown a balloon in Oakland since May 30, 1886, when he carried a bride and groom aloft at Badger Park in East Oakland, with the couple landing on the grounds of Mills College.[15] On February 28, 1909, Van Tassel and C. C. Bradley, a teller from the local branch of Crocker National Bank, ascended in the *Berkeley* from the intersection of College and Alcatraz Avenues in Berkeley at 2:00 p.m. After an hour and a maximum altitude of 15,000 feet, they made a nice landing at a ranch 4

# AERIAL VOYAGE OF FORTY MILES

Captain Van Tassell's Balloon Makes Flight as Planned

Launched at Berkeley, It Finds a Berth Near Bay Point

[Special Dispatch to The Call]
BAY POINT, Cal., Feb. 28.—Captain Van Tassell's balloon, which went up from Berkeley with the captain and C. C. Bradley as passengers, came down three miles northeast of Concord,

## Successful Flight Made By Berkeley Balloon

# MURDER THEORY NOW DISCREDITED

Relatives of Beekman Family View the Tragedy as an Accident

Indications Are That Woman and Children Were Suffocated While Sleeping

BAKERSFIELD, Cal., Feb. 28.—While the efforts of the officers to solve the Beekman tragedy in which five lives were mysteriously lost early Friday morning have thus far been fruitless

The upper picture is a snapshot of the balloon when it was about 2,000 feet in the air. The lower photograph shows the gas bag just before the ascent, with a snapshot of C. C. Bradley (left) and Aeronaut P. A. Van Tassell.

C. C. Bradley and Park Van Tassel with the balloon Berkeley, pictured in the *San Francisco Call* on March 1, 1909. Library of Congress.

miles east of Sunol in Contra Costa County. The ascension was made through the auspices of the Pacific Aero Club.[16]

On April 10, 1909, Van Tassel, Joseph M. Masten, and Knox Maddox departed Oakland in the *Berkeley*, once again landing near Sunol after a three-hour flight and narrowly missing a high-tension line on landing. Their maximum altitude was 7,000 feet.[17] Maddox recalled,

We left Berkeley at 11 o'clock and after reaching an altitude of
1,000 feet encountered favorable inland breezes which carried us on
the course we had planned to sail. Before I entered the basket the
atmospheric conditions were promising and under the guidance of
Captain Van Tassell we had no trouble in maneuvering. We were
caught by a gentle wind as soon as we had risen and drifted over
the fields without any difficulty. Twice we reached an altitude of
7,000 feet. The atmosphere was not cold, on the contrary, we frequently felt warm currents. We had planned to sail over the Santa
Clara valley and land at [Mount] Hamilton, but the arrangements
were altered. At 2 o'clock we landed four miles from Sunol and
experienced no difficulty in descending. My purpose in accompanying Van Tassel was more for observation than for anything else. At
all times the balloon was steady—just as steady as a floor. The trip
was delightful.[18]

By June 1909, Van Tassel had purchased the famous *United States* balloon
from Dick Ferris of Los Angeles for an undisclosed amount of money.[19] Ferris worked in the entertainment industry in Hollywood and had been instru-
mental in the formation of the Aero Club of California.[20]

The *United States* had been flown by Lieutenant Frank Lahm (pilot) and
Major Henry B. Hersey (copilot)[21] to a first-place finish at the international
Gordon Bennett Cup (Coupe Aéronautique Gordon Bennett), held at
Paris, France, in 1906.[22] Spectators had gathered in the famed Tuilieres
Gardens in Paris to witness history's first sponsored air race—a long-
distance gas balloon race. James Gordon Bennett Jr., an American newspa-
per tycoon living in France, sponsored the race, which still bears his name.
Lahm and Hersey covered an amazing 402 miles in twenty-two hours and
fifteen minutes, crossing the English Channel to land at Fylingdales on the
Yorkshire coast. The home country of the winning team was afforded the
honor of hosting the next race, which meant that the 1907 Gordon Bennett
Cup would be held in the United States, with St. Louis as the chosen location. The *United States* was used once again by Hersey and Arthur Atherholt
in the 1907 race.[23] However, at that contest they placed eighth out of nine
contestants. Van Tassel agreed to make a balloon exhibition of the *United*

*States* at Oroville, California, for Independence Day celebrations in 1909. However, on the afternoon of July 4, as the balloon was being filled, it broke free of the netting helping hold it to the ground and sailed aloft, going straight up until it disappeared from sight.[24] The *United States* was recovered eventually, with Van Tassel disposing of the balloon entirely.[25] He already had his sights on a new project.

# 23. CITY OF OAKLAND

IN THE SUMMER of 1909, another balloon was built in Oakland by Van Tassel, under contract to A. Vander Naillen Jr., president of the Oakland Aero Club. The *City of Oakland* was to be used to advertise Oakland in the upcoming Portola Festival and in races with other balloons. Vander Naillen brought the idea of naming the balloon after the city to the Chamber of Commerce, which would then pay for the expense of inflation and use in the festival. Van Tassel was proposed as the pilot, since he too called Oakland home.[1]

(*Left*) Park Van Tassel in his ballooning uniform, circa 1909. Smithsonian National Air and Space Museum (NASM 72–1132).

(*Opposite page, top*) The balloon *City of Oakland* being prepared for launch in downtown Oakland in August 1909. Oakland History Room, Oakland Public Library (F-2280).

(*Opposite page, bottom*) *City of Oakland* just prior to launch, with Park Van Tassel and A. Vander Naillen Jr. on the basket. J. J. Earle Collection, Oakland History Room, Oakland Public Library.

On August 14, 1909, Van Tassel and Vander Naillen Jr. launched in the *City of Oakland* on its maiden voyage.[2] Filling the 80-foot-tall balloon took ten hours. The ceremony included an invocation by the Reverend Nelson E. Saunders and a christening of the balloon with "real" champagne by Jeanne Vander Naillen, daughter of the owner. Dr. C. L. Tisdale served as master of ceremonies. Representing the mayor's office, a Councilman Rufus Vose wished the two pilots Godspeed and a safe return after the christening. With the ropes released, the balloon floated upward, rather miraculously avoiding a set of high-tension lines and the steeple of the First Presbyterian Church near the intersection of Fourteenth and Franklin Streets. At about 1,200 feet, the balloon was carried west out over the Bay, where it floated for several hours. It was Vander Naillen's first flight—and he was in for quite a journey. Van Tassel later recalled for the newspapers:

I AM very sorry that our much anticipated trip had such an unfavorable ending. We had intended to make many valuable observations and notes of atmospheric conditions, and but for a careless act of one of our many enthusiastic and excited friends, whereby we were cut loose before having sufficient ballast, we might have successfully completed our undertaking, as far as the scientific part is concerned. The act was [not] of malicious intent, but was a misunderstanding. When we were trying the balloon I called to the men below to haul us down for more ballast. Imagine my surprise when I discovered that we were loose and soaring upward. However, we could do nothing, so we prepared our thermometers and compasses. Passing northeast, then to the eastward, I dared throw out but a small portion of our ballast, with the result that the hills were barely passed over without striking. I must say that the conditions and the day were an ideal combination for an ascension. The day was calm, but the atmosphere clear and the temperature normal. As we passed over Oakland and its suburbs the picture was beautiful in every respect. Far off I saw a column of smoke rising straight and high, and I said to Vander Naillen; "Van, it couldn't be better, see how still that smoke is? Let us descend a little here." A slight breeze then caught us and blew us still to the eastward, varying at times a point or two, but still holding the general direction. I told my companion to mark the height and temperature. The height was figured at 3000 feet, showing a temperature of 64 degrees Fahrenheit. Striking a humid portion, we rose to 5000 feet, which was the greatest height attained. The country for miles and the encompassing ocean appeared to wonderful advantage from this height. I had taken with us two carrier pigeons. At 1 o'clock sharp I decided to let one go, Vander Naillen first writing the following message: "Who cut us loose without command? Not enough ballast. Offering $100 for a sack of sand: no takers. Balloon behaving splendidly: 1 p. m.—drifting towards Mt. Diablo. All is well 'VANDER NAILLEN'" I watched the bird speed back until it disappeared from view, and wondered whether it would reach the point of departure. Everything was as we would want it. I took several photographs of the country below, including several of Oakland. I think we took about half a dozen altogether. For an hour more we enjoyed the trip. The unexpected happened as we neared the Livermore valley. I had just looked at my watch and noticed the time was five minutes after 2 o'clock, when a gentle eddying and trembling of the cage told us of wind. We had just crossed a high hill, skirted over it, when a terrific gale coming down the valley caught us in its powerful grasp and hurled and tossed and dragged us down to the ground, where we struck with a terrible crash, which temporarily stunned us both. The noise of the wind was great, shrieking through the balloon shrouds.

When we struck the balloon heeled over, and, acting as a sail, dragged the bumping cage, furrowing it through the ground down the hill. We clung to the ropes on the bottom of the cage, putting forth all our strength to keep position. As we crossed a small creek and struck the opposite bank, the basket being practically horizontal, the lower edge struck first, completely overturning us for a second. Here we lost the camera and instruments. The ropes were our salvation, for if they had not been there we would have been thrown out again and again, and probably been killed.

We now began to rise gently, for a short distance, when we were again caught by the wind and dragged over fields, crashing through barb wire fences and cutting into the ground like a plow. I cannot remember how many times we arose and descended, each time striking the ground with a terrific blow. The cage was smashed and worn clear through from the dragging, while the solid oak ring, from which the cage was suspended, was entirely demolished. When we finally landed in a field about seven miles north of Pleasanton the balloon had about collapsed, and we were both bleeding in many places and so weak that we could barely stand on our feet.

C. Orloff, a rancher, first saw our plight, and attempted to assist us by trying to make fast the anchor, but he was unsuccessful. He arrived at the scene and greatly assisted us in getting straightened out. I looked back over the path we had traveled and followed it plainly—a great, broad, devastated track. We had been dragged for about 2000 feet, breaking through half a dozen barb wire fences. Passing slowly and painfully along the way, we gathered up the camera and other instruments, which we found together when we first struck, all being seriously damaged. These and the balloon, which, strange to say, was uninjured, and the fittings we piled upon a wagon one of the farmers brought and had it taken to Pleasanton, where we followed shortly, after having bandaged our bruises at the house of Orloff.

Ralph Coxhead and his companion, C. Brown, had followed us from Oakland, and arrived on the scene in time to take us to Pleasanton for the incoming train. The gale was a fifty-mile wind, and in all of my twenty-nine years of ballooning I have never experienced such a disastrous and terrible adversity; it is the worst experience I have ever had. The balloon itself is first-class in every respect. IT is made of cotton fabric, containing 750 panels in the block system of construction. The capacity is about 45,000 cubic feet.

You see, we were continually thrust down by the eddies and currents that circled through the valley. We could have outdistanced them if, in the first place, there had been sufficient sand, but we dared not throw out more than we did, as we had to keep a certain amount for making a landing, which requires careful and quick controlling of the bag. I shall make another ascension in the same balloon next Sunday from the Aero Club grounds at Sixty-third street and Telegraph avenue. Joseph Hidalgo of San Francisco will accompany me. A strange coincidence with reference to the entire affair was how our second pigeon went

A. Vander Naillen Jr. (center) and Park Van Tassel (lower left) described their harrowing landing in the *San Francisco Call*, August 15, 1909. Library of Congress.

through all the terrible hammering and remained in the little cage uninjured. When I took it out and attempted to send it with a message it could not fly, possibly being dazed with fright. I left it at the farm house. P. A. VAN TASSELL.[3]

Vander Naillen Jr. noted, "It is an experience I shall never forget—one I do not care to go through again, and I am happy to have passed through all with but a few bruises and a stiff leg, outside of the general shaking up."[4] The total flight duration was four hours.

The first annual Aero Show of the newly formed Pacific Aero Club, based in San Francisco, took place on Wednesday, August 18, 1909, at the

Dreamland Rink. The exhibition included static displays of aircraft as well as lectures by prominent members of the club. Professor Joseph Hidalgo spoke on the history of aerial navigation; the lecture was included in a book in 1910.[5] At the Aero Show, Van Tassel exhibited "a pilot balloon," a small balloon that could be used to test air currents before liftoff of a larger balloon.[6] On the night of the exhibition, the Pacific Aero Club challenged the Oakland Aero Club to compete in a balloon race.[7]

The Portola Committee was in charge of the Portola Festival, held in San Francisco from October 19 to October 23, 1909. The festival commemorated the discovery of San Francisco by Gaspar de Portolá, the first Spanish governor of California. It was advertised to be "more magnificent and attractive than either the Mardi Gras of New Orleans or the Veiled Prophets of St. Louis."[8] The Portola Committee offered a silver cup to the winner of two different races, each two hours in duration, with longest distance traveled being the goal.[9] The Portola Cup would be the permanent property of the winning club. On August 22, 1909, Van Tassel made an ascension in the repaired *City of Oakland* with Geneve Shaffer and Joseph Hidalgo, both of the Pacific Aero Club.[10] It was a final test of preparations before the Portola Cup balloon race.

The first Portola race was held on October 10, 1909, and featured balloons from three Pacific Coast clubs: the *City of Oakland* (also known as *Greater Oakland*) of the Oakland Aero Club, the *Queen of the Pacific* (also known as the *Queen City* and named in honor of San Francisco), operated by the Pacific Aero Club, and *Fairy*, owned by A. C. Pillsbury of the Seattle Aero Club.[11] The activities started from the circus grounds at Eleventh and Market Streets in San Francisco, with the true rivalry between the Pacific and Oakland clubs. Somewhat ironically, this wasn't just any rivalry. When the passengers for each balloon had been announced, several women were included. Piloting the *City of Oakland* was Van Tassel, along with passengers Vander Naillen Jr. and Margaret Miller. Piloting the *Queen of the Pacific* was Ivy Baldwin, along with passenger J. C. Irvine, president of the Pacific Aero Club, and Geneve Shaffer. J. C. Mars would fly the *Fairy* in the name of the Seattle Aero Club with no passengers.[12]

Shaffer in particular was heavily engaged in aeronautics, along with her brother Cleve, in the Pacific Aero Club. She had already flown in balloons and

An aerial view of the *City of Oakland* during inflation, photographed from the balloon *Fairy* in San Francisco on October 10, 1909. Smithsonian National Air and Space Museum (NASM A-49912-B).

gliders, and she and Cleve were constructing a powered aircraft that would include a Curtiss motor. But just prior to the race, it was announced to the public that, for unknown reasons, the race would be limited to male passengers, a decision reached by members of the Pacific Aero Club.[13] The decision generated considerable division within the club, especially when it was announced in the local papers that Geneve had backed out of the flight because she was afraid, which was hardly the case.[14] She was allowed to christen the new *Queen of the Pacific* just before the race.

One hundred thousand people gathered to watch the ascension of the three balloons.[15] Problems with inflation left the *City of Oakland* with insufficient buoyancy for additional crew plus ballast, so Van Tassel flew alone. The *Fairy* launched first, at 2:30 p.m., the *Queen of the Pacific* was next at 2:46 p.m., followed by the *City of Oakland* at 3:05 p.m. Less than ten minutes after launch, the *Fairy* was at a height of 8,000 feet to test the upper air currents. Mars discovered that the currents were offshore and pushing the *Fairy* toward the ocean. Coming down to lower altitudes, he piloted the *Fairy* to a landing near Dumbarton Bridge shortly before 6:00 p.m. It was the first bit of land that he encountered after launch.

Van Tassel in the *City of Oakland* also headed in the direction of San Jose but landed in the San Francisco Bay near South City around 8:00 p.m. Having traveled 18 miles but still short of his goal, he was picked up by a boat piloted by Joseph Mesten and Charles Bridley of the Pacific Aero Club.

The *Queen of the Pacific* also followed a heading toward San Jose. An hour later, shortly before the balloon descended into the Bay, a launch party on a boat caught its 300-foot drag rope and rescued the passengers, taking them to shore near San Mateo. Without sufficient room in the boat, the *Queen of the Pacific* was abandoned in the Bay where it landed. A life preserver was attached to the balloon to mark the spot where it went underwater. A long search was made on October 13 to recover the balloon, bring it ashore, and prepare it for another launch.[16]

News of the rescues didn't arrive back to San Francisco until 11 p.m., after considerable anxiety on the part of both clubs.[17] The *Queen of the Pacific* had traveled a distance of 30 miles, winning the race.[18] However, disputes between the Pacific and Oakland clubs arose in the newspapers. Should the winner be declared on total time aloft? Or should the winner be declared on total distance made, irrespective of time?

In light of the troubles in determining who won the first race, a second race was scheduled for October 24, 1909, this time starting from the showgrounds at Sixty-Third Street in Oakland, with a goal of San Jose. In this race, the *Queen of the Pacific* was piloted by Ivy Baldwin, with Geneve Shaffer as passenger, while the *City of Oakland* was piloted by J. C. Mars, with Margaret Miller as passenger. Once again the winds were light and variable, and not much distance could be made. The *Queen of the Pacific* landed about 2 miles from the starting point, with the *Oakland* landing slightly farther away and

(*Opposite page*) The balloon race of October 10, 1909, made front-page news in the *San Francisco Call* the following day. Library of Congress.

# ISLAIS BASIN BOND PROJECT'S GHOST APPEARS

## Lumber Interests' Representatives Ask That Pivotal Lots Be Saved From Dredging

## Seek Merchants' Association's Aid, Agreeing Not to Oppose Harbor Plans

THE ghost of the Islais basin, which haunted the bond issue proposition when the matter was before the voters of the state at the last general election, seems about to materialize again, much to the surprise and astonishment of the proponents of the harbor improvement. Harding and Monroe, representing, it is claimed, the Union lumber company, the Acme lumber company and other concerns, have addressed a plausible letter to the Merchants' association asking the aid of that body in supporting a movement to save from dredging the five pivotal lots at the Kentucky street apex of the India basin, adjoining Islais creek channel. The Merchants' association has circulated the letter among its membership, asking that the members reply by ballot whether or not they favor engaging in the cause of the lumber companies.

### Lumber Companies' Plan

In substance the plan of the lumber companies is practically that which they followed out last year in fighting the first bond issue throughout the state, and also before the legislature in Sacramento, where it maintained an

---

# Mammoth Racing Balloons Plunge Into Waters of Bay

---

# SKY SAILORS RESCUED ALIVE

## Three Rival Aeronauts Taken Off Guy Ropes in Nick of Time by Launch

## PERILOUSLY NEAR TO DRIFTING OUT TO SEA

## Contrary Aerial Currents Put Navigators to Extreme Test for Safety

## QUEEN OF THE PACIFIC RULED WINNER OF RACE

### THE AERONAUTS

J. C. MARS, in the Fairy, piloting the racers.

CAPTAIN IVY BALDWIN and JACK IRVINE, in the Queen of the Pacific.

CAPTAIN P. A. VAN TASSELL, in the City of Oakland.

Overtaken by nightfall, two racing balloons which started in the preliminary race for the Portola cup from the ball grounds at Eleventh and Market streets yesterday afternoon descended into the bay, the three aeronauts being rescued from drowning just a few minutes before the mammoth air crafts settled into the water. The race was between the Pacific and the Oakland aero clubs, the former being represented by

---

expensive lobby to oppose the movement to have the bond issue proposition to be submitted to the voters include the #2 blocks which naturally come in the confines of the basin. The bond project called for a $1,000,000 issue, the money to be expended by the state in the purchase of 63 blocks of submerged land at the Islais creek basin, the land to be dredged and an inland harbor constructed. The lumber interests desire that the five blocks they control—blocks 322-327, inclusive,—be exempt from dredging. It is desired by the interests that they be permitted to construct lumber yards, mills and factories on the five blocks. The companies are willing to sell the blocks to the state at a price to be determined by condemnation proceedings, and then to lease the property from the state, the improvements made by the companies paying for the lease.

### Will Not Fight Bonds

Incidents in the exciting aerial race, and persons who figured prominently in it. In the upper left is the Queen of the Pacific, while to the right is the City of Oakland, being snap shots of the balloons in midair. Below are Rev. H. J. Pierce (left), who offered the prayer before starting, and J. C. Mars, the pilot. In the center are the crews, that of the Queen of the Pacific being on the left, and of the Oakland balloon on the right. The lower photo shows the three balloons being inflated.

---

Captain Ivy Baldwin and Jack Irvine, president of the club, in the new balloon, the Quee of the Pacific, and the latter by Captain P. A. Van Tassell in the City of Oakland.

### Van Tassel Found Helpless

The rescue was made by Joseph Maston and Charles C. Bradley, secretary and vice president, respectively, of the Pacific aero club. They, seeing the direction in which the balloons were traveling and not having received word of their landing, set out in a launch up the bay. On account of the darkness it was extremely difficult to locate them. The City of Oakland was found first. It was about six miles up the bay from Goat Island, absolutely helpless, with its water anchor trailing. Van Tassell had tried for hours to attract the attention of passing vessels, but in vain. He slid down the rope on to the deck of the launch, but was forced to leave the big gas bag

thus winning the second race. A third race was needed to determine the winner of the Portola Cup.[19]

The third and final race took place on October 31, 1909, with both balloons staying aloft for the full two hours. The *Queen of the Pacific* traveled 25 miles, while the *City of Oakland* traveled a half mile farther for the win. Given the interest in and growing memberships of the two rival clubs, Robert Martland of the Oakland Aero Club thought of affiliating with the Aero Club of America. To do so, two hundred or more members were required, and J. C. Mars and Park Van Tassel set out on a campaign to secure that number.[20]

On March 31, 1910, Van Tassel test-flew a new "balloon-dirigible" at Neptune Gardens in Alameda as a part of an aviation meet. Thousands of spectators watched from the grandstand and bleachers.[21] On April 3, Van Tassel and a youngster from Berkeley named Sidney Vincent ascended in the *City of Oakland* at an aviation exposition at Alameda, determined to fly farther than the distance established by the *Queen of the Pacific* the day before on its flight from Alameda to Stockton. But when Van Tassel and Vincent launched, instead of heading east, they headed west toward Redwood City. At one point it seemed they would be carried out to sea when a valve on the balloon became stuck. However, they landed on the side of Scarpet Peak near Half Moon Bay before reaching the shoreline.[22] Van Tassel also offered to make an ascension in Marysville, California, as a part of its Independence Day celebrations, but in the end the city declined.[23]

On May 19–21, 1910, the Pacific Aero Club held its second annual Aero Show in San Francisco. Among the many aircraft displayed, President J. C. Irvine of the Pacific Aero Club exhibited his now "battle-scarred" *Queen of the Pacific* while Van Tassel displayed his new 8,000-foot dirigible, 14 feet in diameter and 63 feet long.[24] At the Emeryville Race Track on July 3–4, 1910, an aviation meet included balloons, parachute drops, and a race between a Curtiss biplane and Farman biplane. Van Tassel was a noted participant at the event, as the theme of the meet was not only to help celebrate Independence Day but also to depict the history of aviation from ballooning to aeroplanes.[25] High winds were a perpetual issue.[26] As a part of the effort, Van Tassel repeatedly attempted to make an ascension in his balloon-dirigible. But the winds precluded the fun.[27]

Later, on October 2, 1910, Van Tassel ascended in the balloon *Diamond* at

Liftoff of the *City of Oakland* with passengers Park Van Tassel and Sidney Vincent from Alameda, California, on April 3, 1910. Smithsonian National Air and Space Museum (NASM A-49912).

Oakland, along with two passengers, men named Mathewson, and Wishar.[28] It was the inaugural flight for the *Diamond*, and Blanche Bonham was given the honor of christening the large balloon with California champagne. Vander Naillen Jr. served as master of ceremonies, and Councilman Harold Everhart of Oakland gave a short speech. At first the balloon drifted south, but then it started moving west toward the Bay. Van Tassel brought the balloon lower and found a westerly current in the direction of Newark. Apogee was at roughly 5,220 feet, and at one time the balloon dropped from 4,900 feet to just 55 feet above the water. At 6:15 p.m. the balloon landed in a marsh 5 miles south of Alvarado, near Hunter's Point. The landing was made in a 35-knot wind and was sufficiently hard that Van Tassel was ejected from the basket on impact, but he and the other passengers were uninjured.[29] News of the adventure made it all the way back to Salt Lake City.[30] Undeterred, and with better air currents, Van Tassel once again launched at Oakland, in October 1910, in an unknown balloon. He made a landing near Alvarado in Alameda County, covering a distance of 20 miles in two hours.[31] At the time, Van Tassel (now age fifty-six) was living with his sister Minnie E. Crew (age sixty-three) in Alameda.[32]

By November 1910, Van Tassel had leased an empty lot on East Nineteenth Street in Oakland and established a service taking seven to eight passengers aloft in his captive balloon *Diamond*. The balloon had a volume of 50,000 cubic feet and was inflated at night from the local city gasworks.[33] He also traveled to Bakersfield to make captive flights with the *Diamond*.[34] In Bakersfield, Van Tassel announced his intention to make a long-distance cross-country flight from Bakersfield to Los Angeles in his balloon-dirigible.[35] He planned to take a newspaper reporter along and possibly two other passengers, but no definite date was set. Also in Bakersfield, Van Tassel made a captive test with the *Diamond* to evaluate a new dirigible engine. But the balloon ended up bursting at 1,500 feet with no passengers on board. According to reports, the balloon burst "as the result of being stopped too suddenly by the engine."[36] Van Tassel's source of additional income was now in tatters.

# 24. GOLDEN YEARS

*another* [handwritten margin note]

IT SEEMS THAT on January 7, 1912, a P. A. Van Tassell married A. F. Barr,[1] *married* [handwritten margin note] with the Reverend Henry J. Ferreira presiding over the service in Oakland, which was likely held at St. Joseph's Portuguese Church. Little is known of Barr or how long the marriage lasted, but with the frequency of Van Tassel's previous marriages, another one is somehow not surprising. [handwritten marks]

Later that spring, on the campus of the University of California at Berkeley, a student-led interscholastic circus was arranged for April 27, including a parade through the streets of Berkeley.[2] Topping off the parade was a balloon ascension by Van Tassel. He had developed another new balloon at this time and intended to make test flights with it at Oakland. However, with some prior ballooning experience, Colonel J. H. Pierce, a sixty-four-year-old friend of Van Tassel's and a citizen of Oakland, served as pilot. Pierce first made a test hop at 3:00 p.m. from the corner of Twelfth and Harrison Streets, with a successful landing at the Piedmont Hills after flying over Lake Merritt. A second flight was arranged. At first the wind took Pierce out toward the Bay but then returned him back toward Oakland. As the balloon continued to descend, he continued to dump ballast overboard. With the shoreline in sight, he landed in the Bay 2 miles from Alameda. He and the balloon were picked up by fishermen and brought back to shore.[3] On Sunday, May 26, 1912, Van Tassel made an ascension at Grove Street Park, following a baseball game by the Oakland Giants and the Pennant Bars. At the time, the Giants were a semiprofessional group of African American ballplayers.[4]

For Independence Day 1912, Van Tassel was hired by O. F. Olsen and other businessmen to make a balloon ascension from the shore of Lake Merritt in the *City of Oakland*. During the ascent, at roughly 12:30 p.m., Van Tassel dropped several souvenirs of the flight to the crowd of spectators below.[5] A man named Clarence R. Townsend of San Francisco made an ascension from Lakeside Park next to Lake Merritt on the same day. With Van Tassel's instruction, he rose to 6,000 feet and then made a journey around the area for two hours. He landed at Hayward, but after landing, the balloon escaped, returning to the sky without him and continuing on to a second landing in Santa Clara. The balloon was found the next day at Bagnart Ranch, where the drag rope snagged a fence post.[6] The following day, the *San Francisco Call* ran a story titled "Balloon Lands; Pilot Is Missing; Thought to Belong to Prof. Van Tassell of Oakland, but Shoes of Woman Is Only Clew."[7] Constables named Lyle and Maloney managed to deflate the balloon and take it to the local court for storage until it could be retrieved. It was later realized to be Clarence Townsend's property.[8] Later in July, Van Tassel traveled to Santa Cruz to help with the planning of a "naval and water pageant" that, among other things, was to include a balloon race.[9] In September 1912, plans were announced for the California Apple Show, to be held October 7–12 in Watsonville. In addition to two US Navy submarines anchored off Port Watsonville for public viewing, Van Tassel was engaged to provide daily balloon ascensions and parachute drops at the show, as well as captive balloon launches for customers. William Ivy was hired to make the parachute jumps from Van Tassel's balloon. However, on the morning of October 10, the inflated balloon tore from its moorings and sailed away. Very fortunately, youngsters who were helping with the ropes let go in time, or else they too could have been carried away.[10] The balloon continued to soar over Castroville and then Hollister, some 20 miles away. According to reports, Van Tassel had planned to take the balloon to the Midwest to partake in a balloon race, but that was no longer possible.[11] It also seemed that while performing at the Watsonville show, a vandal had perforated the balloon with rocks, requiring Van Tassel to make hasty repairs. Displaying balloons for events and entertainment was increasingly difficult.

Van Tassel took a hiatus from ballooning through the winter of 1912. In May 1913 it was announced that Van Tassel would take part in a balloon race between balloonists from northern and southern California as a part of Portola Festival celebrations in October.[12] In late June 1913, it was also announced that Van Tassel would provide a balloon ascension and parachute drop as a part of Independence Day celebrations at Chehalis, Washington. The event was organized by Joseph M. Rieg of Portland, manager of the American Show Print Company. At the time, Van Tassel was billed as "one of the pioneer aeronauts of the country."[13] Reporters also remembered Van Tassel as the first in the Northwest to make a parachute jump.[14] Van Tassel and his balloon arrived in Chehalis a week prior to July 4. The balloon was to be launched from the "old schoolhouse block on Park Street." With Van Tassel now advancing in age, an aspiring young aeronaut, John Edgar, was hired to make the parachute jump instead.[15] Newspapers indicated that Van Tassel and Edgar were considering making a tour of India "to engage in the balloon and airship business."[16]

On July 4, high winds delayed the balloon ascension from 4:30 p.m. to about 6:00 p.m. The repaired balloon *Diamond* rose more than a mile high in the sky, with Edgar jumping and making a perfect descent to a successful landing at Coal Creek, Washington. The balloon continued to float on the wind to the northeast, coming to rest in a large tree, torn and heavily damaged as a result. The balloon was simply abandoned, as the expense of getting it down from the tree was not worth the effort. A planned ascension for Saturday, July 5, was canceled because of the damage to the *Diamond*.[17] Given that the *Diamond* cost several hundred dollars, the good businessmen of Chehalis pitched in to raise enough money compensate Van Tassel for his damages. In return, Van Tassel offered to make a new balloon and call it *Chehalis*, with the first ascension being in that city.[18] It is clear that Van Tassel made another balloon ascension from City View Park near Portland on October 15, 1913, but it isn't clear which balloon was used.[19]

On June 20, 1914, Park's sister Lillie married Yuba Parks[20] at Yuba City, California. It is unclear if Park was in attendance. There are no records of Park Van Tassel making balloon ascensions in 1914, and it is likely that he took time to be with family. However, remembering a life of travel, Van Tassel remained eager to again see other shores. In early 1915, a newspaper announced that Van Tassel would be traveling to Honolulu with two balloons to make flights throughout the Hawaiian Islands.[21] However, just weeks after the announcement, the paper said that Van Tassel would not be providing these exhibitions, as the program for a planned carnival was already full.[22] Despite this, it seems that Van Tassel traveled to Hawaii anyway, bringing the *Queen of the Pacific*, owned by Guy T. Slaughter. Government rules precluded flights near Pearl

Harbor to protect the fortifications from "unlawful mapping," and it remains unclear if Van Tassel ever flew in Hawaii during 1915.[23] However, the balloon was eventually sold to Joel C. Cohen of the Consolidated Amusement Company. On March 25, 1915, the USS *F-4* (originally named USS *Skate*), a US Navy F-class submarine taking part in maneuvers off the coast of Honolulu, sank, becoming the first commissioned US Navy submarine lost at sea. All twenty-one sailors aboard were lost. A large search ensued, and editors of the *Honolulu Star-Bulletin* suggested using Van Tassel's balloon in a captive configuration to try to spot the *F-4* from the air.[24] It remains unknown if the balloon was actually deployed in this manner.

In March 1917, Van Tassel stayed for a time at the Occidental Hotel in Santa Rosa. He was remembered in the local newspaper for his earlier ballooning escapades at Woodward's Gardens in San Francisco and expressed interest in a balloon ascension as a part of the Rose Carnival, which was scheduled for May 1917.[25] Later that month, it was reported that Van Tassel had offered to fly a new "torpedo-shaped" balloon (probably his balloon-dirigible) for $150. The matter was still under consideration by the Rose Carnival organizers into late March,[26] but it is possible that all plans changed when the United States declared war on Germany on April 6, 1917, and entered World War I, as there are no records of Van Tassel actually flying a balloon in Santa Rosa that year. Van Tassel and assistant Vernon Spencer arrived in Reno, Nevada, on March 8 to make arrangements for a balloon flight on Easter Sunday, April 8, 1917, with his "torpedo balloon," with Spencer making a parachute jump from 3,000 feet.[27]

In June or early July 1917, Park made a balloon ascension and parachute jump at Calistoga, California, and attempted to make arrangements to be part of the Napa County Farm Bureau Fair in July 1917.[28] In August 1917, Van Tassel arranged to fly his balloon-dirigible in two appearances at the Almond Festival in Arbuckle, California.[29] The 1918 influenza pandemic further curtailed Van Tassel's activities.

Perhaps recalling his time in India, where schoolchildren would imitate the Van Tassel Troupe with toy parachutes of their own, the inventive but aging Park Van Tassel filed for a US patent on a "mechanical toy" on June 16, 1919. The patent described a toy parachute that was shot into the sky with an elastic band, opened automatically, and fell back to Earth, complete with a

Drawing of a "mechanical toy"—a rubber-band-launched parachute—patented by Park Van Tassel on February 22, 1921 (US patent no. 1,369,504). United States Patent and Trademark Office.

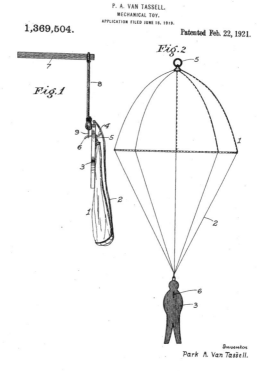

P. A. VAN TASSELL.
MECHANICAL TOY.
APPLICATION FILED JUNE 16, 1919.

1,369,504.

Patented Feb. 22, 1921.

Inventor
Park A. Van Tassell.

*By* Harry P. Schroeder
*Attorney*

suspended weight in the form of a man. US patent no. 1,369,504 was approved on February 22, 1921. It was Van Tassel's only patent. He established the Captain P. A. Van Tassel Toy Balloon Manufacturing Company, a maker of miniature balloon ascension toys, while living at 644 Merrimac Street in Oakland.

In 1919 Van Tassel and a Lieutenant C. M. Williams were hired by the organizers of the Livermore Stockmen's Rodeo for a balloon ascension and parachute descent on Independence Day, Friday, July 4. However, strong winds that day forced the event to be postponed to Saturday and then again to Sunday, the last day of the rodeo. With the balloon about two-thirds full of hot air and smoke, a gust of wind blew it to one side and it caught fire. Freed from its moorings, the unpiloted balloon began to rise and then roll along the ground, directly toward a corral of wild horses, in front of the eyes of thousands of spectators. Wranglers quickly sprang to action to get the horses out of the way while the balloon, bounding along in the wind, bounced 100 feet in the air and over the corral, still on fire. It landed in a hay field nearby, coming to rest near a large haystack. By that time the balloon had nearly burned itself out, but a small fire at the base of the haystack was quickly extinguished by a well-positioned fire truck that just happened to be at the rodeo.[30]

By 1920, Park Van Tassel (now age sixty-seven) was living with his sister Minnie (now age seventy-three) in Alameda.[31] In light of his experience with his balloon-dirigible, he assisted with the development and testing of an aerodynamic advertising balloon to help celebrate the sixty-ninth anniversary of the White House, a retail store in San Francisco. The balloon was funded by the Goodyear Rubber Company, and its shape would allow it to withstand winds up to 30 miles per hour rather than just 16 miles per hour for regular spherical advertising balloons. Van Tassel was placed in charge of its operation.[32] While the Goodyear Company had some experience with large dirigibles, this was one of its first forays into gas blimps. Its first untethered blimp, the *Pilgrim*, the first blimp to fly with helium, debuted later, in 1925. In the fall of 1924, Van Tassel was hired as caretaker of the Robert Martland estate at Glen Arbor, California, on the banks of the San Lorenzo River near Ben Lomond and Santa Cruz. Martland, a wealthy member of the California State Auto Trades Association, maintained a house at Oakland and a summer house at Glen Arbor.[33] Martland was also a member of the Oakland Aero Club and helped arrange for aviation meets in the 1910s.[34] Park Van Tassel's motivation to be in general seclusion at Martland's house in Glen Arbor from 1924 to roughly 1930 is a mystery, but it likely had to do with the need to maintain some amount of income leading up to and through the Great Depression, as he was no longer able to maintain the lifestyle required to continue as an aeronaut.

In 1930 Van Tassel (then age seventy-six) left Glen Arbor and returned to live with his sister Minnie at 9423 B Street in Oakland.[35] Park suffered from heart disease and slowed down. In late September 1930, Van Tassel was interviewed by Wallace Rawles, a reporter from Oakland. The ensuing article about "Capt. Parks Van Tassel" was carried in small papers nationally. The report reviewed parts of his long career in aviation, suggesting that Van Tassel had "dropped in parachutes from balloons in 46 countries."[36] News of his decaying health was also reported by the *Albuquerque Journal*.[37]

Just one month later, on the evening of October 24, 1930, while writing a letter at the dinner table, Park Van Tassel suffered a heart attack and never regained consciousness. His passing made local, state, and national news.[38] Both the local *Santa Cruz Evening News* and the *New York Times* still managed to incorrectly report his name as "Parks Van Tassel," with the *New York Times* incorrectly citing Kansas City as the location of his first parachute jump. Over fifty years of balloon ascensions and harrowing escapades, the aerial magician Van Tassel rather miraculously lived to see his older years. A funeral service was held on October 27, 1930, at 3:00 p.m. at the Grant D. Miller Mortuary in Oakland.[39] In the height of the Great Depression and without much in the way of finances, he was buried in an unmarked grave at Evergreen Cemetery alongside his half-sister Minnie, who had preceded his passing by about three weeks, with Park's sister Lillie surviving both of them.

# EPILOGUE

*⚬ aiding women?*

OVER THE COURSE of his life, Park Van Tassel witnessed an amazing transition in flight. Starting with little knowledge in the art of lighter-than-air flying machines and following his initial success at Albuquerque, he helped introduce ballooning to the West at a time when many had never witnessed lighter-than-air flight. As ballooning became more commonplace, he coinvented the first parachute in the West, his balloon used to drop Thomas Baldwin, and a generation of new exhibitionists jumped onto the method worldwide. One of Van Tassel's many wives, the first woman in the West to make a parachute jump, also leaped from one of his balloons, and he continued to assist other women in both parachuting and ballooning. A photographer bankrolled by William Randolph Hearst took the first aerial photos in the West from one of Van Tassel's balloons. Van Tassel was one of a generation of aerial exhibitionists to perform in the late nineteenth century, focusing on the English-speaking colonies of the British Empire, namely Australia and India.

However, during Van Tassel's time away from the United States, aeronautics advanced at an increasing pace. By the time of his return at the start of the twentieth century, dirigibles and heavier-than-air flying machines were no longer science fiction. The public now considered balloon ascensions and parachute jumps to be more commonplace; women's parachuting still somewhat daring. The public began to be captivated by concepts of powered heavier-than-air flight, and more and more citizens were eager to partake in aviation rather than pay to watch exhibitionists do the same. Citizens experimenting with their own balloons, dirigibles, gliders, and powered aeroplanes began to form clubs. Caught in this dynamic, the middle-aged Park Van Tassel focused on serving as an elder statesman of ballooning for the aero clubs in the San Francisco Bay Area. He dabbled with dirigibles but avoided a transition to heavier-than-air flying machines. Through the challenges of the Panic of 1893, World War I, and the Great Depression, and no longer on the cutting edge of aviation, he was lost from the spotlight. Having survived numerous near-death experiences during his lengthy career in aviation, he was quite fortunate to lead such a long and distinctly different life.

Some associated with Van Tassel continue to be remembered for their many efforts in aviation. For instance, the shrewd opportunist Thomas Baldwin is enshrined in the National Aviation Hall of Fame for his contributions to ballooning, parachuting, dirigibles, and heavier-than-air flying machines. Often hailed as the sole "inventor of the flexible parachute"[1] and after debuting the first dirigible for the US Army, Baldwin also became known as the "father of the American dirigible." These accolades were partially earned for his bravery and abilities as a showman but also largely on the shoulders of others, such as Van Tassel, Greth, and Montgomery, whose relationships to Baldwin have been minimized or forgotten entirely. Baldwin served with honor in World War I, assisting the US Army with lighter-than-air craft. He passed away in 1923 and is buried in Arlington National Cemetery.

John Montgomery is enshrined in the National Aviation Hall of Fame as the first person in the United States to fly in a controlled fashion in a glider and also for his efforts to launch gliders from high-altitude balloons in 1905.[2] However, Montgomery's relationship with Van Tassel was short-lived. Other aviators, such as Augustus Greth, James Price, the Hawker (Viola) sisters, and the Freitas sisters, also remain rather forgotten.

This difference in fame was observable even shortly after Van Tassel's passing. For instance, in 1935, when Congress debated early aeronautics and its application in patents, Roy Knabenshue, the pilot of the *California Arrow* at the 1904 World's Fair in St. Louis, testified at the hearings. He stated to Congress:

> The most beloved of the old timers was Capt. Thomas Scott Baldwin, who was always happy and who made a joke of everything and particularly his own profession. I received a great deal of training under Baldwin. He was known to millions as "Captain Tom," and during the early days was probably the most widely known American airman in existence. He was genial, kindly, generous, and friendly,

and undoubtedly the greatest showman of them all in his particular
line. . . . He was engaged in walking a tight-rope from Seal Rocks
to Cliff House at San Francisco, when he met Prof. Van Tassel, who
was advertised to make a parachute drop from a balloon at one of the
local amusement parks. Tom Baldwin made the first parachute jump
in America out at San Francisco, in January 1885. Tom made an agreement with Van Tassel to make the drop for him, and this, as I say,
was the first parachute drop in America, the first successful parachute
descent.

Later in the proceedings, Knabenshue commented,

Tom Baldwin built the first successful American dirigible which was
flown at the St. Louis Exposition in 1904. . . . Another dear old soul
was Prof. Park A. Van Tassel of Oakland, Calif. It was from his balloon that Captain Baldwin jumped from in San Francisco in 1885. Van
Tassel at the same time as Baldwin made a world tour and returned
to this country and his last stop was Honolulu. He had a young man
travelling with him to make all the ascents and parachute jumps. On
their last engagement at Honolulu, the young man came down in the
bay in full view of the crowd and was devoured by sharks before help
arrived. Of course, this put an end to Van Tassel's experience.[3]

The readers of this book will realize that at the time of Lawrence's tragedy
at Honolulu, Van Tassel's international journey and importance to aviation
were far from over. Knabenshue's lack of accurate and complete information
was not unique. Those in Australia knew little of Van Tassel's previous efforts
in the West. Those in India knew only indirectly of Van Tassel's association
with James Price, there was confusion about the familial relationship of
Gladys and Valerie Freitas to Park Van Tassel, and those in Australia were
easily confused when yet another "daughter," Jeanette Van Tassel, passed in
Dacca. While some recognize Van Tassel as the first to fly in Sri Lanka, his
history before and after those flights remains unknown to many, other than
that Van Tassel had made balloon ascensions and parachute drops for some
time in India. It is ironic that while Van Tassel's efforts as an aerial

exhibitionist often resulted in crowds of thousands of spectators at each stop, his typical frenetic pace from one city to the next left a ragged and incomplete trail for historians to appreciate. While we know Park Van Tassel kept a scrapbook of his adventures, and that scrapbook made it back with him from Asia to California in the early 1900s, it too has been lost to time, a key resource and diary of his experiences. Even the location of his unmarked grave in Oakland remained a mystery until the research that produced this book. It is hoped that with greater appreciation might come greater recognition for Van Tassel and the other daring aerial exhibitionists of his generation.

From the 1930s to the 1960s, aviation historians might have taken greater time to truly understand the relationship of Van Tassel and Baldwin.[4] While some credit Baldwin with the sole invention of the flexible parachute, others co-credit Baldwin and Van Tassel. But very few acknowledge that the initial concept was Van Tassel's, and even fewer focus on Baldwin's co-option of the parachute from Van Tassel, the dirigible from Greth, and the propeller from Montgomery. Without the Internet to make such disparate resources easily available, piecing together such a journey would have surely been difficult for previous historians. It certainly did not help that Van Tassel's last name was spelled many ways in the literature, including "Van Tassell," "Vantassel," "Vantassell," "Van Tassol," and even "Mantasso."

It is hoped that this book helps set the record straight. From his first flight in Albuquerque to his last flights in Oakland, Van Tassel had one of the more amazing life journeys in early American aviation. He would certainly be proud of the accomplishments of parachute jumpers Colonel Joseph William Kittinger II, Felix Baumgartner, Alan Eustace, and others who have jumped from balloons at amazing heights above 100,000 feet to parachute back to Earth safely. For instance, on August 16, 1960, just thirty years after Van Tassel's passing, Kittinger jumped from a balloon at a height of 102,800 feet over Roswell, New Mexico, as a part of the US Air Force's Project Excelsior. At the time, his flight set world records for the highest piloted balloon flight, highest parachute jump, longest free fall, longest drogue fall, and highest speed of a human in the atmosphere, 614 miles per hour. His feats were in part eclipsed more recently by Felix Baumgartner, who jumped by parachute from a balloon on October 14, 2012, from a height of 127,852 feet as part of the Red Bull Stratos project in New Mexico. His speed of 843.6 miles per hour roughly

170 miles south of Albuquerque made Baumgartner the first human to exceed the speed of sound during free fall.[5] Alan Eustace exceeded Baumgartner's height mark by jumping from a helium balloon at an amazing altitude of 135,889 feet, establishing a new world record for the longest free fall: 123,414 feet.[6] However, Eustace's jump involved a drogue parachute and thus was slower and in a different category than Baumgartner's speed record. These amazing accomplishments take the efforts of Van Tassel and Baldwin to the extreme and would have been considered absolutely impossible at the time they were quietly testing their flexible parachute design in private at the Mechanics' Pavilion in San Francisco.

Van Tassel would have been most proud that Albuquerque is now home to the Albuquerque International Balloon Fiesta®, a celebration of beauty and camaraderie of lighter-than-air flight, established by Albuquerque's own Sidney Cutter and many others associated with the Albuquerque International Balloon Fiesta, Inc., which he helped establish. Their efforts are the true reason that Albuquerque has become known as the Balloon Capital of the World. Similarly, three Albuquerque aviators, Benjamin Abruzzo, Maxie Anderson, and Larry Newman, pushed the limits of ballooning with their flight in the *Double Eagle II* from Presque Isle, Maine, to Miserey, France, near Paris, landing on August 11, 1978. It was the first successful transatlantic crossing via gas balloon, a distance of 3,120 miles covered in 137 hours and six minutes. Not long after this success, Abruzzo, Newman, Hiroaki "Rocky" Aoki of Japan, and Ron Clark of Albuquerque became the first to complete a transpacific crossing in their helium-filled *Double Eagle V* with a flight from Nagashima, Japan, to Covelo, California, a distance of 5,768 miles in eighty-four hours and thirty-one minutes. More recently, on January 31, 2015, Troy Bradley of Albuquerque and Leonid Tiukhtyaev of Russia flew their 350,000-cubic-foot *Two Eagles* helium balloon from Japan to Mexico, setting new world records for both distance (6,646 miles) and duration (160 hours and thirty-eight minutes), besting the long-standing *Double Eagle V* record. In true Van Tassel fashion, their landing was in the water off the coast of Baja California.

On March 5, 2005, New Mexico governor William Blane "Bill" Richardson III signed into law Senate Bill 13, sponsored by New Mexico state senator Steve Komadina, a member of the ballooning community in Albuquerque.

Among other things, the bill certified the yucca as the official state flower, the roadrunner as the state bird, and the hot air balloon as the official state aircraft. In 2013 New Mexico state representative Tim D. Lewis introduced House Bill 625 for the creation of a set of Heritage Registration automobile license plates. One of the proposed plates was to honor all New Mexico aeronauts, including Park Van Tassel and his first flight in 1882. Unfortunately, the bill stalled in committee, and the license plates were never approved. We should be proud to remember that Albuquerque and New Mexico's association with balloons started on July 4, 1882, with a young and courageous man named Park Van Tassel. His lifetime association with ballooning and parachuting led to many amazing adventures, including landing in swamps, mudflats, trees, and seas. But despite these difficulties, he persevered, introducing flight to many thousands across the western United States and around the world through daring aerial exhibitions.

# GLOSSARY

aeronaut: A pilot of a balloon or other aircraft

aeroplane (variant spelling): A heavier-than-air fixed-wing aircraft

aerostat: An inflatable aircraft that has no means of lateral propulsion. It either drifts freely with the wind or is tethered to the ground by a long rope or cable.

anchor: In gas ballooning, a hook used during landing for both ballast release and snagging the ground to slow the balloon's forward progress

ballast: In gas ballooning, a weight dropped overboard to aid in control of a balloon's altitude. This generally involves pouring sand from a bag or dropping the entire bag, thus creating an ascent or slowing a descent.

barometer: An instrument that measures atmospheric pressure and is calibrated to indicate altitude above sea level

basket: A balloon's car or gondola, sometimes called a cage, typically constructed of tightly woven rattan or wicker. Baskets are circular or rectangular and carry human cargo and supplies. The sides vary in height from 3 to 5 feet. The basket is often wooden, with skids on the underside.

buoyancy: The tendency of a balloon to rise or float in the air. Buoyancy can be lost when ambient air cools, lifting gas leaks or is released, or weight (including rainwater) is added to the balloon. Buoyancy can increase with the loss of a passenger or ballast.

cabane: A strut or brace, typically on the top of a wing, used for the attachment of stays that hold the wing in a level position

captive flight: Flight in a buoyant balloon held captive to the ground by mooring lines or tether lines—as opposed to free flight, when the balloon is unhampered by anything attached to the ground. For very high captive

flights, say 1,000 feet, the tether lines (cables or heavy ropes) are reeled in
and out by a winch.

carriage: A gondola-type framework rigidly attached below a dirigible's
gasbag to house the pilot and the power plant

coal gas: A flammable lifting gas that is mostly comprised of hydrogen,
methane, and carbon monoxide. It is made by burning coal in a low-
oxygen environment.

dirigible: A horizontally elongated, hydrogen gas–filled airship that is
propelled forward by an onboard engine turning a propeller and is
steered by a rudder. It is somewhat aerodynamically streamlined in that it
has a blunt nose and a pointed tail (stern).

dirigibility: The capability of a lighter-than-air flying machine to be steered
or directed in flight

drag rope: A long, heavy rope that orients a balloon and rip panel to the
wind. It is also used to slow the balloon's descent rate and horizontal
speed. As "recoverable ballast," it helps save other types of ballast.

free flight: When a balloon is buoyant and drifting freely, with no ties
to Earth, and travels through the atmosphere at the same speed and
direction as the wind. If there is no wind, the balloon reaches a state of
equilibrium and hangs motionless over a fixed point on the ground. In
such cases, the pilot may elect to climb higher or drop lower in search of
more suitable wind. The direction and speed of wind vary with altitude
and terrain.

gasbag: A spherical or tear-shaped bag made of tapered strips of muslin
sewn together using a lockstitch. The cloth is interwoven with linen or
silk and made impervious to the release of gas by a light coating of oil.

gas balloon: Historically, a balloon that used coal gas from a municipal
main that normally supplied illuminating or heating gas to connected
customers, or a balloon that used hydrogen as the lifting gas. Hydrogen,
which has much more lifting power than coal gas, could be generated
on-site and piped to the inflating balloon. Modern gas balloons typically
use hydrogen or helium, and may use anhydrous ammonia or methane
for training flights. Filling takes place at the neck, a tapered appendix at
the base of the gasbag, which is designed to receive a filling tube, pipe,
or hose. The neck is tied off after filling but untied after launch to allow
expanding gas to escape, thus preventing rupture.

glider: An unpowered fixed-wing aircraft

guide ropes: handling lines attached to a gasbag and dangling within reach of ground crew members. The ropes are used to steady the balloon during inflation.

hot air balloon: A balloon filled with air, which expands when heated above the ambient temperature and becomes lighter. However, even at 212°F, hot air has only a quarter of the lifting power of hydrogen.

hydrogen gas: A gas that is fourteen and a half times lighter than air, thus providing very good buoyancy. While hydrogen can easily be generated on-site using iron filings and sulfuric acid, it has one major drawback: it is extremely flammable when in contact with oxygen.

moorings: Lines attached to a load ring and anchored to the ground to secure and steady a balloon

netting: A strong net wrapped around a gasbag and secured to a solid-oak load ring, which in turn is attached to the basket by ropes. Netting adds considerable strength to gas balloons. It can also serve as a parachute for the balloon if for some reason the envelope fails.

parachute: A strong, lightweight, dome-shaped canopy used to slow the descent of a suspended person by creating drag through the atmosphere

release valve: A spring-loaded vent at the top of a balloon that can be operated by a rope extending to the pilot in the basket. It can be used as a pressure relief valve when gas expands at high altitude and as a means to deflate the balloon. The valve can become stuck open or closed.

rip panel: A section of a gasbag that is lightly fixed in place. On or near the ground, the pilot can pull a cord to open the rip panel to quickly deflate the balloon. Spectators often viewed this opening as an accidental tear in the balloon fabric, when in fact it was intentional.

smoke balloon: A hot air balloon inflated by suspending a wide-throated muslin bag above burning kerosene-soaked wood, so that hot smoky air fills the balloon. The smoke and soot help seal pores in the fabric so that the balloon holds heat longer. Smoke balloons have no airborne heat source and no disposable ballast—hence no means of flight control. They also have no netting and no basket for passengers. Generally a "smoke jumper" with a parachute is suspended by ropes until he or she jerks the connection loose from the gasbag. (With a gas balloon, the weight of the jumper jerks the line free.) Smoke balloons became popular at fairs and exhibitions as parachutes were perfected. During inflation, hot flying embers in the balloon's interior sometimes set the muslin on fire, which was dangerous if the fire was not discovered until after the pilot signaled, "Let her go!"

trapeze artist: A performer who ascends with a smoke balloon or gas balloon while sitting or hanging on a trapeze suspended from a parachute attached to the balloon. During the ascent, the artist might perform acrobatic acts. At the desired altitude, the artist parachutes back to Earth.

# NOTES

## Preface

1. Richard Holmes, *Falling Upwards: How We Took to the Air* (New York: Vintage Books, 2013), 66–68.
2. Tom Crouch, *The Eagle Aloft: Two Centuries of the Balloon in America* (Washington, DC: Smithsonian Institution Press, 1983), 202.
3. *Weekly Placer Herald*, September 3, 1853.

## Chapter 1

1. *Pierceton Record* 21, no. 15 (February 2, 1899): 4. Rufus Van Tassel was born in 1823 and died on February 2, 1899.
2. Rufus and Nancy are listed in the 1870 US Census with daughter Lillie (four years old). Nancy Connor was born in 1828. Her death date remains unknown.
3. Eliza J. Van Tassel was born in 1846.
4. Clarissa A. Van Tassel was born in 1851.
5. Effie E. Van Tassel was born in 1864.
6. Lillie Van Tassel was born in 1866.
7. "Iowa Marriages, 1838–1934," Family Search, http//familysearch.org/tree/person/details/KX29-PLL(accessed January 21, 2021). Phebe Lorinda Smith was born on January 17, 1847, and died on July 14, 1922.
8. "United States Census, 1880," Family Search, https://www.familysearch.org/ark:/61903/3:1:33SQ-GYBZ-6Y3?i=5&wc=XWD3-PTL%3A1589403245%2C1589404167%2C1589404261%2C1589394944&cc=1417683 (accessed January 31, 2021).
9. John Connor was born in 1783 and died on August 26, 1848.
10. Elizabeth Connor was born in 1790 and died on March 10, 1849.
11. *New York Times*, September 14, 1930; *Popular Aviation*, May 1931, 40; *Oakland Tribune*, October 25, 1930.
12. "Indiana Marriages, 1811–2007," Family Search, https://familysearch.org/ark:/61903/1:1:XXFR-W4R (accessed January 31, 2021).
13. *Cincinnati Daily Star*, June 19, 1876.

14. Ella Block was born in 1863.

15. "California, County Marriages, 1850–1952," Family Search, https://familysearch.org/ark:/61903/3:1:3QSQ-G93H-BV4K?cc=1804002&wc=9653-W3D%3A152598201 (accessed January 31, 2021).

16. *Fresno Morning Republican*, November 24, 1889.

17. Harry Van Tassel was born in November 1879.

18. Forestus Fordyce Martin was born on March 16, 1834 and died on June 1, 1927.

19. *Daily Evening Herald*, April 11, 1874.

20. As noted in the introduction, it was quite common for aerial showmen to adopt the title "Professor" as a part of their marketing.

21. *Sacramento Daily Record-Union*, August 16, 1880.

22. *Sacramento Daily Record-Union*, September 4, 1880.

23. *San Francisco Examiner*, January 22, 1881.

24. *Los Angeles Herald*, July 23, 1881.

25. Dick Brown and Rick Van Tassel, "Albuquerque's First Aeronaut" *Albuquerque International Balloon Fiesta*, 2016, 68; *Albuquerque Daily Journal*, March 30, 1882; *Albuquerque Daily Journal*, May 25, 1882.

26. *Albuquerque Daily Journal*, March 30, 1882; *Albuquerque Daily Journal*, June 15, 1882.

27. *Albuquerque Evening Review*, May 27, 1882; *Albuquerque Daily Journal*, May 27, 1882.

28. *Albuquerque Daily Journal*, February 24, 1882.

29. *Albuquerque Daily Journal*, May 12, 1882.

30. Coal gas was a mixture of hydrogen, methane, and carbon monoxide produced by burning bituminous coal in a low-oxygen environment.

31. Dick Brown, personal communication, 2019.

32. *Albuquerque Evening Review*, July 6, 1882.

33. "Part L. First National Flights," Fédération Aéronautique Internationale, https://www.fai.org/sites/default/files/documents/rpt_l_first_national_flights.pdf (accessed March 5, 2019).

34. William B. Lyon to Corie Bowman, June 29, 1882, Archives and Special Collections at New Mexico State University.

35. William B. Lyon to Corie Bowman, July 3, 1882, Archives and Special Collections at New Mexico State University.

36. William B. Lyon to Corie Bowman, July 4, 1882, Archives and Special Collections at New Mexico State University.

37. William B. Lyon to Corie Bowman, July 5, 1882, Archives and Special Collections at New Mexico State University.

## Chapter 2

1. *Las Vegas Daily Gazette*, July 27, 1882.

2.  *Las Vegas Daily Gazette*, August 2, 1882.
3.  *Las Vegas Daily Gazette*, August 4, 1882.
4.  *Aspen Weekly Times*, August 5, 1882.
5.  *Albuquerque Morning Journal*, August 8, 1882.
6.  *Las Vegas Daily Gazette*, August 9, 1882.
7.  *Las Vegas Daily Gazette*, August 13, 1882.
8.  *Las Vegas Daily Gazette*, August 15, 1882; *Albuquerque Morning Journal*, August 15, 1882; *Albuquerque Morning Journal*, August 16, 1882.
9.  *Las Vegas Daily Gazette*, August 17, 1882.
10. Dick Brown, personal communication, 2018.
11. *Albuquerque Daily Journal*, August 18, 1882.
12. *Las Vegas Daily Gazette*, August 17, 1882.
13. *Las Vegas Daily Gazette*, August 17, 1882.
14. "The Question of the Marshalship," BlongerBros.com, http://www.blongerbros.com/posse/marshalship.asp (accessed December 20, 2017). Lou Blonger's brother Sam Blonger was deputy marshal.
15. Possibly Kitty Blonger.
16. *Albuquerque Morning Journal*, September 12, 1882; *Albuquerque Evening Review*, September 12, 1882; *Las Vegas Daily Gazette*, September 14, 1882.
17. *Albuquerque Morning Journal*, September 20, 1882.
18. *Albuquerque Morning Journal*, September 22, 1882.
19. *Las Vegas Daily Gazette*, September 23, 1882.
20. *Las Vegas Daily Gazette*, September 29, 1882.
21. *Albuquerque Morning Journal*, October 8, 1882; *Albuquerque Morning Journal*, October 10, 1882.
22. *Albuquerque Morning Journal*, November 1, 1882.
23. *Albuquerque Morning Journal*, November 8, 1882.
24. *Sacramento Daily Union*, January 27, 1883.
25. *Las Vegas Daily Gazette*, January 27, 1883.
26. *Las Cruces Sun News*, February 17, 1883.
27. *Las Vegas Daily Gazette*, February 13, 1883.
28. *Las Vegas Daily Gazette*, March 18, 1883.
29. *Albuquerque Morning Journal*, February 6, 1883.
30. *Albuquerque Morning Journal*, February 16, 1883.
31. *Albuquerque Morning Journal*, February 15, 1883.

## Chapter 3

1.  *Las Vegas Gazette*, March 18, 1883.
2.  *San Francisco Examiner*, March 15, 1883.
3.  *Salt Lake Herald*, June 10, 1883.
4.  *Salt Lake Herald*, June 14, 1883.

5. *Salt Lake Daily Tribune*, June 23, 1883.

6. *Salt Lake Herald*, June 24, 1883.

7. *Salt Lake Herald*, July 4, 1883.

8. *Salt Lake Herald*, July 6, 1883, September 5, 1883; *Deseret Evening News*, July 5, 1883.

9. *Salt Lake Herald*, July 4, 1883; *Latter-Day Saints' Millennial Star* 45 (1883): 447; *Deseret Evening News*, May 18, 1907.

10. *Deseret Evening News*, May 18, 1907.

11. *Deseret Evening News*, July 11, 1883.

12. *Salt Lake Herald*, July 21, 1883.

13. *Salt Lake Herald*, July 22, 1883.

14. *Salt Lake Herald*, July 24, 1883.

15. *Salt Lake Herald*, July 14, 1883.

16. *Salt Lake Herald*, July 26, 1883; *Deseret Evening News*, May 18, 1907.

17. *Kansas City Times*, August 28, 1886.

18. *New York Times*, November 27, 1884.

19. *Salt Lake Herald*, July 29, 1883; *San Francisco Examiner*, August 4, 1883.

20. *Salt Lake Herald*, September 5, 1883; *Eugene Guard*, September 15, 1883.

21. *Sacramento Daily Record Union*, November 5, 1883.

22. *Sacramento Daily Record Union*, November 5, 1883; *Willamette Farmer*, November 9, 1883.

## Chapter 4

1. *Daily Alta California*, January 25, 1884.

2. *Daily Alta California*, January 27, 1884.

3. *Las Vegas Daily Gazette*, February 7, 1884.

4. *Daily Alta California*, February 14, 1884.

5. *Sacramento Daily Record-Union*, April 21, 1884; *San Jose Mercury News*, April 22, 1884; *Reno Evening Gazette*, April 22, 1884.

6. *Los Angeles Herald*, May 17, 1884, June 4, 1884.

7. *Los Angeles Herald*, June 15, 1884.

8. *Sacramento Daily Record-Union*, June 16, 1884.

9. *New York Times*, November 27, 1884; *Washington Post*, December 22, 1884.

10. *San Francisco Examiner*, November 15, 1884.

11. *San Francisco Examiner*, December 1, 1884. The World's Industrial Cotton Centennial Exposition of 1884–1885 was also known as the New Orleans World's Fair.

12. *New York Times*, November 27, 1884.

13. *San Francisco Examiner*, November 30, 1884.

14. *Daily Alta California*, December 1, 1884.

15. *San Francisco Chronicle*, December 1, 1884.

16. *Daily Alta California*, December 1, 1884.

17. *San Francisco Chronicle*, December 1, 1884.

18. *Daily Alta California*, December 1, 1884.

19. *Los Angeles Herald*, November 15, 1884; *Daily Alta California*, November 30, 1884; *Sacramento Daily Record-Union*, December 1, 1884; *Reno Evening Gazette*, December 1, 1884; *Daily Alta California*, December 1, 1884; *San Francisco Bulletin*, December 1, 1884; *Santa Cruz Sentinel*, December 4, 1884.

20. *Bismarck Tribune*, December 12, 1884; *Washington Post*, December 22, 1884.

21. *Nature* 34 (August 19, 1888): 371.

22. *Times of India*, September 9, 1886.

23. *San Francisco Examiner*, April 4, 1885.

24. *Daily Alta California*, January 9, 1885.

25. *San Francisco Bulletin*, March 7, 1885; *San Francisco Examiner*, March 9, 1885.

26. *Galveston Daily News*, March 1, 1885.

27. *Huntsville Gazette*, March 14, 1885.

28. *Times Picayune*, March 18, 1885.

29. *Times Picayune*, March 20, 1885.

30. *Times Picayune*, March 20, 1885.

31. *Los Angeles Times*, March 27, 1885.

32. *Times Picayune*, March 20, 1885.

33. *Sacramento Daily Record-Union*, March 20, 1885; *St. Landry Democrat*, March 28, 1885; Daniel W. Perkins, *Practical Common Sense Guide Book through the World's Industrial and Cotton Centennial Exposition at New Orleans* (Harrisburg PA: Hart, 1885).

34. *Bolivar Bulletin*, March 20, 1885; *Reno Evening Gazette*, March 20, 1885; *Galveston Daily News*, March 20, 1885; *Salt Lake Herald*, March 20, 1885; *Magnolia Gazette*, March 26, 1885; *Panola Weekly Star*, March 26, 1885; *St. Landry Democrat*, March 28, 1885.

35. *Galveston Daily News*, March 28, 1885.

36. *Sacramento Daily Record-Union*, March 31, 1885.

37. Clara A. Coykendall was born in 1861.

38. "California, County Marriages, 1850–1952," Family Search, https://www.familysearch.org/ark:/61903/1:1:V48Q-5R8 (accessed January 31, 2021).

39. *Daily Alta California*, April 3, 1885; *Sacramento Daily Record-Union*, April 3, 1885; *San Jose Mercury News*, April 3, 1885; *Santa Cruz Sentinel*, April 5, 1885.

40. *San Francisco Examiner*, April 4, 1885.

41. *Daily Alta California*, May 27, 1885; *Sacramento Daily Record-Union*, May 29, 1885.

42. *San Francisco Examiner*, May 31, 1885.

## Chapter 5

1. *San Francisco Examiner*, July 23, 1885.

2. *San Francisco Examiner*, July 26, 1885.

3. This meant the atmosphere was very humid, probably due to low clouds and fog.

4. *Daily Alta California*, July 23, 1885, July 26, 1885, July 27, 1885; *San Francisco Chronicle*, July 27, 1885; *Sacramento Daily Record-Union*, July 28, 1885.

5. *Sacramento Daily Record-Union*, September 2, 1885, September 4, 1885, September 5, 1885, September 7, 1885; *Daily Alta California*, September 7, 1885; *Sacramento Daily Record-Union*, September 7, 1910.

6. *San Francisco Examiner*, September 20, 1885.

7. *Daily Alta California*, September 17, 1885.

8. *Daily Alta California*, September 17, 1885; *San Jose Mercury News*, September 17, 1885; *Daily Alta California*, September 19, 1885, September 21, 1885; *San Francisco Bulletin*, September 21, 1885; *Daily Alta California*, September 22, 1885; *San Francisco Examiner*, September 22, 1885.

9. *San Francisco Chronicle*, January 10, 1886.

10. *Daily Alta California*, January 5, 1886, January 8, 1886, January 10, 1886, January 11, 1886.

11. *San Francisco Examiner*, January 11, 1886.

12. *Daily Alta California*, January 12, 1886; *San Jose Mercury News*, January 13, 1886; *San Francisco Examiner*, January 12, 1886.

13. *Daily Alta California*, January 28, 1886; *San Jose Daily News*, January 29, 1886; *Daily Alta California*, January 31, 1886.

14. *Daily Alta California*, February 15, 1886.

15. *San Jose Mercury News*, February 1, 1886.

16. *San Jose Mercury News*, February 1, 1886; *San Francisco Bulletin*, February 1, 1886.

17. *Daily Alta California*, February 22, 1886.

18. *Daily Alta California*, March 16, 1886.

19. *San Francisco Examiner*, March 7, 1886.

20. *San Francisco Examiner*, March 11, 1886.

21. *San Francisco Examiner*, May 6, 1886.

22. The Bill Graham Civic Auditorium in downtown San Francisco sits on the site of the former Mechanics' Pavilion.

23. This was far less than the originally planned 600,000 cubic feet of gas.

24. *Arizona Weekly Journal-Miner*, May 12, 1886.

25. *Las Vegas Gazette*, May 26, 1886.

26. *Daily Alta California*, May 6, 1886; *Sacramento Daily Record-Union*, May 7, 1886; *Santa Rosa Press Democrat*, May 7, 1886; *Sonoma Democrat*, May 8, 1886.

27. *Daily Alta California*, May 24, 1886, May 30, 1886, June 1, 1886; *San Francisco Examiner*, May 30, 1886.

## Chapter 6

1. *Los Angeles Times*, June 27, 1886.

2. *Los Angeles Daily Herald*, June 30, 1886.

3. *Los Angeles Daily Herald*, July 3, 1886, July 4, 1886.

4.  *Los Angeles Times*, June 27, 1886.

5.  *San Francisco Examiner*, July 6, 1886.

6.  *Los Angeles Daily Herald*, July 6, 1886.

7.  *San Francisco Bulletin*, July 7, 1886.

8.  *San Francisco Bulletin*, July 7, 1886; *San Jose Mercury News*, March 17, 1886; *American Engineer*, April 1, 1886; *Marshfield Times*, April 9, 1886; *San Jose Mercury News*, May 7, 1886; *Oshkosh Daily Northwestern*, May 15, 1886; *Wellsboro Agitator*, July 13, 1886.

9.  *Scientific American*, June 26, 1886.

10. *English Mechanic and World of Science* 1 (July 30, 1886): 114; *Aberdare Times*, August 7, 1886; *Aberystwith Observer*, August 7, 1886; *Llangollen Advertiser Denbighshire Merionethshire and North Wales Journal*, September 3, 1886; *Auckland Star*, October 16, 1886; *Bruce Herald*, October 22, 1886; *Western Star*, October 23, 1886; *New Zealand Mail*, October 29, 1886.

11. *Geelong Advertiser*, August 18, 1886; *Pall Mall Budget*, August 19, 1886; *Mount Barker Courier and Onkaparinga and Gumeracha Advertiser*, October 1, 1886; *Brisbane Courier*, October 2, 1886; *Emerald Hill Record*, October 6, 1886, October 7, 1886; *Queenslander*, October 9, 1886; *Melbourne Weekly Times*, October 9, 1886; *Emerald Hill Record*, October 11, 1886, October 12, 1886, October 13, 1886; *Border Watch*, October 13, 1886; *Express and Telegraph*, October 16, 1886; *Emerald Hill Record*, October 23, 1886, October 26, 1886, October 27, 1886, October 28, 1886; *Logan Witness*, October 30, 1886; *Daily Telegraph* (Launceston, Tasmania), July 4, 1887.

12. *Albuquerque Morning Democrat*, July 20, 1886.

13. *Colorado Daily Chieftain*, August 8, 1886; *Aspen Daily Times*, August 8, 1886.

14. *Salt Lake Herald*, August 7, 1886.

15. *Fort Collins Courier*, August 12, 1886.

16. *Herald Democrat*, August 10, 1886.

17. *Colorado Daily Chieftain*, August 14, 1886.

18. Sandy Branham, "Over Ninety Years of Ballooning in Colorado," *Ballooning*, Summer 1976, 71–72; Crouch, *Eagle Aloft*.

19. *Kansas City Times*, August 28, 1886.

20. Branham, "Over Ninety Years of Ballooning in Colorado."

21. *Kansas City Star*, August 30, 1886.

22. *Kansas City Star*, August 31, 1886, September 1, 1886.

23. *Daily Alta California*, October 31, 1886.

24. *San Francisco Examiner*, November 1, 1886.

25. *San Jose Mercury News*, November 2, 1886.

26. *Sacramento Daily Union*, November 9, 1886; *San Francisco Chronicle*, November 8, 1886.

27. *San Francisco Chronicle*, November 15, 1886.

28. *San Francisco Examiner*, November 20, 1886.

29. *San Jose Mercury News*, November 20, 1886; *San Diego Union and Daily Bee*, November 21, 1886.

## Chapter 7

1. Thomas Scott Baldwin was born on June 30, 1854, and died on May 17, 1923.
2. Howard Lee Scamehorn, "Thomas Scott Baldwin: The Columbus of the Air," *Journal of the Illinois State Historical Society* 49, no. 2 (1956): 163–89.
3. Scamehorn, "Thomas Scott Baldwin"; Crouch, *Eagle Aloft*; *Hawaiian Gazette*, November 26, 1889; *Arizona Republican*, October 27, 1901; *San Francisco Examiner*, January 22, 1887. Although some sources, such as Scamehorn, suggest that the experiments happened in both 1885 and 1886, others, such as the *San Francisco Examiner* of January 22, 1887, quote Van Tassel as stating that he was working on parachute systems independently before meeting Baldwin. Still others, such as the *Arizona Republican* of October 27, 1901 suggest that Thomas Baldwin, "Ivy Baldwin," and Park Van Tassel met in the summer of 1887 to consider the idea, but jumps already occurring in January 1887 render this concept inconsistent with history. Crouch suggests that Baldwin and Van Tassel purchased the parachute from two local gymnasts who were experimenting with it for an indoor act, with a first test on January 21, 1887.
4. *San Francisco Examiner*, January 22, 1887.
5. *San Francisco Examiner*, January 22, 1887.
6. Scamehorn, "Thomas Scott Baldwin."
7. Scamehorn, "Thomas Scott Baldwin."
8. *Hawaiian Gazette*, November 26, 1889.
9. Rodelle Weintraub, "A Parachutist Prototype for Lina," *Shaw* 8 (1988): 77–84.
10. *San Francisco Chronicle*, January 31, 1887; *Sacramento Daily Record-Union*, February 1, 1887; *Sun* (New York), February 10, 1887.
11. *Sporting Life*, February 19, 1887.
12. *San Francisco Chronicle*, January 31, 1887; *Sacramento Daily Record-Union*, January 31, 1887.
13. William Ivy was born on July 31, 1866, and died on October 8, 1953.
14. *San Francisco Chronicle*, April 4, 1887.
15. *Los Angeles Herald*, April 19, 1887.
16. *San Francisco Examiner*, April 16, 1887.
17. *Photographic News*, July 8, 1887, 419.
18. *Deseret Evening News*, May 18, 1907.
19. *Sacramento Daily Record-Union*, May 28, 1887.
20. *Sacramento Daily Record-Union*, June 2, 1887.
21. *Sacramento Daily Record-Union*, June 9, 1887; *San Bernardino Daily Courier*, June 22, 1887; *Los Angeles Herald*, June 25, 1887, June 26, 1887.
22. *Los Angeles Herald*, June 27, 1887; *Los Angeles Times*, June 27, 1887.
23. *Los Angeles Herald*, June 28, 1887.
24. *Los Angeles Herald*, June 28, 1887.
25. *San Bernardino Daily Courier*, June 29, 1887.
26. *Sacramento Daily Record-Union*, July 5, 1887; *Los Angeles Herald*, July 5, 1887.
27. *Sacramento Daily Record-Union*, July 7, 1887; *San Francisco Chronicle*, July 17, 1887.

## Chapter 8

1. The Santa Clara Valley Agriculture Society Fair was also known as the San Jose Fair. The choice of San Jose was interesting, as it was also Clara's hometown.

2. *San Jose Mercury News*, July 23, 1887; *Daily Alta California*, July 28, 1887; *Reno Evening Gazette*, July 29, 1887; *Santa Cruz Sentinel*, July 30, 1887; *San Jose Mercury News*, July 30, 1887; *Pacific Rural Press*, August 6, 1887; *Marin Journal*, August 11, 1887.

3. *New York Times*, September 14, 1930.

4. *Santa Cruz Sentinel*, August 19, 1887; *Daily Alta California*, August 19, 1887; *San Francisco Chronicle*, August 19, 1887.

5. *San Jose Mercury News*, January 26, 1888; *San Francisco Examiner*, January 26, 1888.

6. *Los Angeles Herald*, February 15, 1888, February 16, 1888.

7. *Los Angeles Herald*, February 21, 1888.

8. *San Bernardino Daily Courier*, February 23, 1888.

9. *Coronado Mercury*, March 10, 1888.

10. *Coronado Mercury*, March 21, 1888.

11. *Coronado Mercury*, March 31, 1888. One wonders how anyone on the ground would have been able to discern the difference between 1 mile and 1.5 miles above the surface.

12. *Coronado Mercury*, April 3, 1888.

13. *Coronado Mercury*, April 12, 1888, April 13, 1888.

14. *Coronado Mercury*, April 14, 1888, April 16, 1888.

15. *Los Angeles Times*, July 5, 1888.

16. Crouch, *Eagle Aloft*.

17. *Los Angeles Herald*, July 2, 1888.

18. *Los Angeles Times*, July 5, 1888; *Los Angeles Herald*, July 2, 1888, July 6, 1888.

19. It is unlikely that the actual volume of gas in the balloon was 250,000 cubic feet, as the previous *Eclipse* and *City of London* held about 80,000 cubic feet and the *Monitor* held closer to 150,000 cubic feet. It may have been that 250,000 cubic feet of gas was used to fill the balloon, but with all the leaks over the time required to fill it, this number was larger than the balloon's actual volume.

20. *Los Angeles Herald*, July 2, 1888; *Salt Lake Herald*, July 15, 1888.

21. *Lyttelton Times*, February 14, 1889.

22. *Fair Trade*, August 3, 1888.

23. *Los Angeles Herald*, July 2, 1888.

24. *Los Angeles Herald*, July 12, 1888.

25. *Los Angeles Herald*, July 12, 1888.

26. *Los Angeles Times*, July 27, 1888.

27. *Reno Evening Gazette*, August 21, 1888; *San Jose Mercury News*, August 15, 1888, August 17, 1888, August 18, 1888; *Santa Cruz Sentinel*, August 19, 1888; *Daily Alta California*, August 20, 1888; *San Jose Mercury News*, August 20, 1888; *Santa Cruz Sentinel*, August 21, 1888; *Sacramento Daily Union*, August 21, 1888; *Reno Evening Gazette*, August 21, 1888; *San Francisco Examiner*, August 20, 1888.

28. *San Jose Evening News*, August 25, 1888.

## Chapter 9

1. *Morning Oregonian*, September 10, 1888.
2. *Morning Oregonian*, September 24, 1888.
3. *Morning Oregonian*, September 28, 1888.
4. *Sacramento Daily Union*, September 24, 1888; *San Jose Mercury News*, September 24, 1888; *Morning Oregonian*, September 24, 1888, September 25, 1888, September 26, 1888; *Santa Cruz Sentinel*, September 29, 1888.
5. *Morning Oregonian*, September 28, 1888.
6. *Morning Oregonian*, September 28, 1888; *Evening Capital Journal*, September 28, 1888.
7. *Morning Oregonian*, October 15, 1888.
8. *Evening Capital Journal*, October 15, 1888; *San Jose Mercury News*, October 15, 1888.
9. *Morning Oregonian*, October 26, 1888.
10. *San Jose Evening News*, November 15, 1888.
11. Turn Verein was a German American social organization that promoted health, exercise, and well-being.
12. *Seattle Post-Intelligencer*, November 2, 1889.
13. *Auckland Star*, December 10, 1888, December 20, 1888.
14. *Auckland Star*, December 11, 1888, December 24, 1888.
15. *Morning Oregonian*, January 2, 1889; *Daily Alta California*, January 3, 1889; *Evening Capital Journal*, January 3, 1889; *Morning Oregonian*, January 3, 1889; *Reno Evening Gazette*, January 5, 1889.
16. *San Jose Mercury News*, February 8, 1889.
17. *San Francisco Chronicle*, February 11, 1889.
18. *Daily Alta California*, February 11, 1889; *Los Angeles Times*, February 11, 1889; *San Francisco Chronicle*, February 11, 1889; *Daily Alta California*, February 12, 1889; *Los Angeles Daily Herald*, February 11, 1889; *Los Angeles Times*, February 11, 1889; *San Francisco Chronicle*, February 11, 1889.
19. *Santa Cruz Sentinel*, February 14, 1889.
20. *Press Democrat*, March 27 1889.
21. *Auckland Star*, March 23, 1889.
22. *Press Democrat*, March 27 1889, March 31, 1889; *Healdsburg Tribune*, April 6, 1889; *Sonoma Democrat*, April 6, 1889; *Press Democrat*, April 12, 1889.
23. *San Francisco Chronicle*, April 21, 1889.

## Chapter 10

1. From 1875 to 1893, Garfield Beach Resort Pavilion was the premier resort on the shores of the Great Salt Lake, with direct trains running six times daily from Salt Lake City in 1888. Located near the present-day town of Lake Point, the large resort unfortunately burned down in 1904.
2. *Salt Lake Herald*, May 22, 1889.

3. *Salt Lake Herald,* May 22, 1889.
4. *Salt Lake Herald,* May 22, 1889; *Standard,* May 23, 1889.
5. *Salt Lake Herald,* May 23, 1889.
6. *Salt Lake Herald,* May 23, 1889, May 24, 1889, May 25, 1889.
7. *Salt Lake Herald,* May 26, 1889.
8. James William Price was born on May 15, 1871, and died on September 21, 1921.
9. *Salt Lake Herald,* May 26, 1889, May 29, 1889.
10. Ruby Marana Hawker was born on November 23, 1873, and died on February 15, 1935.
11. No evidence of a familial relationship between James William Price and Ruby Marana Hawker has been found, although two of Hawker's Australian sisters also became parachute jumpers. Hawker was also known as Ruby Horaker and later, after marriage, Ruby Hastings.
12. James W. Price's mother's maiden name was Sisk.
13. *Chicago Tribune,* May 5, 1888.
14. *Mentone Gazette,* May 19, 1888.
15. He was incorrectly called Professor Rice in newspapers.
16. *St. Paul Daily Globe,* September 10, 1888.
17. *Salt Lake Herald,* June 4, 1889.
18. *Nebraska State Journal,* August 19, 1900.
19. *Salt Lake Herald,* June 5, 1889, June 11, 1889.
20. *Salt Lake Herald,* June 4, 1889.
21. *Butte Semi-weekly Miner,* July 10, 1889.

## Chapter 11

1. *Albuquerque Morning Democrat,* June 30, 1889; *Albuquerque Journal,* June 27, 1889.
2. *Salem Daily News,* December 9, 1889; *Thomas County Cat,* December 12, 1889.
3. *Santa Fe Daily New Mexican,* July 8, 1889.
4. *Sacramento Daily Union,* July 5, 1889.
5. *Los Angeles Times,* July 19, 1889; *San Bernardino Daily Courier,* July 25, 1889; *Los Angeles Herald,* July 27, 1889; *San Bernardino Daily Courier,* July 27, 1889; *Daily Alta California,* July 29, 1889.
6. *San Francisco Bulletin,* July 29, 1889.
7. *Hawaiian Gazette,* November 26, 1889; *Los Angeles Herald,* August 2, 1889; *Los Angeles Times,* August 2, 1889; *Los Angeles Herald,* August 4, 1889, August 5, 1889.
8. *Fresno Morning Republican,* August 10, 1889, August 11, 1889, August 13, 1889.
9. *Hawaiian Gazette,* November 26, 1889.
10. *Hawaiian Gazette,* November 26, 1889.
11. *Hawaiian Gazette,* November 26, 1889.
12. *Fresno Morning Republican,* August 20, 1889.
13. *Fresno Morning Republican,* August 21, 1889, August 25, 1889.

218 Notes

14. *San Jose Mercury News*, August 26, 1889; *Fresno Weekly Republican*, August 30, 1889; *San Francisco Chronicle*, August 25, 1889.

15. *San Francisco Examiner*, October 4, 1889.

16. *San Jose Mercury News*, October 11, 1889.

17. *San Jose Mercury News*, October 11, 1889; *San Francisco Examiner*, October 11, 1889, October 13, 1889.

## Chapter 12

1. *Daily Alta California*, October 21, 1889; *San Francisco Examiner*, October 20, 1889.

2. *San Francisco Examiner*, October 20, 1889.

3. Ancestry.com. "Hawaii, U.S., Arriving and Departing Passenger Lists, 1843–1898," Ancestry.com, https://www.ancestry.com/search/collections/61078 (accessed February 10, 2021).

4. *San Francisco Examiner*, October 20, 1889.

5. *San Francisco Examiner*, October 20, 1889.

6. "Hawaii, Passenger Lists, 1843–1898," Ancestry.com; *Daily Bulletin* (Honolulu), October 28, 1889.

7. *Daily Bulletin* (Honolulu), October 28, 1889; William J. Horvat, *Above the Pacific* (Fallbrook, CA: Aero Publishers, 1966).

8. Robert C. Schmitt, "Some Transportation and Communication Firsts in Hawaii," *Hawaiian Journal of History* 13 (1979): 105; *Daily Bulletin* (Honolulu), November 4, 1889; *Hawaiian Gazette*, November 5, 1889.

9. *Hawaiian Gazette*, March 5, 1889, April 9, 1889.

10. *Hawaiian Gazette*, November 26, 1889.

11. The Punchbowl is known to Hawaiians as Puowaina, a place of ritual sacrifice.

12. *Hawaiian Gazette*, November 12, 1889.

13. *Hawaiian Gazette*, November 24, 1889.

14. *Sacramento Daily Union*, November 24, 1889.

15. *Hawaiian Gazette*, November 24, 1889; *Los Angeles Herald*, November 24, 1889.

16. *San Jose Mercury News*, November 23, 1889; *Helena Independent*, November 24, 1889; *Daily Morning Astorian*, November 24, 1889; *Salt Lake Herald*, November 24, 1889; *Seattle Post-Intelligencer*, November 24, 1889; *Oregonian*, November 24, 1889; *Sun* (New York), November 24, 1889; *New York Times*, November 24, 1889; *Los Angeles Times*, November 24, 1889; *Fresno Morning Republican*, November 24, 1889; *Daily Independent*, November 25, 1889; *Boston Post*, November 25, 1889; *Galveston Daily News*, November 25, 1889; *San Jose Mercury News*, November 25, 1889; *Greenock Telegraph and Clyde Shipping Gazette*, November 25, 1889; *Stattfordshire Sentinel*, November 25, 1889; *South Wales Echo*, November 26, 1889; *Victoria Daily British Colonist*, November 26, 1889; *Arizona Weekly Journal-Miner*, November 27, 1889; *Butte Semi-Weekly Journal-Miner*, November 27, 1889; *Los Angeles Times*, November 30, 1889; *Livingston Enterprise*, November 30, 1889; *Cardiff Times*, November 30, 1889; *Dalles Times-Mountaineer*, November 30, 1889; *Salem Daily*

*News*, November 30, 1889; *Weekly Independent* (Elko), December 1, 1889; *Sun*, December 1, 1889; *Mesilla Valley Democrat*, December 3, 1889; *Salem Daily News*, December 4, 1889; *New York Times*, December 8, 1889; *Salem Daily News*, December 9, 1889; *New Zealand Herald*, December 9, 1889; *Auckland Star*, December 9, 1889; *New Zealand Times*, December 10, 1889; *West Australian*, December 11, 1889; *Diss Express*, December 20, 1889; *London North News and Finsbury Gazette*, December 21, 1889; *Daily Independent* (Elko), January 17, 1890; *Phillipsburg Herald*, January 24, 1890; *Tombstone Epitaph*, February 22, 1890.

17. *San Francisco Examiner*, February 17, 1890.

18. *Pacific Commercial Advertiser*, November 5, 1891.

19. *Salem Daily News*, December 9, 1889.

20. Liliuokalani, *Hawaii's Story by Hawaii's Queen* (Boston: Lothrop, Lee and Shepard, 1898): 204.

21. *Los Angeles Herald*, November 24, 1889; *Sacramento Daily Union*, November 24, 1889; *Santa Cruz Sentinel*, November 24, 1889; *Press Democrat* (Santa Rosa), November 24, 1889; *Daily Alta California*, November 24, 1889; *Seattle Post-Intelligencer*, November 24, 1889; *Sacramento Daily Union*, November 25, 1889.

22. *Salt Lake Herald*, July 5, 1893.

23. *Daily Bulletin* (Honolulu), April 15, 1893; *Pacific Commercial Advertiser*, February 24, 1896.

24. *Daily Alta California*, November 30, 1889.

25. *Leader* (Melbourne), December 28, 1889.

26. *Salem Daily News* (Ohio), November 30, 1889.

27. *San Francisco Examiner*, February 17, 1890.

# Chapter 13

1. *Daily Bulletin* (Honolulu), November 25, 1889; "Hawaii, U.S., Arriving and Departing Passenger Lists, 1843–1898," Ancestry.com, https://www.ancestry.com/search/collections/61078/ (accessed January 31, 2021).

2. *Auckland Star*, December 7, 1889, December 9, 1889; Errol W. Martyn, *A Passion for Flight: New Zealand Aviation before the Great War.* Vol. 1: *Ideas, First Flight Attempts and the Aeronauts 1868–1909* (Christchurch: Voplane Press, 2012).

3. *Daily Telegraph* (Sydney), December 13, 1889; *Argus* (Melbourne), December 9, 1889.

4. *Sydney Morning Herald*, December 23, 1889.

5. *Evening Bulletin* (Sydney), February 18, 1896.

6. *Sydney Morning Herald*, December 17, 1889; *Evening News* (Sydney), December 21, 1889.

7. *Bendigo Advertiser*, December 21, 1889.

8. *Bendigo Advertiser*, December 21, 1889.

9. The Bondi Aquarium was also known as the Royal Aquarium and Pleasure Grounds. It was an amusement park located at Tamarama Beach near Sydney.

10. *Argus* (Melbourne), December 23, 1889; *Evening Journal* (Adelaide), December 23, 1889; *Brisbane Courier*, December 23, 1889; *Sydney Evening News*, December 23, 1889; *Sydney Morning Herald*, December 23, 1889; *Morning Bulletin* (Rockhampton), December 24, 1889; *Telegraph* (Brisbane), December 24, 1889; *Adelaide Observer*, December 28, 1889.

11. *Australian Star*, December 23, 1889.

12. *Australian Star*, December 23, 1889; *Pacific Commercial Advertiser*, January 11, 1890.

13. *Sydney Morning Herald*, December 25, 1889.

14. *Sydney Evening News*, December 27, 1889.

15. *Australian Star*, December 27, 1889.

16. *Australian Star*, April 23, 1890.

17. *Australian Star*, April 23, 1890; *Daily Telegraph*, April 24, 1890; *Age* (Melbourne), April 24, 1890.

18. *Sydney Morning Herald*, December 28, 1889.

19. *Leader* (Melbourne), December 28, 1889.

20. *Daily Telegraph*, December 30, 1889.

21. *Sydney Morning Herald*, January 3, 1890, January 4, 1890.

22. *Sydney Morning Herald*, January 9, 1890.

23. *Australian Star*, January 10, 1890.

24. *Australian Star*, January 13, 1890.

25. *Newcastle Morning Herald and Miners' Advocate*, January 22, 1890; *Maitland Mercury and Hunter River General Advertiser*, January 23, 1890.

26. *Newcastle Morning Herald and Miners' Advocate*, January 24, 1890.

27. *Sydney Morning Herald*, July 2, 1885.

28. *Sydney Morning Herald*, June 1, 1889.

29. *Sydney Evening News*, April 30, 1892.

30. *Sydney Evening News*, December 9, 1889, December 6, 1889, December 11, 1889, December 24, 1889, December 31, 1889.

31. *Newcastle Morning Herald and Miners' Advocate*, January 24, 1890.

32. *Newcastle Morning Herald and Miners' Advocate*, January 25, 1890.

33. *Australian Star*, January 28, 1890; *Newcastle Morning Herald and Miners' Advocate*, January 28, 1890.

34. *Sydney Evening News*, January 28, 1890; *Newcastle Morning Herald and Miners' Advocate*, January 29, 1890.

35. *Newcastle Morning Herald and Miners' Advocate*, January 29, 1890; *Sydney Morning Herald*, January 29, 1890; *Maitland Mercury and Hunter River General Advertiser*, January 30, 1890; *Sydney Mail and New South Wales Advertiser*, February 1, 1890; *Advocate* (Melbourne), February 1, 1890; *Queensland Times, Ipswich Herald and General Advertiser*, February 4, 1890.

36. *Maitland Mercury and Hunter River General Advertiser*, February 1, 1890.

37. *Maitland Mercury and Hunter River General Advertiser*, February 1, 1890; *Newcastle Morning Herald and Miner's Advocate*, February 1, 1890; *Maitland Mercury and*

*Hunter River General Advertiser*, February 1, 1890; *Katoomba Times*, February 1, 1890.

38. *Newcastle Morning Herald and Miners' Advocate*, February 3, 1890; *Evening News* (Sydney), February 3, 1890; *Maitland Mercury and Hunter River General Advertiser*, February 4, 1890.

39. *Evening News* (Sydney), February 6, 1890; *Newcastle Morning Herald and Miners' Advocate*, February 7, 1890; *Referee* (Sydney), February 5, 1890.

## Chapter 14

1. *Newcastle Morning Herald and Miners' Advocate*, February 7, 1890.

2. *Maitland Mercury and Hunter River General Advertiser*, February 8, 1890; *Newcastle Morning Herald and Miners' Advocate*, February 8, 1890.

3. *Sydney Morning Herald*, February 10, 1890; *National Advocate* (Bathurst), February 10, 1890; *Newcastle Morning Herald and Miners' Advocate*, February 10, 1890; *Australian Star*, February 10, 1890; *Mercury* (Hobart), February 11, 1890; *Telegraph* (Brisbane), February 11, 1890; *Maitland Mercury and Hunter River General Advertiser*, February 11, 1890; *Mount Alexander Mail* (Victoria), February 11, 1890; *Brisbane Courier*, February 13, 1890; *Toowoomba Chronicle and Darling Downs General Advertiser*, February 13, 1890.

4. *Newcastle Morning Herald and Miners' Advocate*, February 13, 1890. The empty canister associated with this medal survives at the National Library of Australia and can be found in the Crome Collection (MS 1925, Folio-Box 140, Item 69). It is labeled "Van Tassell balloon ascent, 1890."

5. *Australian Star*, February 17, 1890.

6. *Australian Star*, February 17, 1890.

7. *Referee*, February 19, 1890.

8. *Weekly Times*, February 22, 1890.

9. *Barrier Miner*, February 17, 1890; *Darling Downs Gazette*, February 24, 1890.

10. *Daily Telegraph*, February 24, 1890.

11. *Sydney Morning Herald*, February 24, 1890.

12. *Australian Star*, February 24, 1890; *Sydney Mail and New South Wales Advertiser*, March 1, 1890; *Scone Advocate*, March 1, 1890; *Brisbane Courier*, March 3, 1890; *Age*, March 6, 1890.

13. *Australian Star*, February 24, 1890.

14. *Australian Star*, February 24, 1890.

15. *Australian Star*, February 24, 1890.

16. *Daily Telegraph* (Launceston), February 24, 1890.

17. The Friendly Societies' Grounds were at the present-day location of Olympic Park in Melbourne.

18. *Age*, March 6, 1890; *Mount Alexander Mail*, March 7, 1890.

19. *Age*, March 6, 1890.

20. *Age*, March 6, 1890.

21. *Age*, March 6, 1890.

22. *Sydney Morning Herald*, March 6, 1890.

23. *Wagga Wagga Advertiser*, March 8, 1890; *Morning Bulletin* (Rockhampton), March 8, 1890; *Queenslander*, March 8, 1890; *Morning Bulletin*, March 11, 1890; *Maryborough Chronicle, Wide Bay and Burnett Advertiser*, March 11, 1890; *Mackay Mercury*, March 18, 1890; *Southern Queensland Bulletin*, April 26, 1890.

24. *Express and Telegraph*, March 14, 1890; *Adelaide Observer*, March 15, 1890; *Advertiser* (Adelaide), March 20, 1890.

25. *Inquirer and Commercial News*, March 26, 1890.

26. *Sydney Morning Herald*, March 8, 1890. At her home in Oakland, California, Clara very likely had no idea her name was being mentioned in Australian newspapers by her "daughters" and her now estranged husband, Park.

27. *Evening Journal*, March 10, 1890.

28. *Evening Journal*, March 10, 1890; *Argus*, March 10, 1890; *Newcastle Morning Herald and Miners' Advocate*, March 14, 1890.

29. *Argus*, March 10, 1890.

30. *Ballarat Star*, March 13, 1890.

31. *Daily Telegraph*, March 10, 1890; *Geelong Advertiser*, March 10, 1890; *Sydney Morning Herald*, March 10, 1890.

32. *Age*, March 10, 1890.

33. *Border Watch*, March 12, 1890.

34. *Geelong Advertiser*, March 10, 1890.

35. *Ballarat Star*, March 14, 1890.

## Chapter 15

1. *Geelong Advertiser*, March 10, 1890.

2. *Australian Star*, March 10, 1890.

3. *Ballarat Star*, March 11, 1890.

4. *Age*, March 17, 1890.

5. *Ballarat Star*, March 17, 1890.

6. *Ballarat Star*, March 17, 1890; *Bendigo Advertiser*, March 17, 1890; *Argus*, March 17, 1890.

7. *Ballarat Star*, March 17, 1890.

8. *Bendigo Advertiser*, March 27, 1890.

9. *Bendigo Advertiser*, March 28, 1890.

10. *Bendigo Advertiser*, March 28, 1890; *Age*, March 28, 1890.

11. *Bendigo Advertiser*, April 1, 1890.

12. *Mercury*, April 1, 1890.

13. *Bendigo Advertiser*, April 2, 1890.

14. *Bendigo Advertiser*, April 3, 1890.

15. *Age*, April 3, 1890.

16. *Bendigo Advertiser*, April 3, 1890.

17. *Bendigo Advertiser*, April 7, 1890, April 11, 1890.

18. *Bendigo Advertiser*, April 11, 1890.

19. *Bendigo Advertiser*, April 11, 1890.

20. *Express and Telegraph*, April 23, 1890; *Evening Journal*, April 23, 1890.

21. *Evening Journal*, April 24, 1890; *South Australian Register*, April 24, 1890; *Adelaide Observer*, April 26, 1890.

22. *Express and Telegraph*, April 24, 1890; *Advertiser*, April 24, 1890.

23. *Express and Telegraph*, April 24, 1890; *Advertiser*, April 24, 1890.

24. This value is likely incorrect relative to the capacity of 77,000 cubic feet.

25. *Evening Journal*, April 25, 1890; *Express and Telegraph*, April 26, 1890.

26. *Evening Journal*, April 23, 1890.

27. *South Australian Register*, April 26, 1890.

28. Patricia Sumerling, *The Adelaide Park Lands: A Social History* (Kent Town, South Australia: Wakefield, 2011).

29. *Express Telegraph*, May 5, 1890.

30. *Express Telegraph*, May 5, 1890; *Australian Star*, May 5, 1890.

31. Sumerling, *Adelaide Park Lands; Inquirer and Commercial News*, May 23, 1890.

32. *Evening Journal*, May 5, 1890.

33. *Daily News*, May 5, 1890; *Brisbane Courier*, May 5, 1890; *Evening News*, May 5, 1890.

34. *Evening Journal*, May 7, 1890, May 8, 1890; *Express and Telegraph*, May 7, 1890.

35. *Evening Journal*, May 12, 1890.

36. *Evening Journal*, May 12, 1890; *Express and Telegraph*, May 12, 1890.

37. *Evening Journal*, May 12, 1890.

## Chapter 16

1. *Geelong Advertiser*, May 13, 1890.

2. *Geelong Advertiser*, May 14, 1890.

3. *Geelong Advertiser*, May 14, 1890.

4. *Geelong Advertiser*, May 14, 1890.

5. *Geelong Advertiser*, May 16, 1890.

6. *Geelong Advertiser*, May 23, 1890; *Maryborough Standard*, May 22, 1890; *Age*, May 22, 1890.

7. *Colac Herald*, May 27, 1890; *Kyneton Observer*, May 31, 1890.

8. *Brisbane Courier*, May 14, 1890.

9. *Brisbane Courier*, May 19, 1890.

10. *Brisbane Courier*, May 21, 1890.

11. *Daily Telegraph* (Sydney), May 23, 1890.

12. *Queensland Times*, May 24, 1890.

13. *Daily Telegraph* (Sydney), May 23, 1890; *Brisbane Courier*, May 23, 1890.

14. *Bendigo Advertiser*, May 24, 1890.

15. *Bendigo Advertiser*, May 30, 1890.

16. *Bendigo Advertiser*, June 2, 1890.

17. *Brisbane Courier*, May 26, 1890.

18. *Daily Northern Argus*, May 27, 1890; *Goulburn Evening Penny Post*, May 27, 1890.

19. *Brisbane Courier*, May 27, 1890.

20. *Australian Star*, May 27, 1890; *Daily Telegraph* (Sydney), May 27, 1890; *Morning Herald and Miners' Advocate*, May 27, 1890; *Maryborough Chronicle, Wide Bay and Burnett Advertiser*, May 27, 1890; *Evening Journal*, May 27, 1890; *South Australian Register*, May 27, 1890; *Barrier Miner*, May 27, 1890; *Daily Telegraph* (Sydney), May 27, 1890; *Age*, May 27, 1890; *Mackay Mercury*, May 27, 1890; *Geelong Advertiser*, May 27, 1890.

21. *Brisbane Courier*, May 29, 1890.

22. *Brisbane Courier*, May 29, 1890.

23. *Telegraph*, May 31, 1890.

24. *Telegraph*, June 2, 1890; *Brisbane Courier*, June 2, 1890.

25. *Telegraph*, June 2, 1890; *Brisbane Courier*, June 2, 1890; *Queensland Times, Ipswich Herald and General Advertiser*, June 3, 1890.

26. *Telegraph*, June 2, 1890.

27. *Brisbane Courier*, June 2, 1890.

28. *Brisbane Courier*, June 4, 1890; *Daily Telegraph* (Sydney), June 4, 1890.

29. *Maryborough Chronicle, Wide Bay and Burnett Advertiser*, June 5, 1890.

30. *Brisbane Courier*, June 7, 1890; *Daily Telegraph* (Sydney), June 7, 1890.

31. *Maryborough Chronicle, Wide Bay and Burnett Advertiser*, June 9, 1890.

32. *Maryborough Chronicle, Wide Bay and Burnett Advertiser*, June 9, 1890.

33. *Maryborough Chronicle, Wide Bay and Burnett Advertiser*, June 9, 1890.

34. *Maryborough Chronicle, Wide Bay and Burnett Advertiser*, June 9, 1890.

35. *Maryborough Chronicle, Wide Bay and Burnett Advertiser*, June 9, 1890.

36. *Daily Northern Argus*, June 13, 1890.

37. *Lorgnette*, June 7, 1890.

38. *Daily Northern Argus*, June 16, 1890.

39. *Morning Bulletin* (Rockhampton), June 16, 1890.

40. *Daily Northern Argus*, June 16, 1890.

41. *Daily Northern Argus*, June 16, 1890.

42. *Brisbane Courier*, June 27, 1890.

43. *Daily Telegraph* (Sydney), June 24, 1890.

44. *Brisbane Courier*, June 26, 1890.

45. *Brisbane Courier*, June 26, 1890.

46. *Brisbane Courier*, June 27, 1890.

47. *Brisbane Courier*, June 26, 1890.

48. *Newcastle Morning Herald and Miners' Advocate*, June 26, 1890.

49. *Daily Telegraph* (Sydney), June 28, 1890.

50. *Maryborough Chronicle*, June 30, 1890.

51. *Northern Miner*, July 10, 1890.

52. *Brisbane Courier*, July 10, 1890; *Telegraph*, July 10, 1890.

53. While it is remarkable that a street was named in her honor despite the public debate, it is ironic that the street name itself, Vantassel, is in error relative to Park Van Tassel's name. The street name is one word instead of two and does not include the double *l* that was common at the time. It also honors Gladys, whose last name was actually Freitas, and is a remembrance of the many twists and turns associated with the entire Van Tassel experience in Australia.

54. *Toowoomba Chronicle and Darling Downs General Advertiser*, July 1, 1890; *Singleton Argus*, July 2, 1890.

55. *Warwick Examiner and Times*, July 2, 1890.

56. *Northern Miner*, July 4, 1890.

57. *Northern Miner*, July 4, 1890.

58. *Week*, July 12, 1890.

59. *Barrier Miner*, July 17, 1890.

60. *Yorke's Peninsula Advertiser*, July 25, 1890.

61. *Barrier Miner*, July 17, 1890.

62. *Daily Telegraph* (Sydney), October 18, 1890.

63. *Bathurst National Advocate*, October 18, 1890.

64. *Bathurst National Advocate*, October 21, 1890.

65. *Bathurst National Advocate*, October 23, 1890.

66. *Bathurst National Advocate*, October 24, 1890.

67. *Bathurst National Advocate*, October 25, 1890.

68. *Bathurst National Advocate*, October 31, 1890; *Freeman's Journal*, November 1, 1890.

69. *Daily Telegraph* (Sydney), September 29, 1890; *Sydney Morning Herald*, October 2, 1890, October 8, 1890; *Daily Telegraph* (Sydney), October 18, 1890; *Australian Star*, October 25, 1890.

## Chapter 17

1. *Singapore Free Press and Mercantile Advertiser*, August 27, 1890.

2. *Daily Telegraph* (Sydney), October 18, 1890.

3. *Singapore Free Press and Mercantile Advertiser*, August 27, 1890.

4. *North-China Herald and Supreme Court & Consular Gazette*, May 30, 1890.

5. *North-China Herald and Supreme Court & Consular Gazette*, September, 19, 1890; *London and China Telegraph*, October 27, 1890.

6. *Singapore Free Press and Mercantile Advertiser*, October 9, 1890; *North-China Herald and Supreme Court & Consular Gazette*, October 3, 1890.

7. A colloquial term for a day laborer.

8. *Singapore Free Press and Mercantile Advertiser*, October 22, 1890.

9. *North-China Herald and Supreme Court & Consular Gazette*, October 3, 1890; *Yomiuri Shinbun*, October 12, 1890.

10. The term *hi-yah* is actually Anglicized slang for *aiya*, an exclamatory phrase common in China, expressing surprise, blame, dismay, shock, or fear.

11. *North-China Herald*, October 17, 1890.

12. *North-China Herald*, October 17, 1890.

13. *Singapore Free Press and Mercantile Advertiser*, December 10, 1890.

14. *San Francisco Chronicle*, July 21, 1901.

15. *Daily Advertiser*, January 3, 1891.

16. *San Francisco Chronicle*, July 21, 1901.

17. *San Francisco Chronicle*, July 21, 1901.

18. *Times of India*, March 2, 1891.

19. *San Jose Mercury News*, January 31, 1891.

20. *Times of India*, January 28, 1889.

21. *Times of India*, January 4, 1878.

22. *Times of India*, January 16, 1889, January 18, 1889, January 28, 1889.

23. *Straits Advocate*, March 16, 1889.

24. *Times of India*, March 7, 1889, March 23, 1889.

25. *Times of India*, April 11, 1889.

26. Amitabha Ghosh, "The First Indian Aeronaut," *Indian Journal of History of Science 27*, no. 3 (1992): 291–308; Abhijit Gupta, "First Solo Balloon Flier," *Telegraph* (Calcutta), August 8, 2010.

27. *Straits Times Weekly Issue*, May 14, 1890.

28. *Japan Weekly Mail*, October 11, 1890; *North-China Herald and Supreme Court & Consular Gazette*, October 24, 1890, October 31, 1890.

29. *North-China Herald and Supreme Court & Consular Gazette*, November 14, 1890.

30. *South Wales Daily News*, November 15, 1890; *Japan Weekly Mail*, November 22, 1890.

31. *Otago Daily Times*, January 22, 1889; Errol W. Martyn, *A Passion for Flight: New Zealand Aviation before the Great War*. Vol. 1, *Ideas, First Flight Attempts and the Aeronauts 1868–1909* (Christchurch: Volplane Press, 2012).

32. *Japan Weekly Mail*, December 20, 1890.

33. *Flintshire Observer Mining Journal and General Advertiser for the Counties of Flint and Denbigh*, November 12, 1891. It should be noted that descriptions of this event attributed the near disaster to an "invisible whirlwind." This was a very early description of the hot-air currents that later became known as thermals.

34. *Inquirer and Commercial News*, March 6, 1891.

35. *Times of India*, December 16, 1891.

36. *Times of India*, December 16, 1891; *Queenstown Free Press*, January 8, 1892.

37. Believed to be no relation to the Joseph Lawrence who passed away in Hawaii.

38. *Times of India*, January 4, 1892.

39. *North-China Herald and Supreme Court & Consular Gazette*, December 26, 1890.

40. *Morning Call*, August 16, 1890.

41. *Los Angeles Herald*, September 12, 1890.

42. *North-China Herald and Supreme Court & Consular Gazette*, December 26, 1890; *Morning Call*, August 16, 1890.

43. *Times of India*, February 26, 1891.

44. *Times of India*, March 14, 1891.

45. *San Francisco Chronicle*, July 21, 1901; *Daily Advertiser*, April 15, 1891; *Homeward Mail from India, China, and the East*, April 20, 1891; *North-China Herald and Supreme Court & Consular Gazette*, April 24, 1891.

46. *San Francisco Chronicle*, July 21, 1901.

47. *Morning Bulletin* (Rockhampton, Queensland), June 18, 1891.

## Chapter 18

1. *Morning Olympian*, September 14, 1891; *Times of India*, October 9, 1891.

2. *Evening Capital Journal*, September 15, 1891; *Times of India*, November 10, 1891.

3. *Morning Olympian*, September 15, 1891.

4. *Daily Advertiser*, November 11, 1891.

5. *Morning Olympian*, September 14, 1891.

6. *Morning Olympian*, September 14, 1891.

7. *Times of India*, October 9, 1891.

8. *Morning Olympian*, September 14, 1891; *Evening Capital Journal*, September 15, 1891; *Morning Olympian*, September 15, 1891.

9. *San Francisco Chronicle*, April 17, 1891.

10. *San Francisco Chronicle*, July 21, 1901.

11. *Homeward Mail from India, China and the East*, October 26, 1891.

12. *San Jose Mercury News*, September 25, 1891.

13. *Times of India*, October 17, 1891.

14. *Times of India*, October 14, 1891, October 15, 1891, October 16, 1891.

15. *Times of India*, October 16, 1891

16. *Times of India*, October 14, 1891.

17. *Times of India*, October 19, 1891.

18. A term for a peasant farmer.

19. *Times of India*, October 28, 1891.

20. *Daily Advertiser*, November 11, 1891.

21. Stephen M Edwardes, *The Bombay City Police* (Oxford: London, 1923).

22. *San Francisco Chronicle*, July 21, 1901.

23. *North-China Herald and Supreme Court & Consular Gazette*, November 20, 1891.

24. *San Francisco Chronicle*, July 21, 1901.

25. *Inter Ocean*, December 22, 1891.

26. *Times of India*, January 20, 1892.

27. *Times of India*, January 20, 1892.

28. *Times of India*, February 15, 1892.

29. Possibly George A. Meears from Van Tassel's time in Utah, but this remains unconfirmed.

30. *Times of India*, February 15, 1892.

31. *Times of India*, February 15, 1892.

32. *Homeward Mail from India, China and the East*, March 7, 1892.
33. *Times of India*, February 18, 1892.
34. *Homeward Mail from India, China and the East*, February 29, 1892; *Western Daily Press*, March 4, 1892.
35. *Nottingham Evening Post*, March 4, 1892; *Aberdeen Evening Express*, March 5, 1892; *Glasgow Evening Post*, March 5, 1892; *Falkirk Herald*, March 12, 1892; *Aberdeen Press and Journal*, March 16, 1892; *L'Aeronaute: Moniteur de la Société* 5 (March 1892); *Pyrenees Journal*, March 12, 1892.
36. *Flintshire Observer Mining Journal and General Advertiser for the Counties of Flint and Denbigh*, March 10, 1892.
37. *Singapore Free Press and Mercantile Advertiser*, April 5, 1892.
38. *Singapore Free Press and Mercantile Advertiser*, April 5, 1892.
39. At the time of her flight, Dacca was part of India, but it is now part of Bangladesh, so Jeanette's flight is considered the first by a woman in Bangladesh's history.
40. *Dundee Evening Telegraph*, March 19, 1892; *Illustrated London News*, March 26, 1892; *Pacific Commercial Advertiser*, April 7, 1892; *Yorkshire Evening Post*, April 12, 1892; *London Daily News*, April 12, 1892; *Evening Herald* (Dublin), April 13, 1892; *Liverpool Mercury*, April 13, 1892; *East Anglian Daily Times*, April 13, 1892; *Exeter and Plymouth Gazette*, April 13, 1892; *North Wales Chronicle*, April 16, 1892; *Homeward Mail from India, China and the East*, April 19, 1892; *Yorkshire Evening Post*, April 12, 1892; *Aberdeen Evening Express*, April 13, 1892; *North Wales Chronicle and Advertiser for the Principality*, April 16, 1892; *Flintshire Observer Mining Journal and General Advertiser for the Counties of Flint and Denbigh*, March 21, 1892; *Pearson's Weekly*, March 26, 1892.
41. *Markdale Standard*, May 12, 1892.
42. *Markdale Standard*, May 12, 1892.
43. *Singapore Free Press and Mercantile Advertiser*, April 6, 1892.
44. *Singapore Free Press and Mercantile Advertiser*, April 6, 1892.
45. *Evening News* (Sydney), March 21, 1892.
46. *Singapore Free Press and Mercantile Advertiser*, April 6, 1892.
47. *Evening News* (Sydney), March 21, 1892.
48. *Evening News* (Sydney), April 30, 1892. The astute reader will recall that only Gladys toured with Park Van Tassel through Southeast Asia, not Valerie as suggested in this letter to the editor. Research for this book turned up no confirmation of Gladys's possible jumps in Germany.
49. *Singapore Free Press and Mercantile Advertiser*, April 26, 1892.
50. *Times of India*, March 22, 1892.

## Chapter 19

1. *Homeward Mail from India, China and the East*, August 3, 1892.
2. Edith Ann Nowlan was born in 1874.

3. *Brisbane Courier*, March 13, 1893; *South Wales Daily Post*, March 4, 1893; *Singleton Argus*, April 15, 1893; *Daily Telegraph* (Sydney), March 24, 1893; *Australian Star*, February 15, 1893.

4. Robert Recks, "Appendix4-CL, First Balloon Flights by Country and Date," Who's Who of Ballooning, http://www.ballooninghistory.com/whoswho/appendix4CL.html (accessed January 13, 2021).

5. Crouch, *Eagle Aloft*.

6. "Prelude," Sri Lanka Air Force, http://airforce.lk/pages.php?pages=prelude (accessed January 13, 2021); "Ferguson's Seylon Directory," History of Ceylon Tea, https://www.historyofceylontea.com/ceylon-publications/fergusons-directory/1942-fergusons-ceylon-directory/pdf/resources/1942-fergusons-ceylon-directory.pdf (accessed January 13, 2021); *Ceylon in Our Times, 1894–1969* (Sri Lanka: Ceylon Cold Stores, 1969), 20.

7. *Ceylon in Our Times*, 20.

8. *San Francisco Chronicle*, July 21, 1901.

9. *San Francisco Chronicle*, July 21, 1901.

10. *San Francisco Chronicle*, July 21, 1901.

11. *Times of India*, December 7, 1895.

12. Van Tassel previously used the same name on a balloon while stationed in San Francisco.

13. *Times of India*, December 9, 1895.

14. *Inter-Mountain Republican*, February 11, 1907.

15. *Singapore Free Press and Mercantile Advertiser*, March 2, 1897.

16. *Times of India*, January 15, 1898, January 22, 1898.

17. "The North Point Annual. No. V January 1900," St. Joseph's School North Point, https://www.sjcnorthpoint.com/annuals/North%20Point%20-%201899.pdf (accessed January 13, 2021).

18. An Indian soldier serving under British or other European orders.

19. *Times of India*, March 16, 1900.

## Chapter 20

1. Lillian Mary Hawker was born on May 7, 1872, and died on February 27, 1933.

2. *Auckland Star*, March 8, 1894, March 26, 1894, March 27, 1894, April 5, 1894.

3. *Evening News* (Sydney), December 31, 1895.

4. *Evening News* (Sydney), December 31, 1895.

5. *Evening News* (Sydney), December 31, 1895.

6. *Evening News* (Sydney), December 31, 1895.

7. Ethel Harriet Hawker was born on September 28, 1876, and died on September 26, 1935.

8. *Rock Island Argus*, May 15, 1895; *Dalles Daily Chronicle*, May 15, 1895.

9. *Freeland Tribune*, March 30, 1896.

10. *Evening Herald* (Shenandoah, PA), December 11, 1895; *Indianapolis Journal*, December 11, 1895; *Salt Lake Herald*, December 11, 1895.

11. *San Francisco Call*, December 10, 1895.

12. *San Francisco Call*, December 10, 1895.

13. *San Francisco Call*, January 20, 1896.

14. *San Francisco Call*, January 20, 1896.

15. *San Francisco Call*, February 3, 1896.

16. *San Francisco Call*, April 25, 1896, April 27, 1896.

17. *San Francisco Call*, July 25, 1896, July 26, 1896.

18. *Pacific Commercial Advertiser*, February 29, 1896.

19. *Australian Star*, January 9, 1896.

20. *Australian Star*, January 9, 1896.

21. *Pacific Commercial Advertiser*, February 29, 1896.

22. *Pacific Commercial Advertiser*, February 18, 1896; *Hawaiian Star*, February 19, 1896, February 20, 1896; *Pacific Commercial Advertiser*, February 22, 1896. This location is south of present-day Kamehameha Highway, east of Lehua Avenue, and primarily north of Interstate H-1.

23. *Hawaiian Star*, February 21, 1896.

24. *Hawaiian Gazette*, February 25, 1896.

25. *Hawaiian Gazette*, February 25, 1896.

26. *Hawaiian Gazette*, February 25, 1896.

27. *Pacific Commercial Advertiser*, March 3, 1896.

28. *Honolulu Evening Bulletin*, September 2, 1896.

29. *Honolulu Evening Bulletin*, September 2, 1896.

30. Scamehorn, "Thomas Scott Baldwin."

31. A time of year that now features the Albuquerque International Balloon Fiesta®.

32. Kim Veseley, Dick Brown, Tom McConnell, and Paul Rhetts, eds., *The World Comes to Albuquerque* (Albuquerque: Rio Grande Books, 2011), 18.

33. Scamehorn, "Thomas Scott Baldwin."

34. *Selangor Journal*, January 12, 1894.

35. *Cardigan Observer and General Advertiser for the Counties of Cardigan, Carmarthen and Pembroke*, July 17, 1897.

36. "Unionville Fair—September 17th, 18th, and 19th, 1895," Heritage Place Museum, http://www.lynmuseum.ca/2016/12/26/unionville-fair-september-17th-18th-19th-1895/ (accessed May 19, 2019).

37. *Bennington Semi Weekly Banner*, September 6, 1895.

# Chapter 21

1. *San Francisco Chronicle*, July 9, 1901; *San Jose Mercury News*, July 10, 1901; *San Francisco Chronicle*, July 21, 1901.

2. *San Jose Mercury News*, July 10, 1901.

3. *San Francisco Chronicle*, July 21, 1901.

4. *San Francisco Chronicle*, July 21, 1901.

5. "Correspondence of Lord Kelvin," Kelvin Library, https://zapatopi.net/kelvin/papers/letters.html (accessed January 31, 2021).

6. *Newark Advocate*, April 26, 1902.

7. Joseph Leconte, "The Problem of a Flying Machine," *Popular Science Monthly* 34 (November 1888): 69–76.

8. *Scientific American*, July 31, 1869.

9. Gary F. Kurutz, "'Navigating the Upper Strata' and the Quest for Dirigibility," *California History* 58, no. 4: 334–47.

10. Aluizio Napoleão, *Santos-Dumont: Conquest of the Air* (São Paulo, Brazil: Associação Brasileira de Ultraleves, 1997).

11. *Scientific American*, November 7, 1903.

12. *Scientific American*, November 7, 1903; "Airship Flies over San Francisco," *Popular Mechanics* 5, no. 4: 309.

13. *San Francisco Call*, April 24, 1904; *Santa Cruz Sentinel*, April 24, 1904.

14. *San Francisco Call*, April 24, 1904.

15. *San Francisco Call*, April 24, 1904.

16. *Press Democrat* (Santa Rosa), April 24, 1904.

17. *San Francisco Call*, April 24, 1904.

18. *San Francisco Call*, April 24, 1904.

19. "Greth's Eight-Mile Airship Trip," *Scientific American*, May 14, 1904.

20. "Greth's Eight-Mile Airship Trip."

21. The similarity of the design of Baldwin's *California Arrow* and Greth's *California Eagle* should not be lost on the reader.

22. Craig Harwood and Gary B. Fogel, *Quest for Flight: John J. Montgomery and the Dawn of Aviation in the West* (Norman: University of Oklahoma Press, 2012).

23. Gary Fogel and Craig Harwood, "John J. Montgomery's Circulation Theory of Lift," January 2, 2016, Aerospace Research Central, https://doi.org/10.2514/6.2016-1159.

24. Harwood and Fogel, *Quest for Flight*.

25. Thomas S. Baldwin, "I Will Fly over and under the Brooklyn Bridge," *World Magazine* (supplement to *New York World*), November, 27, 1904.

26. Thomas S. Baldwin, "The High Seas of Space," *National Magazine* 28, no. 4 (July 1908): 457–60.

27. The reader will also notice the similarity between the names of Baldwin's *California Arrow* and Greth's *California Eagle*.

28. Harwood and Fogel, *Quest for Flight*.

29. J. Mayne Baltimore, "The New Baldwin Airship," *Scientific American* 91, no. 9 (August 27, 1904): 147.

30. Baldwin, "High Seas of Space."

31. Patent no. 851,481, granted April 23, 1907.

32. *San Francisco Chronicle*, June 8, 1904; *San Francisco Call*, June 25, 1904.

33. Harwood and Fogel, *Quest for Flight*.

34. While the Wright brothers were the first to demonstrate powered heavier-than-air flight, in December 1903, they did so in a very private manner and continued to experiment largely in private through 1905. Using a glider and a balloon for launch at altitude, Montgomery's public exhibition in April 1905 was the first flight by a heavier-than-air flying machine ever witnessed by the American public.

35. "Battle of the Airship Men Goes Merrily On and On and Now's in Court," *San Francisco Examiner*, June 2, 1905.

36. *Oakland Tribune*, July 5, 1905.

37. *Oakland Tribune*, July 5, 1905.

38. *Oakland Tribune*, July 5, 1905.

## Chapter 22

1. *Salt Lake Telegram*, February 11, 1907.

2. *Salt Lake Telegram*, February 11, 1907; *Inter-Mountain Republican*, February 2, 1907.

3. *Inter-Mountain Republican*, February 11, 1907.

4. *Salt Lake Telegram*, February 11, 1907.

5. *Salt Lake Telegram*, February 11, 1907.

6. *Salt Lake Telegram*, February 11, 1907.

7. *Salt Lake City Herald*, June 18, 1907.

8. *Deseret Evening News*, June 19, 1907; *Inter-Mountain Republican*, June 20, 1907.

9. *Inter-Mountain Republican*, June 20, 1907.

10. *Los Angeles Herald*, August 10, 1907; *San Francisco Call*, August 10, 1907; *Pacific Commercial Advertiser*, August 27, 1907.

11. *San Francisco Call*, September 24, 1907.

12. *Los Angeles Herald*, July 21, 1907.

13. Gary B. Fogel, "The Aero Club of California: Initial Years (1908–1909)," Aerospace Research Central, January 6, 2019, https://doi.org/10.2514/6.2019-2196. The Aero Club of America later became the National Aeronautic Association, while the Aero Club of California became the Aero Club of Southern California. Both organizations continue to exist today.

14. *Oakland Tribune*, January 21, 1909.

15. *Oakland Tribune*, January 21, 1909.

16. *Aeronautics*, March 1909, 100; *San Jose Mercury News*, March 1, 1909; *San Francisco Examiner*, March 1, 1909.

17. *Aeronautics*, June 1909, 208; *San Francisco Chronicle*, April 12, 1909.

18. *San Francisco Chronicle*, April 12, 1909.

19. *Aeronautics*, July 1909, 10.

20. Fogel, "The Aero Club of California."

21. A resident of Santa Fe, New Mexico, Hersey had also helped form New Mexico's

contingent of the First Cavalry of Rough Riders, assisting Theodore Roosevelt in the Spanish-American War before Roosevelt became president.

22. "1st Coupe Aéronautique Gordon Bennett—Paris (FRA) 1906," Fédération Aéronautique International, https://www.fai.org/page/gb-1906 (accessed January 15, 2021).

23. "2nd Coupe Aéronautique Gordon Bennett—St. Louis (USA) 1907," Fédération Aéronautique International, https://www.fai.org/page/gb-1907 (accessed January 15, 2021).

24. *San Francisco Chronicle*, July 6, 1909; *Los Angeles Times*, July 6, 1909.

25. *Aeronautics*, September 1909, 107.

## Chapter 23

1. *Oakland Tribune*, July 14, 1909.

2. *Aeronautics*, October 1909, 164; *Oakland Tribune*, August 14, 1909; *San Francisco Chronicle*, August 13, 1909; *San Francisco Examiner*, August 14, 1909; *San Francisco Chronicle*, August 15, 1909.

3. *Oakland Tribune*, August 15, 1909.

4. *Oakland Tribune*, August 15, 1909.

5. Joseph Hidalgo, *History of Aerial Navigation: Lecture Delivered by Professor Joseph Hidalgo before the Pacific Aero Club of San Francisco, January 1, 1910* (San Francisco: Prof. J. Hidalgo, 1910).

6. *Aeronautics*, October 1909, 134.

7. *San Francisco Chronicle*, August 18, 1909; *San Francisco Chronicle*, October 4, 1909.

8. *Pacific Municipalities* 21, no. 1 (September 1909): 142.

9. Hidalgo, *History of Aerial Navigation*.

10. *Aeronautics*, September 1909, 107.

11. *Los Angeles Times*, October 10, 1909.

12. *San Jose Mercury News*, October 10, 1909.

13. *San Francisco Chronicle*, October 10, 1909.

14. *San Francisco Chronicle*, October 10, 1909.

15. *Oakland Tribune*, October 11, 1909.

16. *San Jose Mercury News*, October 14, 1909.

17. *Oakland Tribune*, October 11, 1909.

18. Hidalgo, *History of Aerial Navigation;* Cleve T. Shaffer, "San Francisco-Oakland Race," *Aeronautics*, December 1909, 222.

19. *Oakland Tribune*, October 26, 1909.

20. *Oakland Tribune*, October 26, 1909.

21. *San Francisco Call*, April 1, 1910.

22. *San Francisco Call*, April 4, 1910.

23. *Sacramento Union*, May 29, 1910.

24. *Aeronautics*, August 1910, 53.

25. *San Francisco Call*, June 30, 1910.

26. *San Francisco Call*, July 4, 1910.

27. *San Francisco Call,* July 4, 1910, July 3, 1910.
28. *San Francisco Call,* September 21, 1910.
29. *San Francisco Call,* October 3, 1930.
30. *Salt Lake Telegram,* October 3, 1910.
31. *Aeronautics,* December 1910, 218.
32. "United States Census, 1910," Family Search, https://familysearch.org/ark:/61903/1:1:MV2S-2KK (accessed January 31, 2021).
33. *Morning Echo* (Bakersfield), November 18, 1910.
34. *Oakland Tribune,* November 17, 1910.
35. *Oakland Tribune,* November 17, 1910; *San Francisco Chronicle,* November 18, 1910.
36. *Morning Press* (Santa Barbara), November 24, 1910; *Santa Cruz Sentinel,* November 24, 1910; *San Francisco Chronicle,* November 24, 1910.

## Chapter 24

1. "*California, Marriage Records from Select Counties, 1850–1941.*" Ancestry.com, https://www.ancestry.com/search/collections/8797/ (accessed January 31, 2021).
2. *San Francisco Call,* April 27, 1912.
3. *San Francisco Call,* May 5, 1912.
4. *San Francisco Call,* May 26, 1912.
5. *San Francisco Call,* June 23, 1912; *Oakland Tribune,* July 4, 1912; *San Francisco Call,* July 4, 1912.
6. *San Francisco Call,* July 6, 1912.
7. *San Francisco Call,* July 5, 1912.
8. *San Francisco Call,* July 6, 1912.
9. *San Francisco Call,* July 15, 1912.
10. *San Francisco Chronicle,* October 11, 1912.
11. *San Francisco Chronicle,* September 9, 1912; *Orchard and Farm* 24, no. 10 (October, 1912): 17.
12. *Los Angeles Times,* May 19, 1913.
13. *Chehalis Bee Nugget,* June 20, 1913; *Centralia Daily Chronicle,* June 21, 1913.
14. *Chehalis Bee Nugget,* June 20, 1913.
15. *Chehalis Bee Nugget,* July 4, 1913.
16. *Chehalis Bee Nugget,* July 4, 1913.
17. *Chehalis Bee Nugget,* July 11, 1913.
18. *Centralia Daily Chronicle-Examiner,* July 8, 1913.
19. *Morning Oregonian,* October 15, 1913.
20. Yuba Parks was born in 1852.
21. *Honolulu Star-Bulletin,* January 13, 1915.
22. *Honolulu Star-Bulletin,* January 22, 1915.
23. *Aerial Age* 1 (May 10, 1915): 177.
24. *Honolulu Star-Bulletin,* March 26, 1915.

25. *Press Democrat,* March 20, 1917.

26. *Press Democrat,* March 30, 1917.

27. *Reno Gazette Journal,* March 8, 1917.

28. *Napa Journal Sun,* July 15, 1917.

29. *Sacramento Union,* August 17, 1917.

30. *Oakland Tribune,* July 7, 1919.

31. https://familysearch.org/ark:/61903/1:1:MH39–6N2

32. *Oakland Tribune,* April 30, 1923.

33. *Santa Cruz Evening News,* February 25, 1925.

34. *Los Angeles Herald,* January 9, 1910.

35. "United States Census, 1930," Family Search, https://familysearch.org/ark:/61903/1:1:XCN2-N3J (accessed January 31, 2021).

36. *Tyrone Daily Herald,* September 25, 1930.

37. *Albuquerque Journal,* September 21, 1930.

38. *Santa Cruz Evening News,* October 25, 1930, October 29, 1930; *New York Times,* October 25, 1930; *Oakland Tribune,* October 26, 1930.

39. *Oakland Tribune,* October 26, 1930.

## Epilogue

1. "Baldwin, Thomas Scott," National Aviation Hall of Fame, http://www.nationalaviation.org/our-enshrinees/baldwin-thomas (accessed February 22, 2020).

2. "Montgomery, John Joseph," National Aviation Hall of Fame, http://www.nationalaviation.org/our-enshrinees/montgomery-john-joseph/ (accessed February 22, 2020).

3. *Hearings on H.R. 4523, Before the Comm. on Patents,* 74th Cong. 103 (1935) (statement of Roy Knabenshue).

4. Charles J. V. Murphy, *Parachute* (New York: G. P. Putnam and Sons, 1930); Peter Hemery, *The History of Australian Aviation* (Sydney: Australia News and Information Bureau, 1945); *CHIRP* (journal of the Early Birds of Aviation), January 1, 1951; Charles Harvard Gibbs-Smith, *The Aeroplane: An Historical Survey of Its Origins and Development* (London: H. M. Stationary Office, 1960); T. W. Willans, *Parachuting and Skydiving: A Personal Account of the History and Technique* (London: Faber & Faber, 1964); *Technology and Culture: The International Quarterly of the Society for the History of Technology* 9 (1968): 257.

5. "Baumgartner's Records Ratified by FAI," Fédération Aéronautique Internationale, https://www.fai.org/news/baumgartner%E2%80%99s-records-ratified-fai (accessed February 22, 2020).

6. "Record: Alan Eustace (USA)," Fédération Aéronautique Internationale, https://www.fai.org/record/17338 (accessed February 22, 2020); "Record: Alan Eustace (USA)," Fédération Aéronautique Internationale, https://www.fai.org/record/17339 (accessed February 22, 2020).

# INDEX

Page numbers in italic text indicate illustrations.